EXISTENTIAL PSYCHOLOGY
From Analysis to Synthesis

EXISTENTIAL PSYCHOLOGY

From Analysis to Synthesis

IGOR A. CARUSO

PALM PUBLISHERS

1964
PALM PUBLISHERS, MONTREAL

Original edition *Psychoanalyse und
Synthese der Existenz*, Vienna, Verlag Herder. Translated by Eva Krapf.

First published in Great Britain 1964

Library of Congress Catalog Card Number: 64-15436
© 1964 Herder and Herder, Incorporated
Printed in Great Britain

CONTENTS

FOREWORD

THE author of this book does not in any way intend it to be an 'Introduction to Depth Psychology'. It is, rather, meant to be a critical review, both of the theoretical roots of present day depth psychology and of some of its practical effects. A review of this kind is not a systematic enquiry into the whole field of our discipline. On the other hand it is not confined to a negative criticism, but is intended to make a constructive contribution. In any case this book, even in its theoretical discussions, has its origin in practice—or rather in thoughts originating from practical work.

Some of my articles, scattered over a number of reviews and periodicals from 1946 onwards, already contain a certain amount of preparatory work, as well as what might be termed preliminary sketches for parts of this book. This preparatory work in fact reflects the slow process of 'thoughts about practice' to which I have just alluded. Thus the attentive reader will probably find much that is familiar; the more so since, during these years of preparation, I have seen a number of my ideas confirmed and completed through research carried out by others. Gratefully, I recall that one of these publications even went so far as to express regret that I had not yet co-ordinated my preparatory essays into a whole; yet this very acceptance and use of my ideas has held me back from hasty publication, until such time as I could feel that my thinking *as a whole* was sufficiently mature. I am anxious, therefore, that this book should be discussed as freely as possible—*as a whole*—by which I do not mean that I am presenting the world with a ready-made panacea, excluding other ideas. I should be more pleased if a few of the facts and theories set out here led readers and critics to draw a number of different conclusions, than if the many facts and theories led always to one and the same, fundamentally preconceived, conclusion.

A few words on terminology may not be amiss here. In the context of the subject here treated, I mean by 'analysis' a process essentially invented by Freud and used to investigate the unconscious: the free association of such contents of the psyche as dreams and spontaneous ideas. However, though I use this term to mean this technique, I do not mean it to include the whole corpus of theory, explanation and popularisation of Freud, elaborated by that master's more orthodox disciples. Jung also claimed to be working with 'analysis'; so do a number of other people, including, in all modesty, the author of this book and his Research Group for Depth Psychology in Vienna. I am very sorry to be forced to appear, to many readers, as yet another heretic of psychoanalysis, but I cannot accept its dogmatism: in fact, the real heresy would lie in just such a dogmatism of non-dogmatic, partial truths; that is of statements which are neither wholly truth nor error. All heresy, indeed, is totalitarian; but the curse of totalitarianism lies heavily on the present age, and therefore also on its psychology.

The author of this book, then, is neither a Freudian nor a Jungian nor an Adlerian; but neither is he an eclectic, and certainly not the 'pope' of a new psychoanalytic 'Church' or sect: he does not wish to obstruct the path of free discovery, either for himself or others. For this very reason he has a great desire to express his gratitude to his 'training analyst', V. E. von Gebsattel, who understood how to create and stimulate in him the love for freedom.

VIENNA, 1951.

Note

All the author's references to publications in the footnotes have been left as cited in the original Austrian edition. A list of English translations of the main works has, however, been appended on p. 228 for this English language edition.

INTRODUCTION

1. *The defection from the hierarchy of values*

FOR thousands of years, psychology was a branch of philosophy. The subject of psychology, the study of man, was subordinate to the total world view, that is to a hierarchy in which God, the world and all it contains, and man with his own characteristics, feelings and thoughts, had not yet been wrenched apart but formed a coherent whole.

Thus, while it was possible to approach the total structure of human knowledge from different angles, the enquirers would be sure to arrive at the same world view in the end, as long as certain consistent rules of thought were observed. In this unity of knowledge concerning the soul of man, always related in certain essential ways to the world, his fellow men and God, metaphysics was the logical and living result of the contemplation of nature. Man as the subject of psychology was unimaginable outside a stable system of relationships and values.

Medieval society was as yet unaware of man as an object of knowledge, divorced from this frame of reference; nor indeed did it conceive of any object of knowledge singled out of the world view. The process of fragmentation began when the world order became centred on man. As a result of humanism, man's relation to an order above him came to be neglected and ignored; the main emphasis of evaluation has changed accordingly. All values were primarily placed in relation to man. But this meant that man's loneliness increased. He was no longer sheltered within the hierarchy of values; indeed, in his Promethean optimism, he believed that he himself could establish and embody the highest values. He thus came to see as absolute values what he had previously regarded as relative, mutable and transitory.

The dawn of humanism, the Reformation and the rise of modern democracy, contributed to the twofold process of relative values becoming absolutes and, in direct consequence, of absolute values becoming relative ones. It was not only man who, in loosening or even breaking the ties of his metaphysical relationships, became free and autonomous; the absolutised values of freedom and science themselves became independent of man. A curious centrifugal movement resulted. Man's liberation from his Creator was the prelude to the absolute independence of all creatures, including his own; economic and political theories, for instance, turned into ends in themselves. Depending on whether he tended to confer absolute value on an abstract individual or on an abstract society of individuals, man fell a prey to nihilism or to totalitarianism. Indeed, the more he placed himself at the apex of the hierarchy or scale of values, the more uncertain became his relationship with the world. It was as if politics, economics, technology and art were all in some way becoming independent of him and threatening to enslave him—which is exactly what happened during the disasters that marked the first half of our century.

God was 'dead'. His place was taken by total man, with his reason and his urge towards enlightenment. Soon man became superman; but this entailed the appearance of subman. This divorce is, paradoxically, implicit in the very belief in progress. Between the wars it was the fashion in certain reactionary circles to deny the reality of progress, yet progress has brought forth great things. Through such ideas as liberty, equality, fraternity, humanity has helped gradually to free the weak, the poor and the sick. Women have become emancipated, and so have whole nations and races; the goal of this gradual liberation was greater justice, health, and happiness. But the *hubris* of this uprooted, immanent, absolutised concept of humanity was soon to reveal itself. Humanism in the service of total man toppled over into its own contradiction and disavowal, and progress went into a terrifying decline; alongside a purely formal progress came the murder of liberty and human dignity, the extermination of the helpless, mass murder, total war, concentration camps, the atom bomb—all the vast misery and dread of this century.

Since man opted out of the traditional scale of values, it

was the relation to values in the first place that became 'immanent', the values themselves were no longer regarded as objective, but as depending purely on his human and subjective point of view. But soon not only the relation to values, but values themselves became 'immanent'. Man came to believe that his position did not depend on the hierarchy of objective values, but the position of the values on him. Thus from a being that recognized values, he became a being that determined them. The world order now depended not on objective truth but on man's judgment or utility. This naturally led to the denial of obedience, to a *non serviam*. Whom, indeed, should antonomous man obey but his reason or his interest or his desire for power? Unfortunately, reason and interest and the desire for power are, precisely, very relative things; and despite its goodwill, mankind was soon forced to realize that it is not yet in a position to build a valid order out of such materials. Man was able to devise various systems of order; but these systems, relative as they are in themselves, soon put forward totalitarian claims. For who was to establish their relativity if there was no longer any frame of reference to objective values?

We shall see that psychology also underwent this development, absolute and relative values changing places. Psychology is a gauge of the intellectual current, since its chosen subject is man himself, who overturns and re-evaluates the scale of values. Thus psychology was also drawn into the centrifugal movement; it investigated man's less essential characteristics, taken in isolation from the rest (as in experimental psychology) or else it reduced all the values it could find in the human soul to immanence, and then declared them to be superstructures based on human reason or human interest, or human urges. Like the rest of human order, the psychology of man also fell a victim either to scepticism or to the totalitarian exaggeration of its own conclusions. Either it saw man as an endless repetition of one and the same model, or it saw the whole world as being full of 'exceptional cases' instead of living men and women.

2. *The historical background of modern psychology*

It is characteristic of the situation of man today that contemporary psychology is in the process of undergoing a profound change. The twentieth century may well be termed the 'psychological century; the unprecedented flowering of psychology during this period has rapidly degenerated into a peculiar rankness. Present day man is in a bad way. The process we have outlined above (absolute values becoming relative and relative ones absolute) seems to have reached a provisional and highly paradoxical state. At no time in history has man believed himself to be the absolute centre of the world quite as much as he does today; and yet at no time in history was he quite so relative, so powerless, so endangered. It is therefore quite understandable that psychology should be the keystone in the structure of modern science; but it also becomes clear, for the same reasons, that the picture of man given by modern psychology is extraordinarily incomplete and relative. It is, accordingly, impossible to speak of a unity in psychology. Broadly speaking, psychological research can be divided into two streams, which both succeed each other in time and run parallel to each other. One of them concentrates on the uniqueness and significance of man, the other tries to find a common denominator for what is specifically human on the one hand and the general laws of nature on the other. On the whole, professional psychiatrists and careful observers would probably agree that contemporary psychology has returned to a position less inimical to spiritual concepts than was the case only fifty years ago. It is possible to observe tentative efforts towards overcoming that split in the image of man to which we have already referred. This is especially true in depth psychology, which, although it uses the tools of traditional psychoanalysis, is far more cautious and far less categorical in presenting its conclusions than was the case in Freud's day.

Psychology, originally an offshoot of philosophy, became a discipline of natural science some decades ago. At first it seemed no longer to have anything in common with Aristotelian-Thomist theory; like other natural sciences, psychology proposed to regard as credible only what had been empirically proved. It appeared possible to keep psychology and one's general outlook on life in separate, watertight compartments. Psychology sought objectivity and neutrality. Man, however, is in the first instance a subject, and he lacks neutrality with regard to himself; so that a certain doubt is cast at the very outset on the possibility of a neutral science of man about man. Old-fashioned psychology, and we are already entitled to apply that adjective to the psychology of, say, before the first World War, could not but acknowledge this difficulty; but since it saw the model for all science in the objective experiments of physics, it regarded introspection (the subject looking into himself) as highly suspect, and preferred to arrange repeatable experiments with man as an object.

It is all too easy, and therefore unfair, to smile at the dryness of experimental psychology. All research consists of patient minutiae. But if we compare the investment in terms of time and means with the actual results achieved by experimental psychology, we are amazed at their paucity, and above all by the fact that they never seem to be about man himself, but only about his peripheral activity. The image of man derived from experimental psychology is like those personal descriptions to be found in passports: if the photograph were not there, all we should have is exact information about the holder's height and a few meaningless generalities. In experimental psychology, man became a robot whose reactions were very carefully measured, but about whose soul the professional psychologist knew far less than did, for instance, the witch-doctor of an African tribe. Since psychology admitted only what was measurable and repeatable, it suffered from a peculiar 'psychophobia'. This weakness was further enhanced by the fact that the artificial isolation from any kind of basic outlook on life became itself a concealed outlook on life. The resolute attempt to avoid value judgments amounted to a prejudice. Indeed one of the most foolish prejudices of old-fashioned psychology was the equation of the psyche with the consciousness on the one hand, and its reduction to the physiological correlate on the other.

Affective or emotional life in particular was hardly the concern of this method of research. Emotions can neither be reliably measured nor experimentally repeated. Moreover reason regards them with suspicion and often considers them undesirable. Yet sometimes they avenge themselves in strange and insidious ways: they dictate rules of conduct to the reason and blind its consciousness to such an extent that it remains unaware of the real motives of its behaviour. The ancient truth, namely that consciousness is influenced by emotional forces which it is too blind to perceive, was surely already well known to the educators of the Stone Age; but it was lost to modern psychiatrists some of whom, even today, still speak of psychology as 'the science of conscious experience'. The ideological foundation of a crumbling social order supported this delusion, which itself reinforced hypocrisy and formalism; yet another piece of evidence that unconscious desires also leave their traces on consciousness.

3. Freud's Revolution

Psychology, however, underwent a revolution, which preceded the great social revolutions by a few years; its prime mover was Sigmund Freud. It took him several decades to convince at least some psychiatrists that human actions are neither the product of pure reason nor mere reactions and reflexes, but complicated results of transformed affectivity. Affectivity, he maintained, was the mainspring which set human development in motion. Long before a baby's consciousness awakens, his way of acting is determined by affective experiences, and long after the proud consciousness has ostensibly become the cause of human activity, the latter is still imperceptibly influenced by old affective experiences. Affectivity itself, however, is directed towards pleasure: the whole of man's maturing and developing is nothing but the tension and adaptation between the urge towards pleasure and the social order. Fossilized remains of the unsatisfied urge towards pleasure are repressed from consciousness through identification with the representatives of the social order; but, working from the unconscious, they continue to have largely the same effects. In fact Freud's observations, as though by magic, made it possible to find a common denominator for all that was discordant, dark, and incomprehensible in the human psyche.

Freud was a merciless observer and had a genuine talent for analysis; but like his opponents the experimental psychologists, he believed physics to be the model of all sciences. Also, in his system the apparent neutrality of the empiricist conceals a certain definite outlook on life. The reduction of all the works of man to the pleasure principle was based on the fact that the pleasure sphere is the oldest tangible stratum of human development. From this Freud concluded that all the strata of human existence are causally determined by this oldest layer; this was the fallacy in his philosophical thinking. His *hubris* did not principally lie in the utter confusion between life-urge and sexuality—Freud himself was a severe and pessimistic puritan—but, although his thinking did transform man from the robot of the experimental psychologists into a living being with pulsating drives and urges, it did nothing to reinstate him in an ordered world. Man was still left to himself, without objective values, without a fixed frame of reference. His being was simplified to the extreme: the most primitive stratum was supposed to explain all the others; the life of drives and urges contained within itself all the manifold exchanges between man and the world; all values were now to be regarded as immanent. The dark side of humanism, which had placed man at the centre of the world but had neglected his relation to a Creator, now tended to isolate him more and more. Since man carried his own laws within him, he must perforce either fall a prey to solipsism or be sacrificed to the good of the species through totalitarianism.

Sigmund Freud was, perhaps, the last great humanist. His system carried both dangers within itself: the reduction of all values to immanence and the relentless demands of modern society. In the works of this upright and freedom-loving man we can detect the first faint signs of the anthill-state, and perhaps still more clearly the philosophy of despair in a world without values, as it was later to be preached by certain existentialists. It is a rewarding exercise to study a portrait of Freud, for we shall then understand better how this man, with his penetrating eyes and the bitter lines round his mouth, starting from the pleasure principle, finally arrived at the view that the purpose of all life is death.

Yet we owe a debt of reverence to him. That great sceptic had his own fanaticism—he was a fanatic for truth. Three German-speaking Jews have in our time changed utterly, down to the depths, the image of our social order, the very structure of the universe and the image of man: Marx, Einstein and Freud. All three contributed to raise man and to humiliate him deeply, to increase his self-reliance as well as his insecurity; it is because of these three men that we live in an age of social upheaval, of

the re-evaluation of the totality of the cosmos, and in a psychological age. It would be madness to attempt simply to undo
their influence and that of their successors, but the problems
they left us are not easy to cope with.

There was no need to emphasize, then, that present-day psychology would be unthinkable without Freud. Neither, however,
could we imagine the present age without psychology. Even after
the Freudian revolution it still retained two basic aspects, one
predominantly sociological, the other more individualistic:
Alfred Adler in his 'individual psychology' and the 'socializa-
tion' of Freud's depth-psychology. This was his inarticulate protest against the immanence of Freudian values, and in fact he
achieved a practical system of psychologically based social
adaptation.

Carl Gustav Jung, on the other hand, concerned himself very
little with Adler's vaguely socialising efforts. He bade a final
farewell to the analogies derived from energetics on which both
Freud's system of instincts and Adler's utilitarian scheme were
based. His purpose was to penetrate to the very core of man, to
the hidden treasure in the depth of his soul, in order to reach
the frontier that guards the inexpressible mystery of his being.
It was also the first time that a scientist succeeded, through the
painstaking labour of a lifetime, through patient analysis of the
psychological facts, in plumbing the depths and scaling the
heights hitherto only guessed at by philosophers and poets. Jung
was forced to conclude that the veil of the unconscious concealed
not only the child's unsatisfied pleasure-urge, but also immeasur-
able realms of archaic experiences common to the whole of
mankind. Bees achieve amazing things by means of specific instinct; but they have renounced individuality, each is merely the
organ of the collective. Man, on the other hand, strives towards
individuation, towards utmost consciousness, which is, however,
dialectically related to the psychological capabilities of the
species as a whole. The great problem of man's life, accordingly,
is whether he shall be unknowingly at war with the collective
unconscious which governs his species and be broken in the process, or whether, on the contrary, he shall be instinctively aware
of its voice, clarify it through his consciousness and make use of
it for the development of his personality.

The revolutionary feature of Jung's complex psychology is that he discovered by empirical means certain important functions of the unconscious which determine the individual's relationships to the opposite sex, to society, to the dark side of his own reason and morality. These functions of the psyche Jung called poetically 'anima' (or in women 'animus'), 'persona' and 'shadow'. But there is also a psychological function, the most important of all, which governs the individual's relationship to the opposite sex, society and the reverse of his reason and morality, which Jung calls the 'Self'. With commendable modesty, Jung resisted all attempts to go beyond the frontiers of empirical psychology and further to define this 'Self'; but it must be admitted that there is a certain gnostic element in this description. To abstain from conclusions just at the point where they might shed essential light on the facts themselves is to be neutral only in appearances. Jung's 'Self' is numinous, it is the highest good and infinity. The observant reader may wonder: is it God? Is it the first original 'ground' of the soul? Is it the soul which, like Narcissus, makes God in its own mirror image?

Certainly Jung's psychology does not purport to be a theology. But it may admit of a sober conclusion which points to the possibility of restoring the psyche in its solitude into a frame of value references. For if all archetypes are functions of the psyche, responsible for the mutual effects between it and its objects, the central archetype itself cannot be but an illusion. 'What is illusion?' Jung retorts, rephrasing Pilate's question. Our disjointed age cannot believe in illusions, which is the greatest illusion of all. What kind of serious symptom is it of our thinking and feeling when the exponent of the pleasure principle has to subordinate life to the death-urge, when the teacher of 'individual' psychology has to find his criteria exclusively in society, and when the explorer of the collective unconscious discovers the eternal treasure in the very depths of an all-embracing reflected image?

Man cannot find himself unless at the same time he can find expression for his relationships; conversely, he cannot achieve genuine relationships as long as he is not conscious of himself. This is the dangerous paradox of modern psychology, which is being discovered step by step in our time. It appears that psychology evolves towards a universal and comprehensive image.

4. *Results and new questions*

If we consider contemporary depth psychology we shall find first of all the results of the work done before the first World War or between the wars. They are the fruits of Freud in psycho-analysis, and of his great disciple and opponent, C. G. Jung. Other depth psychologists, among them Adler and some others, have contributed to the multi-coloured mosaic of sometimes con-tradictory and one-sided systems. The work of L. Szondi, for instance, should especially be mentioned. Its theoretical founda-tion is still largely hypothetical, but its practical significance is already assured. Szondi investigates the role of fate in psycho-logical development by tracing it back to the kinship uncon-scious, to the psychological and biological kinship between in-dividual and instinctive life. In general depth psychology shows man as a self-sufficient being or species, establishing values through his socialised consciousness, which is born in the dark regions of the instincts, or the collective unconscious. These values may either be purely the products of his psychological history, or they may be recognised and confirmed by that his-tory; psychology need concern itself only with the *solus ipse* or, at most, the community. The claim of all these systems to repre-sent the whole of psychology is somewhat strange. Yet it must be conceded that a simple selection, a tolerant mixture of all systems, is wrong, because there should be *one* truth, *one* anthro-pology concerning men. But none of these systems is an anthropology in this sense, however well each may, taken by itself, apprehend and even affect certain structures; for instance in psychotherapy, where each school has its own record of suc-cesses and failures.

The same exclusiveness has also coloured certain newer trends, particularly those which proclaimed the emergence of the 'whole' man. Among these are various forms of depth psychology which have been influenced by existentialist thought. They represent reactions brought about by the second World War, which were directed against the denigration of the spirit. Charles Baudouin, a Geneva psychologist, aptly observed in this connec-tion that more is lost than gained by replacing depth psychology with its subordination to laws and rules, with an existential outlook without a psycho-physical foundation. The nihilism of the psychological age cannot be overcome by a stoic heroism. The experience of 'being thrown into the world' can entail conscious responsibility only if one is quite clear both about the part played by determination and about the scale of values in the world. Yet the existentialist reaction was a necessary one. Classical depth psychology saw man as a (presumably) strictly determinate being. Its method required retrospective analysis to trace his motives back to the discovery of causes. This meant that unfree conditioning alone, rather than free motivation, came to be expressed. Concepts like 'decision' and 'responsibility' can be meaningful only if seemingly free motives are not determined by unrecognised complexes.

The question which a new generation of psychologists will ask is not so much whether man is a determinate being or responsible, as *how* his specific freedom *within* the psychophysical determinants can best be represented and used within a unified and unequivocal anthropological framework. Scientific method does not seem quite adequate here, because man is not an object like other objects, but a self-contemplating subject capable of determining values. To take all aspects into account, even those which cannot be quantitatively or causally determined, is already perhaps to philosophise (Baudouin); but anthropology necessarily includes some such activity. Thus a *universal, integral* depth psychology overlaps into the realms of both philosophy and science. All human success and failure has two aspects: a causal, determinate aspect, and one that is purposive and value conscious.

In the first part of this book we shall be concerned in detail with one example of our theory, which is neurosis, that disease typical of our age. We shall see that neurosis cannot be explained and understood from one single viewpoint. We shall also attempt to show that classical depth psychology, itself being the product of modern mental attitudes, shows symptoms of neurosis. Indeed, depth psychology has tried to define and treat neurosis from an isolated point of view. Constitutional disposition, repressed and unsublimated urges, a social compensation of the inferiority feeling, inadequate integration of the shadow, these are some of the partial explanations. But one could also inquire into their existential value or lack of value. Every symptom has a definite cause, yet at the same time it is bound up with destiny, and in the last analysis constitutes a choice made in a situation of conflict. In neurosis, however, this choice is at logger-heads with reality and hampers the harmonious development of man. We shall endeavour to show that it is like clinging to values which should normally already have been outgrown. It thus represents a defection from the necessary values of our existence. It is what I would define as life-heresy, the fallacy of regarding relative values as absolutes. Above all it is the neurotic choice of immanent-egotistical claims by the immature individual which turns 'myself' into an absolute value. But at the same time neurosis is a self-punishment, a cry of the repressed conscience, and this is its positive existential aspect.

Although depth psychology originated in the retrospective analysis of the neurotic symptoms, it also regarded the significance of the immanent historical development of the individual as an absolute. Thus it fell into the very same false absolutes which constitute the existential significance of the neurotic symptom. To this extent depth psychology partakes of the totali-tarianism of our time—the absolute authority conferred on a partial truth; and of its nihilism—the immanent character assigned to truth itself. Many reactions against the old psycho-analysis were in turn 'anti-absolutes', a process familiar to us from the whole picture of contemporary life.

Totalitarianism and nihilism are the two aspects of a single fall from the true scale of values. Not only in politics, but in every field of human thought and endeavour, the problem today is to retrace our link with the hierarchy of true values.

Part I

The Problem

Chapter One

CONFUSION IN DEPTH PSYCHOLOGY

5. *The 'nothing but' solution*

IT has become a commonplace after half a century of passion-
ate debate to say that Freud achieved the most accurate analysis of psychological processes. His method is genuinely an
analysis, the reduction of a complex whole into its component
parts. This means that it is based on the same assumptions as,
for instance, reflexology or associational psychology. This method
can be fully accepted from a utilitarian point of view and has,
moreover, proved its worth by numerous successes. We must,
however, draw the essential distinction between the method itself
and the conclusion that the whole is merely the sum total or
product of its parts. The nineteenth century cherished this illusion: for instance, as soon as it was possible to prove that man is
made up of chemical elements, it was at once stated that man is
nothing but a sum of chemicals; when uninterrupted evolution
from the anthropoid ape to *homo sapiens* became highly probable, it was promptly said that man was essentially indistinguish-
able from the apes. Freud was a research worker of outstanding
merit, but he was a poor philosopher. He discovered the chain
of causation from the smallest everyday mistakes back to the
unconscious elements in our psyche; and from this he concluded
that a reductive explanation also permitted a prospective one,
with which conclusion Jung came to disagree. In philosophy
Freud was attracted to Schopenhauer and Nietzsche, and to the
German materialist philosopher G. T. Fechner. He remarked
himself in his 'self-portrait' that he had a 'constitutional incapacity' for philosophy.

Reductive analysis leaves no room for chance; and indeed,

according to Freud, everything must be explained in terms of rigid determinism:

> He (the indeterminist) will certainly answer: 'Oh, that is not worth explaining; these are little coincidences. What does he mean? Does he intend to affirm that there is any event, however small, which escapes from the chain of universal occurrence, which might just as well not have been as it is?' If a single link in the chain of natural determinism is thus broken, the whole scientific outlook falls to the ground. We might do well to remember the consistency of the religious outlook that 'not a sparrow falls to the ground without God's special will'.[1]

Here Freud unwittingly touched upon a very complicated matter, with which we shall deal later (Section 6) under the name of 'coincidental correspondence' (A. Auersperg): what in reductive analysis appears strictly determined may still, in certain cases, be the working of the free spirit, or even that of divine intervention. Freud defends himself against this possibility: 'The trouble is', he says (op. cit., p. 42), 'that they harbour the illusion of spiritual freedom and are unwilling to give it up. I am sorry to say that on this point I find myself in complete disagreement with them.'

This 'complete disagreement' is based on the fact that psychological associations are always determined by a previous event; that in other words there are in the life of the psyche no groundless, indifferent or replaceable phenomena. Thus in the matter of associations which lead from the dream image to the complex, Freud attacked the indeterminists, and also rejected free will:

> In the main, however, they—the indeterminists—are in the wrong. They are greatly mistaken when they regard as arbitrary the assumption that the dreamer's next association must necessarily lead him, directly or indirectly, to what he is after, when they suppose that the association might just as well be quite desultory and without any connection with the object of the search, and when they believe that it is merely an expression of my faith in God if I expect it to be otherwise. I have already once taken the liberty of pointing out to them that they have a deeply-rooted belief in psychological freedom and arbitrariness—a belief which is, however, quite unscientific and must yield to the claims

[1] Sigmund Freud, *Vorlesungen zur Einführung in die Psychoanalyse*, 5th edition, 1926, p. 21.

of a determinism which also governs the life of the psyche. I must ask you to respect the fact that the patient has thought of this particular thing and of no other. But I am not pitting one faith against another. It can be proved that the association produced by the patient is not arbitrary, not indeterminable, not unconnected with what we are looking for.[2]

Thus every individual destiny is completely predetermined. Let us take, for example, two people, two young girls of equivalent disposition (supposing that were possible); one of them is the daughter of the janitor, the other the daughter of the master of the house. The latter will probably find it easier to sublimate her instincts, and this is the explanation of apparent 'freedom':

> The difference between the two destinies, despite similar experiences, stems from the fact that the *ego* of one girl had undergone a development that did not take place in the other. The janitor's daughter regarded sexual activity later as natural and unobjectionable as in childhood. The master's daughter had experienced the effects of education and accepted its requirements. Her ego had thus built up ideals of feminine purity and integrity incompatible with sexual activity; her intellectual education had lowered her interest in the feminine role assigned to her. Through this higher moral and intellectual development of her *ego* she came into conflict with the claims of her sexuality.[3]

In Adler's individual psychology, at least as it is often presented, the deterministic conception of mental life is not very clearly expressed. Indeed, individual psychology claims to provide not causal but final explanations, which imply that the orientation of life is determined by its 'secret goal'. This 'secret goal', however, is also a sort of figurative image, a continuous compensation for inferiority feelings; and the task of education, or of psychotherapy, is to bring individual aspirations into harmony with society.

> The child's whole capacity for education depends on this feeling of inadequacy. The future thus becomes for him the region that will bring him compensation.[4] Just as an inadequate organ creates an intolerable situation which gives rise to a number of attempts at compensation until the organism once more feels able to meet the

[2] Op. cit., p. 104.   [3] Op. cit., p. 367.
[4] Alfred Adler, *Praxis und Theorie der Individualpsychologie*, 2nd edition, Munich 1924, pp. 9–10.

demands of its environment—in the same way the child's soul in its uncertainty is looking for that source of strength which is to overcome his feelings of insecurity.[5]

If we were looking, in a short-sighted manner, for a psychotherapy as a way of objective confirmation of faith in God and spiritual values, we might regard C. G. Jung's complex psychology and his analytical therapy as being intrinsically suitable for a psychology concerned with values. Of course for Jung as for Freud, the soul can only be represented in terms of energy. Yet for Jung faith in God is no mere sublimation of the sexual instinct, but one of the inborn characteristics of each soul, an archetype. Depth psychology cannot but recognize this archetype. Education, leadership and psychotherapy must know all and promote the human powers necessary for the development of the personality in accordance with their purpose and goal.

> Probably everyone carries a way of life within himself, an irrational form for which no other superior form exists. This can, of course, be no objection to proceed as far as this is possible to normalize and rationalize. If this therapy is sufficiently successful, we can probably leave it at that. If it is unsuccessful, the therapy will have to adapt itself as best it may to the patient's irrational data. Here we must follow nature as our leader, and what the doctor does then is not so much treatment as the unfolding of the creative seeds lying within the patient.[6]

It looks as if this work, which goes beyond the confines of natural science, would require criteria and standards which cannot be derived from psychology itself, but only from metaphysics. But what does Jung's divine archetype mean? His archetypes are, without exception, myths, that is symbolic representations of the collective unconscious mirrored in the individual psyche—'an accumulation of value (= libido) in the unconscious'.[7]

The 'creative seeds' within man are therefore the seeds of a subjective myth. It can be readily imagined to what boundless

[5] Op. cit., p. 53.
[6] C. G. Jung, *Seelenprobleme der Gegenwart*, Zurich 1932, pp. 95-96.
[7] C. G. Jung, *Die Beziehungen zwischen dem Ich und dem Unbewussten*, Zurich 1945, p. 164. The equation between value and libido is Jung's own!—*Author's note.*

relativism, to what pure solipsism the intelligent and patient psychologist will attain, in carefully leading the soul through the labyrinth of the collective unconscious to the divine archetype.

It may be called an illusion—he says[8]— but what is illusion? From what point of view can we describe something as an illusion? Is there anything, for the soul, which we may describe as an *illusion*? . . . What we call illusion is perhaps a spiritual fact of enormous significance[9] . . . In using the concept 'God' we are merely formulating a definite psychological fact, that is, the independent superiority of certain psychic contents, which expresses itself in their capacity to thwart the will, obsess consciousness and influence moods and actions. It will arouse indignation that an inexplicable mood, a nervous disturbance or even an uncontrolled vice should in some sense be a manifestation of God; but religious experience in particular would suffer an irreparable loss if such things, even when they appear bad, were to be artificially distinguished from autonomous psychological contents. To minimize them with a 'nothing-but' explanation is a fallacious euphemism; it can only push them away out of sight, and the advantage gained is generally only an apparent one—merely a somewhat changed illusion . . . The conception of God as an autonomous psychological content turns God into a moral problem—which is admittedly very uncomfortable. But if this problem does not exist, then God cannot be real either, for then he no longer intervenes in our lives at any point. If he does not pose a moral problem, he is nothing but a piece of historical mumbo-jumbo, or of philosophical sentimentality. It is possible, by completely discarding the notion of a 'Divine Being' and keeping strictly autonomous contents, to remain within the bounds of intellectual and empirical decorum; but it means glossing over something which, psychologically, is indispensable; for only the use of the concept of a 'Divine Being' can accurately express the actual way in which we experience the effects of autonomous contents . . .

It would therefore seem advisable in searching for the divine archetype, to approach the impressive structure of Jung's depth psychology with due caution. In his thinking the great Zurich psychologist would resist having to relate the autonomous con-

---

[8] *Seelenprobleme der Gegenwart*, Rascher, Zurich 1931, p. 113.
[9] *Die Beziehungen zwischen dem Ich und dem Unbewussten*, Rascher, Zurich 1939, pp. 203–205.

tent which he has discovered in the soul to an objective being; but in so doing he robs himself of the last possibility of overcoming neurosis. He may be right in saying that the divine archetype is a reflection of the collective unconscious, but this statement, like Freud's theory of sublimation, requires a metaphysical foundation if the existential problem of superstition is to be freed from its vicious circle.

6. *The symbolism of scientific language and 'coincidental correspondence'*

Depth psychology followed in the wake of the change in the human image. As we have seen, however, the human image was gradually taken out of its system of relationships, and thus became unique among other objects of knowledge. All scientific disciplines became individual problems, and, following the rise of natural science, developed a preference for the modes of thought and the terminology of the natural sciences. Left to itself depth psychology has built up a kind of short-circuited view of the world, which was supposed to co-ordinate its conclusions and enable them to illuminate each other. This abortive view of the world, itself the result of the causal-deterministic findings of the scientific method, could not but become causal-deterministic in its turn. On the other hand, the far-reaching discoveries of depth psychology have themselves influenced the whole of our century's thinking and have enormously furthered research. The achievements of depth psychology in the realms of education and therapy have enabled it to overcome great opposition; but it has itself helped to assimilate the image of man still further to the modes of thought pertaining to natural science.

However, just as phylogenetic discoveries in no way invalidate man's special position in creation, the causal-deterministic findings of psychology do not invalidate the unique character of the human spirit. The principle of causality is generally valid for the finite and the transitory; it is necessarily present in all modes of being endowed with potentiality; without, however, having *a priori* the character of an essential necessity. Yet the necessity of causation in general should never be confused with physical or biological causation. It should be emphasized that psychology, in drawing a connection between higher and primary phenomena, may never reduce the former to the latter. 'The concept of the unconscious enables us to discover a continuity in psychology which is, however, not an identity . . . One thing must not be reduced to another, as for example art to sexuality, love to biological drives, personality to the individual, but each may be represented as forming part of a continuity.[10]

Everything that we have experienced is effective for the whole of the rest of our lives. Thus, psychoanalysis shows us that past experience is and must be contained in all ensuing experience as a kind of a formal co-determinator: but this form of determination could also take place in another field (for example on the level of freedom), and thus things might also be different. It is one thing to show, as does psychoanalysis: 'It is thus, because it was thus'; and quite another thing to say: 'Since it was thus, it could under no circumstances be otherwise'—a statement which no form of psychoanalysis could prove. In following the process of development, freedom remains; and this is not in contradiction with depth psychology. If we unravel a process in physics, we can determine retrospectively that it had to take place thus and not otherwise; but the same retrospective determination cannot apply, for example, to genetics. The supernatural character of grace, then, is to be interpreted even more decisively as a principle of life which does not shape our ends from past experience but works directly from the eternal present. What the psychoanalyst classifies as neurosis, that is as an illness, can in certain circumstances be for the priest or spiritual adviser the decisive phase on the way towards sanctification.

The example shows that it is not possible to compare the different aspects of one and the same fact, because they are essentially different. From the biogenetic and psychogenic angle of this sort of scientific investigator, the supernatural appears as a *deus ex machina*. In any case it is pointless to deduce the supernatural from analytic observation of the natural order.

The scepticism with which our age regards any kind of metaphysics clearly appears in the psychoanalytical school and its

[10] Charles Baudouin, *Découverte de la Personne*. Quoted by Georges Parcheminey, 'Le Problème de l'Ambivalence' in *Amour et Violence—Etudes Carmélitaines*, Bruges-Paris 1946, p. 43.

ramifications, together with mechanistic images such as the 'stream' of consciousness, feelings being 'pent up' or 'repressed', the libido being 'displaced', or the pleasure-principle being trophically 'adjusted'; and it appears more particularly in the overvaluation of experience as against life itself. According to depth psychology the ego is contained, as a variable not specially capable of extrapolation, in the stream of conscious and unconscious experience. Similarly such figures as father, mother, beloved, are modes of experience, which are shaped and valued in relation to historically determined basic reactions, which have themselves been shaped by previous experience. Even the archetypes of Jung's spiritual philosophy are as it were self-evolved and not encounters with a Being that exists above us, around us and in us. The materialistic approach, together with the impossibility of investigating the higher levels of being with merely scientific means, has led psychology to the dangerous fallacy of denying the very existence of a higher level—that is, of denying the whole of man's spiritual and supernatural life, and in particular his freedom; or at the very least regarding these things as immanent.

It is true that biological methods have shown the dependence of man on the concatenation of his psychological reactions and, beyond this, on his own constitution and his psycho-physical environment: the spirit of man is largely dependent on his body. The fallacy lies in interpreting this broad dependence as an absolute determination, and declaring that man is determined purely and simply by the concatenation of his reactions. Yet in every free act of choice the *whole* man, including his constitution, takes part in the decision. His constitution, therefore, and also the influence of his environment, are among the determining factors in every decision. In itself, however, the individual constitution is not an exhaustive cause of free decision, even though its effect is most significant in every free act. A free act is, in the last resort, brought about by conscious recognition of a motivation. It is through motivation that an indifferent and largely determined act becomes, in the end, a free act.

Depth psychology has evolved so-called 'teleological' or 'finalistic' explanations, but in actual fact these are just as deterministic as the causal ones. Instead of a concatenation backwards, it is directed forwards and the chain of causation being of course maintained.

Indeed it could hardly be otherwise, since psychology, which once occupied a subordinate position in the system of relationships, has now become an autonomous and self-sufficient discipline. Accordingly it soon came to use strictly empirical methods modelled on those of natural science. Psychology, which obviously relies more on subjective feelings than other disciplines, was expected to show an 'objectivity' akin to that of the exact sciences. But our century has carried the emphasis on the natural sciences, which purport to teach only what they can prove, to the extreme of saying: 'From now on, you shall believe only what you know.' And what do you know? 'That which is incontrovertibly proven.' But only what is generally valid, what is 'objective', is considered to be 'proven'. That is why the concept of objectivity is so important in modern thought. In what follows we shall attempt to discriminate between this concept, which pertains to exact science, and the corresponding ontological system.

The findings of exact science are 'objective'. This, however, merely means that the life of the mind is subjective, that is, contained in the ego, and must be carefully distinguished from our outward-directed efforts at cognition, in which we work together with our fellow-men and which are termed scientific or *objective*. 'Subjective' accordingly describes *intra*-individual perception, and 'objective' the *inter*-individual form of expression through which we manage to make ourselves understood among each other, but which can never enable us to reach the intangible core of things. The most exact scientific method can never grasp either the true essence of things or their existential significance for the experiencing subject; these can only be translated into a generally valid technical language. It is of basic importance, therefore, not to confuse the phenomenalistic terminology used by the exact sciences with ontology, the science of being. Thus, for instance, in any discussion on causality, a distinction must be drawn between the terminological concept of 'appearance' (which logically includes that of 'cause'), and our perception, which in the ontological sphere may at best enable us to conclude on the probable isomorphic relation between two appearances. Between the logical pairing of concepts 'cause-appearance', and the probable ontological isomorphism 'two perceptions', there is a significant connection which, however, should not necessarily be interpreted as absolute, that is, as one of uninterrupted causation. Prince Alfred Auersperg called this relation coincidental correspondence,[11] and it became important under this name in Victor von Weizsäcker's work on the *Gestaltkreis*.[12] Coincidental correspondence simply means:

> If I offer the senses a physical arrangement determined in such and such a way, I get a certain definite perception. Nothing can be definitely affirmed beyond the coincidence itself, which is rooted in coherence (in the impermanent unity in which a subject is ordered with regard to his environment—*Author's note*), and there is no transformation-machine to manufacture perception or experience out of the stimulus. This leaves the way open for neuro-physiology to supply the missing causal link between stimulus and the life of sensation.[13]

The methodology of natural science enables us to describe series of coincidental correspondences, inasmuch as we have at our disposal stylized ways of measuring phenomena and translating them into mathematical language. The sentence: 'The temperature in this room is 66°', expresses neither the essence of the warmth itself nor my own perception of the warmth, but translates a factual situation into a symbolic language (the better the thermometer, the better the translation). But then neither does the sentence: 'Religious feelings are the result of sublimation' express either the essence of God or the actual nature of religious feelings. It systematizes a quite hypothetical causal connection between structural characteristics of the soul, which is regarded as an object. It is evident that metaphysical matter can be neither measured nor exhaustively described, proven nor denied by the methods of natural science; the utmost such methods can do is establish coincidental correspondences between different series. The findings of natural science are necessarily causal and deterministic, but this does not mean that causal determination is the only possible way of arranging data in relation

---

[11] Prince, A. Auersperg and H. Buhrmester, Z. *Sinnesphysiol*, 96, 1936.
[12] V. von Weizsäcker, *Der Gestaltkreis*, Leipzig 1940.
[13] V. von Weizsäcker, op. cit., p. 149.

to each other. If the symbols of physics, energy, the atom, quantums and so on, are not in themselves hypostatic or essential, psychological concepts such as libido, displacement, pent-up feelings, sublimation, projection, introjection, derived from such physical models, are even less so.

The inter-individual way of exact science, which is termed 'objective', leads us to a knowledge of the structures of the world of objects. Indeed, only structural characteristics can be translated into 'objective', generally understandable language. Every 'objective' statement is a translation, as accurate as possible and yet very much simplified, stylised and dependent on method, of a coincidental correspondence (but never of an exhaustive identity!) between intra-individual perception and inter-individual interpretation.

Physics, the most thoroughly charted of all sciences as regards both methodology and content, provides a test for the possibilities of our cognition. Physics is a science of observation, a strictly *a posteriori* science, a methodolgy for the ordering of our perceptions according to certain structural points of view. This makes it the best possible preparation for a philosophy; but in itself it possesses no philosophical conclusiveness. Thus, for instance, the incalculable individual movements of electrons do not philosophically invalidate the principle of causality, any more than classical physics can philosophically invalidate freedom.

We may therefore recapitulate as follows: the objectivity of physics, as was indeed already recognized by the 'Vienna Circle' of Schlick's disciples, is *not* the same thing as metaphysical objectivity: it simply means the inter-individual approach. The method of exact science does not attain the nature of things, but concerns itself with the general structural substratum of *intra*-individual perceptions, which it attempts to arrange methodically. Each member of the series thus evolved stands in a relation of coincidental correspondence to subjective perception.

The evergrowing preoccupation with 'objectivity', however, evidently tends to replace metaphysical objectivity by the objectivity of physics, that is by a merely *inter*-individual approach. This is pushed to the extreme of believing only what can be 'objectively' proven. Mankind seems to have lost the shelter of belief; perhaps this is the crisis of our time, the cause of the

B

general feeling of insecurity which makes psychotherapy more necessary than ever before.

7. *The unreliability of the norm*

Depth psychology primarily had its origin in the observation of mentally sick persons from the point of view of natural science. It immediately claimed a methodology akin to natural science, and took energetics as its model. Freud's depth psychology, like Janet's already in part, and even Jung's, is built on a model derived from physics and energetics, which, as we have seen, is far from absolutely valid when applied to psychology.

The generalised application of the natural science approach to depth psychology led inevitably to an inadequate philosophy. Good and healthy have become synonyms, even though we do not know what we actually mean by mental health. In practice, an attempt is made to answer the question by means of a third synonym, which is sought in the pleasure-principle. The answers given by the different therapeutic schools to the question: 'What is meant by mental health?' can all more or less be reduced to the following formula: 'Mental health means to be at peace with oneself.' This formula implies, however, that the criterion of mental health is the pleasure of the psyche's biological bearer, not her metaphysical principle. The expression 'to be at peace with oneself' is far removed from metaphysics; it denotes a condition of pleasurable balance, whether intra- or inter-individual.

This application of the pleasure principle is a fallacious generalization; it gives to the findings of medical psychology based on natural science an unmerited absolute value. As a result people who suffer on account of their deviation from an abstract average norm, or whose deviation causes suffering for society, are declared to be psychopathic or neuropathic personalities. This distinction may be made from practical motives or by conscious application of the pleasure principle; either way it is enormously significant. Peaceful synthesis remains, indeed, the objective of every soul; but this is an ideal hardly attainable in this world, and least of all by 'scientific' means. But does this mean that a man who struggles with himself, who doubts and occasionally despairs, who is torn apart and yearns for peace and oneness, is necessarily 'mentally ill' because he is overcome by pain or grief?

Does he automatically become 'healthy' if his pain is removed or his grief overcome by *any* means? Should he in the interests of his 'recovery' be freed from his conflict in all circumstances? Are not pain and sorrow sometimes far more essential to the health of the soul than 'peace', meaning here pleasure? Particularly for the psychiatrist and for the priest, 'help often consists in making man aware of the anguish he disowns, or even in first surrendering him to his anguish.'[14]

If, however, in view of the unreliability of the pleasure principle for the evaluation of norms we seek some other mathematically verifiable criterion, the solid ground of biology has to be left behind altogether; for instance in the definition evolved by one of the leading scholars in this field, which has been incorporated into countless handbooks:

> Understandably enough, psychiatry cannot make use of a norm based on value, the specific content of which lies outside the realm of scientific discussion. We will therefore confine ourselves to the average norm . . . From the point of view of the average norm, we can now define abnormal personalities as follows: Abnormal personalities are variations, deviations from an average of human personalities, an average which we perceive though we cannot exactly define it. The deviations may be upwards or downwards, may entail a personality richer or poorer than the norm. This means that it is quite unimportant whether a particular deviation from the average norm is regarded as positive or negative from an ethical or social point of view. Seen from the point of view of the average norm, the saint and the poet are as abnormal as the criminal; all three lie outside the average of personality. It is obvious that all personalities which are in any way remarkable, peculiar, notable in any aspect of their being, must be included in this definition . . . If we wished to represent all abnormal personalities, ours would be an immeasurable task. What we actually do is select two groups which we define as psychopathic personalities. We say: Psychopathic personalities are those abnormal personalities which suffer from their abnormality or from whose abnormality society suffers. This delimitation is an arbitrary one and is made on purely practical grounds.[15]

[14] V. E. von Gebsattel, *Christentum und Humanismus*, Klett, Stuttgart, p. 63.
[15] Kurt Schneider, *Die Psychopathischen Persönlichkeiten*, 8th edition, 1946, pp. 2–3.

Mental health is thus evaluated according to a purely abstract norm. With this conception of mental health there is considerable danger of failing to distinguish essentially between a deviation upwards and a deviation downwards. Thus even depth psychology uses the statistical norm (which in any case is not easy to determine) as a criterion of health. All mental conditions and events which show a deviation from the average balance of the libido, from average capacity for adaptation, from average development of the urges—in other words, all conditions and events which show conflict, tension and suffering—are only too easily explained away as pathological and then cheerfully 'removed', 'resolved', 'analysed away' or 'compensated' by psychotherapy.

Jung noticed that 'we are profoundly dissatisfied if, for instance, we ascribe a poem of Goethe's to his mother complex, or we try to define Napoleon as a case of male protest or explain St Francis of Assisi in terms of sexual repression.'[16] This dissatisfaction is justified and necessary; it is almost an illustration of the thesis that not every dissatisfaction is neurotic, whereas a superstitious and complacent satisfaction would be so. However, it would be equally fallacious to use the spirit as a pretext to disown its biological basis, and to try to shut one's eyes to the fact that sexual repression, which may certainly explain neurosis, can also be present in spiritual achievement. But it does not exhaustively explain the spiritual achievement, and there lies the difference. The close relationship existing between neurotic restlessness or neurotic inhibitions and Augustinian unrest or existentialist anxiety, or between a psychopathic condition and mystical ecstasy, or between psychological infantilism and the 'Little Way' of St Teresa of Lisieux, all this merely means that there is a 'coincidental correspondence' between the data of natural science and the spiritual reality. If we seek a compromise here we shall be forsaking orderly method for chaos. It is not easy to establish a differential diagnosis, for frontiers can be traced only on a single level, whereas the same factual situation presents itself to the theologian and to the biologist according to orders on different levels.

---

[16] C. G. Jung, *Seelenprobleme der Gegenwart*, Zurich 1936, p. 311.

Since all psychological typologies are derived from pathology, they have an understandable but dangerous tendency to evaluate everything from a psychopathological point of view. The 'normal' person, as we have seen, tends to become a colourless abstraction or even a mere sociological function; or else the concept of normality is diluted in an effort to emphasize its relationship to the nearest pathological type. It is not enough to say that 'schizothymous-cyclothymous', 'introvert-extrovert' represent normal values, or that 'the urge of self-assertion' means the urge to perfection, or that 'libido' includes all energy, including spiritual energy; these concepts remain confusing and restrictive and sometimes have a distinctly morbid flavour. 'Science' even tends to burden the 'super-normal' with the same terminology as the 'sub-normal', because it 'deviates' from an abstract norm; thus, for instance, religious grace, if not the whole of religion, is simply fobbed off with pathological terminology.

Understandably enough, this unjustified pretension on the part of psychopathology increases when the saint or the genius genuinely does not stand in the 'normal middle' but, as we have seen, reacts according to his or her natural type in an 'abnormal' direction, or even shows neurotic symptoms. Geniuses and saints, being 'super-normal' people, are not infrequently prone to excessive reactions; and *a priori* it can also be imagined that a neuropathic constitution predisposes to overwhelming experiences which, however, can also be genuine and healthy. Indeed the way towards the development of genius or towards holiness does sometimes lead through a neurosis, which reveals a special tension. It is a mistake to describe everything which in such cases lies outside the abstract norm as 'neurotic' or 'psychopathic'. Since, however, this is what usually happens in practice, we arrive at the untenable situation in which 'science' is particularly eager to detect 'neurotic' symptoms in the 'super-normal' and supernatural—oblivious that so far no one has been able to evolve any satisfactory biological concept of mental health. The value judgments used in this connection, all of them still very tentative, are drawn from sociology, politics, or any view of the world that happens to catch the scientist's fancy.[17]

[17] Cf. Alex von Müralt's courageous book, *Wahnsinniger oder Prophet?*, Zurich, Europa-Verlag, 1946, particularly Sections III and IV.

8. *An example of confusion: freedom and conditioning*

If one had complete knowledge of the hereditary and past history of a person, and even of his 'archetypes', 'hidden purposes' and all the other concepts of teleological depth psychology, it would of course be possible partly to explain his present and predict his future. Classical depth psychology, however, assumes that in these circumstances the present could be entirely explained, and the future entirely predicted; it regards its knowledge of man as totalitarian, what Jaspers called 'total knowledge'. It is from such assumed total knowledge that the illusion stems of total understanding, the explicable act being substituted for the free act. Yet it is possible to imagine a free act which is at the same time in full and spontaneous accord with the subject's constitution and past history. Naturalistic psychology would regard that act as a clear proof of total conditioning. However the freedom of the act does not reside in a violation of past development, indeed a sudden discrepancy between constitution and development could give rise to most effective compulsion. If there is such a thing as being free, it takes place on a higher level than the psychophysical level. A free act can make use of constitution, past and environment as bases for mental advance. According to this view every free act would be biological action, but something else as well. Naturalistic psychology cannot see beyond biology; the extreme indeterminist on the other hand tends to ignore it. Their debate is conducted with concepts from entirely different levels of being, and can go on for ever without either side convincing the other.

The determinists in the realm of psychology have overlooked one disturbing fact. They regard man as a 'driven' creature, and indeed causal investigations of depth psychology have shown that man is in fact driven, even in the most unexpected ways. But the very recognition that we are under compulsion adds a foreign element to the statement itself. A piece of mechanism that is driven, presumably even an animal that acts according to its instincts, cannot have the feeling of compulsion. Since for the animal compulsion is simply its fated mode of existence, it is unable to stand outside and become conscious of it.

Thus if the findings of exact science fully convince me that there is and can be no freedom, this conviction is only possible because I look beyond my allegedly strictly conditioned form of existence and recognize that there is no freedom. This is absurd because, if I were really confined within the conditioned mode of existence, it would be the only possible and apprehensible mode for me.

Since in differentiating between compulsion and freedom we are dealing with different orders and levels of human existence, instinct and decision may at the same time be factors in action, not just compulsion or just freedom alone. Moreover, in picturing a free act we should not imagine the decision as occurring side by side with instinct. In his compulsion man moves within his own particular mode of existence; to this extent he is therefore, while under compulsion, within the instinct as such, a being *sui generis*. In his decision, on the other hand (again we mean within the decision itself, not besides or before it) man is not pure spirit, nor entirely responsible. Animals are conditioned in a different way. The error of the determinists, therefore, lies in ignoring the qualitative difference between two forms of compulsion.

'Psychological analysis'—this term, as we shall see, comprises the phenomenality of compulsion in a wider sense than classical psychoanalysis, and is indispensable in order not to measure man by theoretical, and sometimes theoretically unrealistic, criteria of freedom. If, then, the Aristotelian Thomist theory of the mind-soul, *anima forma corporis*, has its validity, if matter and form are aspects of one essence, then we must pay regard to the specifically human element in every field. Psychology is not in a position to apprehend human matter without the essential link with its form, or human form without the essential foundation of matter.

The urges of the anthropoid ape most deceptively resemble human urges, and yet they are not human urges, for man, in his urges, and even in his aberrations, is not an animal, but man.

The famous Gestalt psychologist W. Köhler spent some years living among chimpanzees at the research centre at Teneriffe. He tells of one occasion when he wanted to investigate how far chimpanzees are accessible to purely altruistic emotions. Supposing a chimpanzee is still hungury, is he capable of sharing his food with a yet hungrier one?

A male chimpanzee called Sultan was confined, on a starvation diet, to a special cage. A female chimpanzee called Chego—the most intelligent and best-natured of all—would squat down, as soon as she had received her ration of bananas, in her accustomed place, a few steps away from the bars of Sultan's cage. Turning her back to Sultan, Chego began to chew energetically, smacking her lips with satisfaction. Sultan, who had received nothing, began to complain, softly at first, then louder and louder, he scratched his head and rump agitatedly, stretched out his arms towards Chego, picked up pebbles and straws and threw them, as chimpanzees do, in the direction of his wishes; at last he began to jump up and down on his side of the bars with the utmost impatience, screaming as if tormented. Suddenly the female chimpanzee got up, gathered a handful of bananas, took a few steps towards Sultan, handed him the bananas through the bars of the cage, and then returned eagerly to her interrupted meal. Of course after this experience the prisoner repeated his complaint emphatically on the next day, and he actually managed to get fed five days running, in the same way and by the same animal.[18]

What is remarkable, however, is the observation which Köhler added:

> On the sixth day, the big female remained quite unconcerned, however much the male might agitate; probably she had lost interest in him, for on the sixth day began the cold phase of Chego's sexual cycle (as was also evident from other objective criteria) and she reverted to her previous behaviour only after it ended. (*Op. cit.*)

It is not known whether Freud ever knew of this observation. He would have enjoyed it enormously, since no more obvious corroboration of his doctrine of the sublimation of urges could be devised. Where there is no urge to be sublimated, because the urge is repressed, in this example through the disappearance of the sexual urge, there can be no valuable, social, altruistic achievement. Let no one object that this is so only with the anthropoids, that man is not subject to this natural law. Both the practice of depth psychology, and the mere theoretical reflection on whether the phenomenological history of the ennobling and socialising process of the primitive urge should be the same in man and in the higher apes, will show us that there can only be a single line

[18] *Psychologische Forschung*, Vol. I, 1–2, 1921.

from the first step of sublimation in the case of Köhler's female chimpanzee to the highest spiritual achievement of human selflessness.

The psychologists who try to explain human achievement without reference to the vital urge or *libido* are, quite simply, blind. On the other hand, it is essential to remember that this single straight line means, in Charles Baudouin's words, 'a continuity, but by no means an identity'. The female chimpanzee decided upon an altruistic action. Take a selfless action by a human being, in which the original urge is to all appearances unrecognizable, since it is to a large extent already directed towards objects which are in themselves incompatible with its simple satisfaction, let us admit by all means that this selfless action requires the urge insofar as it claims the whole person; after all, it does not take place in a theoretical vacuum. It may be objected that man can work against his urges and sacrifice them, but has not the chimpanzee done just that? And was it not shown by Freud himself that an urge will not be sacrificed unless the sacrifice yields a higher, sublime satisfaction?

This is our problem: the profound contradiction between urge and decision in every human action can be explained neither by the denial of the decision nor by the denial of the urge. The former school of thought affirms, once again in Baudouin's words, the existence of identity on the grounds of continuity. The latter is aware that there can be no question of identity and, with equal short-sightedness, denies the existence of continuity. The former think they have solved the riddle of man if the word 'urge' is used at least once in every sentence. The latter seem to recognize no other names apart from 'spirit' and 'responsibility'.

The chimpanzee could make no statement about her responsibility. Her mode of existence has been laid down for her; she could not base her altruistic actions on choice, on answering the question: 'Shall I follow my original or my sublimated urges?' We do not know how far our human freedom would have been involved in such a situation. For an evaluation of human conduct the mystery of conscience might be significant; in a situation of this kind a human being could have decided upon one line of action. Of course he could have acted otherwise. He could have lied to himself, which the chimpanzee was unable to do. A human being might, for instance, in obedience to the imperative of his conscience, have shared his food with his hungry neighbour, but at the same time he might have been able to repress the original urge towards the selfish satisfaction of his needs; he might have driven his urge into the unconscious; just because it could not be brought into accord with its challenge. An urge of this kind, which does not agree with the ideal image of the self, would be repressed and would thenceforth, unnoticed by the subject, become the seed of future neurosis.

It is true that Sigmund Freud's psychoanalysis regards the 'ego' as a secondary function formed in order to bring about a compromise between the blind demands of the 'id' and the claims of the surrounding world. The 'ego' tries, in its own interests, to do justice both to the urge and to the social law; in this it is assisted by the so-called 'super-ego', by which the Freudians replace conscience. The 'super-ego' is simply a social structure, derived from the fear of the ego, which naturally dreads the prospect of being crushed between the claims of the objective world and of its own urges. For safety's sake it identifies itself with certain models, first of all with the father-image, which is turned into an unconscious ideal. Thus in the last resort, the super-ego is a function of social fear. The growing ego seeks a support in the ideals which are offered to it, and which in themselves contain no guarantee of objective value. The ideal may very well attach itself to a model which, objectively speaking, is negative and should be rejected. Thus the child of a criminal may model his ego-ideal on the criminal, provided he is impressed by his father's personality and can be protected by him from the threat of the outside world. To confuse Freud's super-ego with the conscience is therefore tantamount to a denial of the conscience itself, for the super-ego is a psychologically immanent, essentially relative function.

It should be said at this point that reductive analysis of psychological processes yields completely satisfactory proof of the effectiveness of this dynamic function in every human psyche. From earliest childhood man seeks protection against an alien and menacing world by identifying himself with certain power factors of this world. Even as adults people identify themselves with the claims of society. The civil servant thinks and feels like a civil servant, the actor like an actor, the ruler like a ruler, the burglar like a burglar. Eventually a sort of crust grows up to cover the individual personality; reactions become mechanical, and a certain transformation takes place, the results of which are also often confused with conscience. In reality, however, the individual is conforming to the unconscious emotional world of a class, caste or group; and this crust of conformity, a mask covering the individual face, is compared by C. G. Jung with that other mask worn by the ancient mimes that was called *persona*. 'Persona' is necessary to society, which cannot tolerate nakedness; but it is merely a caricature of the personality, in fact a mask.

According to this scheme both the conscience and the ideal formed by it must be regarded as externally conditioned reactions, merely the sum of the limitations which the ego must accept in order to survive. There can be no doubt that this view corresponds to a fact which, however, has been generalized and arbitrarily incorporated into a relativistic, mechanistic-materialistic attitude. The Swiss psychotherapist Alphonse Maeder points out[19] that, though Freud himself was a great and severe stoic, his own scepticism and profound pessimism about man had led to one-sidedness. The conscience is identified with the super-ego, which tyrannises over man's individual personality. C. G. Jung notes that this approach corresponds to Freud's own introvert type of personality, and that Adler held a directly opposite viewpoint. Adler's conscience was identified with society, with the 'social sense' which is presented as absolutely worth striving for. Thus both masters of depth psychology remain the prisoners of psychologically immanent forces.

Meanwhile it is beginning to be generally recognized today that contemporary psychology and psychopathology has been unable to pose the problem of human conscience, at any rate in adequate terms. This recognition is enormously important for the re-evaluation of scientific criteria. In other words there is an inner voice telling the psychologist that a science which claims to study man, inclusively with all his heights and depths, must be in a bad way if it never takes into consideration what it is that makes him man in the first place. Contemporary psy-

[19] A. Maeder. 'De la psychanalyse à la psychosynthèse', in *L'Encéphale*, No. 8, 1926, 579–589.

chology is not so much a psychology without a soul as a
psychology without man. But as long as psychology claims to be
merely a sort of humanistic outgrowth of biology, and even seeks
to guarantee the 'scientific approach' by imitating the model of
physics, it is bound to have a scientific blind spot in viewing the
core of the human condition, which can neither be measured nor
expressed in quantitative terms. To be human is a quality of
being, and this quality, which is what makes man to be a man
rather than some other kind of creature, can by its very nature
never be expressed as the quantitative sum of biological characteristics. This peculiar quality, unmeasurable in scientific terms,
is precisely the conscience.

Nineteenth-century psychology had no conception at all of
conscience and short-sightedly replaced it by consciousness. Even
the dynamic psychology of the first half of the twentieth century
carefully avoided having to take the notion of conscience seriously, and circumscribed it with the help of biological metaphors
such as the super-ego. But the evil which produces the bad conscience in man cannot be cured by a theory which denies or
suppresses conscience. Thus scientific treatment of conscience is a
result due and increased by the evil itself. It is at the same time
the symptom, disease and attempted treatment.

The social limitation of the ego is probably necessary for
human existence. But it cannot be identified with conscience;
rather, social limitation is a function of conscience, or more
accurately it is the observable phenomenon produced by a reality
which cannot be scientifically analysed. Things which cannot be
attributed to a tangible analysable cause, and yet which appear
true to the insight, can be neither proved nor disproved by
analysis. Certainly the super-ego has a utilitarian function, which
is to fit the individual into society. This shows that the super-ego
has something in common with instinct : it is a limitation of the
urge for the sake of individual life, a chance enabling the urge
to continue in sublimated form. Yet one wonders how is this
chance guaranteed? And again one wonders, since one level
cannot be reduced to another, whether conscience is not a condition for the formation of the super-ego, even though the superego will not always cover or be able to replace conscience.

9. *An example of confusion: Transcendent Relation and Spiritual Immanence*

Analysis enables us to draw immediate conclusions only concerning the central function of conscience, as when Jung's analytical psychology discovers innate images or 'archetypes' which represent universal functional potentialities of the soul. The 'self' underlying these archetypes refers to a reality which, though sheltered in the depths of the soul, is yet experienced as surpassing all finite things. It is a functional capacity which, since it exists, presupposes a transcendental being.

Jung's inspired achievements suggest, however, even today that, like Columbus, he discovered a continent without realizing what he had found. Columbus thought he had reached the Indies. Jung, whenever he refers to the numinous archetype, which in 'fear and trembling' discloses the *mysterium tremendum* in the depths of the soul, he always concludes with the somewhat embarrassed modesty of modern scientists who will tell us that only verifiable data are the objects of science. Jung can prove that 'fear and trembling' which man exhibits when confronted with mystery. But fear and trembling of what? The answer, says Jung, does not concern science. Thus the most acute psychologist of our time is as helpless on the borders of the newly discovered continent as any other son of this scientific age.

Psychopathology is even less capable of dealing with man's transcendental links. We have seen above (Section 3), that psychopathology and the systems of depth psychology derived from it, tend to confuse the 'super-normal' with the 'sub-normal'. It is obviously quite impossible even to approach the core of religious experience by means of this concept of the norm. For instance, it is a hopeless task to evaluate religious experience, grace or 'holiness', with the means of depth psychology. A genuine religious experience may well evince symptoms which the psychologist regards as neurotic or psychopathic. Even neurosis can be so transcended by religious means as to become the raw material of genuine perfection; but the criteria of spiritual perfection will not coincide with those of psychology.

It is possible, for instance, to imagine a situation in which 'holiness' would provide a genuine transcendental solution of the

existential problem, instead of the solution which, in the face of
reality and with similar symptoms, constitutes neurosis. As the
saint is never wholly perfect he too may succumb to neurosis;
but the fact that he overcomes it may be evidence of his sanctity.
If the grace of God permeates man's whole physical-spiritual
nature we can readily suppose that it might produce certain psychological conflicts in man, not least because it awakens transcendental desires. This brings us to the symptomatology of desires.

Everyone reacts in his own way to the object of a strong desire.
He will react within the framework of his own psychological
type. The style of his reaction will depend on whether his type
corresponds, in pathology, to the hysterical or to the compulsive-
neurotic, or some other type. The saint, whom grace has inspired
with an other-worldly desire, would also react according to his
style of life, including so-called pathological traits; for example,
with emotional incontinence or with anxiety-laden scruples. The
outside observer may tend to diagnose neurotic symptoms; but
what is actually taking place is not a neurosis at all, but the
emergence of a genuine solution to the conflict that has arisen, a
new decision.

The person whose desires are directed at the things of this
world likewise reacts according to type, and, if the object of his
desire be unattainable, may produce genuine neurotic symptoms,
because in fact there is for him no transcendental solution.

For depth psychology, the symptoms in both cases are identical; accordingly, in the first case it may produce harmful effects
on the existential conflict; in the second case it may have a healing effect but without finding a fitting transcendental solution.

Every neurosis is an attempt to 'overtake'. A link of the causal
chain is being omitted, as for instance in cases of imagined
pregnancy. Temporal, spatial or ethical conditions, or even individual limitations, are by-passed. Identifications, regressions,
infantilism, fixations, conversions and other categories of neurosis are the results. By jumping over the natural links, the
patient arrives at symbolic wish-fulfilment, for instance in empty
activities. These symbolic wish-fulfilments are in conflict with
reality; in order to be able to satisfy his desire, even if only
symbolically, the neurotic refuses to recognize part of reality.
He wants to cling to his mother's breast, or identify himself with

his father, or enjoy sexual satisfaction which seems to him forbidden. He may want to avoid unpleasant situations or refuse to be a loser in any circumstances. The symbolic fulfilment of his wishes will bear the mark of his constitution, it will develop along a typical 'hysterical', 'compulsive-neurotic' direction.

Grace too might make it possible to overleap links of the causal chain that leads in the direction of the transcendental desire. From a natural point of view this corresponds to a state of emergency, which may sometimes also be characterised by symbolic wish-fulfilment (identification with the Saviour, re-experiencing the Passion, stigmata, etc.). This symbolic wish-fulfilment may also bear a constitutional mark; but in the last resort it is not in conflict with reality, but on the contrary in accord with the highest reality.

In practice psychopathology and depth psychology regard every symbolic wish-fulfilment as rooted in neurosis, since religion is explained as 'illusion' or neurosis over-compensation or a product of the collective unconscious (a *pars pro toto* explanation, since religion in fact contains elements of symbolism, compensation and of the collective unconscious). However, the symbolic fulfilment of a 'this-worldly' wish is in conflict with reality, insofar as it tries to overleap reality, whereas the symbolic fulfilment of an 'other-worldly' wish can become reality by means of grace.

Whatever it is, we have shown that depth psychology in evaluating man's place in a hierarchy of values, lacks the means of knowing how far this hierarchy actually determines reality. If we succeed in showing that a knowledge of the objectivity of the hierarchy of values is essential and centrally important in our efforts to understand man, we shall have to reassess the methods and technique of depth psychology. We shall need, as W. Daim has pointed out, a re-evaluation of psychoanalysis.[20] And this can best be illustrated by that 'black death' of our time known as neurosis. It is analogous to a fall from the hierarchy of values, as we hope to show in the following two chapters.

[20] W. Daim, *Die Umwertung der Psychoanalyse*, Vienna, Herold, 1951.

Chapter Two

THE NEGATIVE ASPECT OF NEUROSIS:
RELATIVE VALUES AS ABSOLUTES

10. *The existential lie*

TO wish for contradictory things, not to be able to decide, is a psychological attitude which may lead to neurosis. Neurosis then becomes an apparent solution: 'not having to decide'; always leaving the way open for retreat; satisfying irreconcilable desires, even if only symbolically. To this extent neurosis is a negation of the whole, of the 'either-or' dilemma, whether for good or for evil. The good man flirts with an evil principle, the bad man wants to enjoy the advantages of goodness as well. This everlasting tension between the desire for an ideal end and the desire for satisfaction may lead to an intolerable situation. It is tempting to try to annihilate the tension by stifling or repressing a bad conscience. Modern psychology has shown, however, that no dynamic psychological current can be annihilated; if it is covered up or repressed it will reappear by devious ways and transform the unbearable bad conscience into aggression—either into aggresion against the ego, which may lead to self-torture, to Kierkegaard's 'sickness unto death', or into aggression against the surrounding world, and in particular against those of its representatives who play some part in the disturbed mental life. This aggression in its turn heightens the pangs of conscience, and the aggressive person is thus caught in a vicious cycle.

Modern psychology explains the origin of neurosis from certain aberrations in development, which originally sometimes seem unimportant: a grudging or harsh, unloved upbringing as much as exaggerated affection or nervous disposition on the part of the parents, may be responsible for the child's sense of insecurity, and determine his aggressiveness for life.

The daughter of respectable parents, who had never done anything wrong, declared one day during an interview: 'I've had a bad conscience ever since I can remember!' Exactly the same words were used by an elderly unmarried woman suffering from severe guilt feeling, despite the fact that her whole life had been devout and self-sacrificing.

The French psychoanalyst Françoise Dolto recently published a collection of cases which she had encountered in her capacity as educational adviser. The material shows how small mistakes in education can burden a child's conscience and turn it into a neurotic. For example: a six-year old boy, brought up among people of little understanding, who was undernourished during the war, acquired a heavy sense of sin and a feeling of revolt because he had been accused of nothing less than blasphemy. In catechism classes children were taught to address Jesus in the Sacrament in poetic terms: 'Jesus, rising sun! Jesus, fair flower!' The boy, however, as later investigations were to show, had never seen the rising sun, and his city environment gave him few chances to see flowers. He longed for a meal which would include vegetables, then scarce, and particularly for carrots and onions; and, to the fury of his teacher, replaced the poetic invocations by 'Jesus, carrot! Jesus, onion!' 'He expected this Jesus-food,' Françoise Dolto remarks, 'to appease all his trials, still his hunger, help him to be free.' But adult lack of comprehension turned him into a moral leper, who was sent to the consulting-room as a hard case.[1]

The special relationship between guilt and neurosis can also be seen in the light of the unsurmounted childish fantasies of neurotics. Orthodox psychoanalysis regards neurosis as a regression to stages of libidinous development which should normally have been transcended; similarly individual psychology sees it as a pattern of life that became fixed and immovable in early childhood. But the infantile attitude is also apparent on the level of the neurotic's ethical ideas. Jean Piaget, who studied the origin of rules of social conduct and ideas of ethical duty in children, observed a succession of two different ethical systems. At first, until the age of seven or eight, there is a 'heteronomous'

[1] *Trouble et Lumière, Etudes Carmélitaines*, Bruges-Paris, p. 53-55.

or naïvely realistic ethic; duties are conceived as magically imposed from outside. An 'autonomous' ethic based on renunciation and the sense of duty develops only much later.[2]

In a study on the development of ethical ideas in children[3] the present author has attempted to show that the two stages, formalistic morality and ethical conviction, do not succeed each other quite as neatly as Piaget believes, but largely overlap and fade into each other. It was found, however, that the repression of personal responsibility is the characteristic feature of infantile ethical thinking. It is also well known that a morality based on magic is characteristic of so-called primitive thinking. The neurotic, whose development has been arrested at an infantile stage, will remain particularly so with regard to ethical thinking, superstition and magic. Ethical laws appear to him to be imposed from without, and neurosis as a kind of magic formula which will enable him to evade them.

Psychology and pedagogy have already shown considerable interest in the fact that, for the child, punishment has a magical effect which presupposes guilt but also to a large extent expiates it. We have descriptions of cases of neurotic children who actually provoked the most severe punishments in order to rid themselves of guilt. We know even of normal children, arrested at the stage of magical thinking, who sometimes measure their guilt exclusively according to the extent of the punishment. If a child is severely punished for something he did with no intention of wickedness, this must mean his action was a very bad one; if he is not punished for something, then either the offence never took place at all, or it must be punished in order to be expiated.

All these features recur in the neurotic guilt-system. The unpleasant symptom of neurosis is a self-punishment for guilt, precisely on the principle that the extent of punishment determines the extent of guilt, and shall serve as expiation. If the guilt, which one would rather not admit to oneself, is to be pushed out of existence, the punishment must be heaped on some other guilt as a kind of scapegoat. In this way it is believed that irreconcilable aims can be attained: first, the expiation of guilt through self inflicted punishment; second, the refusal to recognize the

---

[2] Jean Piaget, *Le Jugement moral chez l'Enfant*, Paris, Alcan, 1932.
[3] *Archives de Physiologie*, Neuchatel, XXIX, 114, 1943.

actual guilt by substituting for it, as self-punishment, either some other or even a fictitious guilt.

Thus the cause of neurotic disturbances of the conscience is always to be sought in the suppression of childhood conflicts. In the case of adults the intolerable burden has long since been repressed into the unconscious. A bad conscience emerges in a roundabout way, as it were in symbolic language, and produces symptoms which are difficult to interpret.

Mrs O. Z., thirty-four years old, intelligent and warm-hearted, but over sensitive and easily depressed, suffers from a classic compulsive neurosis. If, in cleaning her house, she has not replaced a piece of furniture in exactly the same position as before, she imagines that some harm may befall her husband, who is away at the front. She also fears that she may have filled her letters to him with curses and insults instead of expressions of tenderness, and accordingly tries to get her letters back from the post office after she has mailed them.

The patient has been married twice. Her first husband was considerate, but unreliable and unfaithful. She believes that she never thinks of her first husband, and that she is utterly in love with the second, who is reliability itself. Analysis uncovers her unconscious longings for her first husband, and, beyond these, certain childhood experiences and desires of which the object is her father, and later a boy who committed an offence against her when she was nine years old.

This patient is mistaken in her placing of her conflict. She believes that she no longer thinks of her first husband, nor of her first emotional and sexual experiences. She feels, on the whole quite justifiably, that she is a model of virtue. She is reluctant to admit to herself that even virtuous people may be tempted, and yet she feels guilty. From this vague feeling of guilt comes her self-inflicted punishment—the neurotic phobia. But the self-punishment has no healing effect because the patient has erected her own virtue into an absolute. She no longer recognizes her own little human weaknesses; she wants to know herself as perfect by definition, and not even subject to temptation.

Another example:

Miss L. K., twenty-eight years old, has just recovered from nephritis and still suffers from 'psychogenic *retentio urinae*.

Causal analysis meets with a profound resistance. Intelligent and sensitive, the patient finds difficulty in adapting herself to her sphere of life (small shop in a Tyrolese village). She is engaged to her late sister's husband, whom she respects without loving him; intercourse leaves her cold. The engagement has certain financial advantages: Miss L. K. used her symptom as a means of enslaving her husband, and, above all, to avenge herself for disappointed pretensions and infatuations. Yet at the same time she felt guilty about it, repressed her guilt together with her childish conflicts, and transferred the feeling of 'being dirty' from the ethical to the physical sphere. She preferred to live in fear of contagion, thereby punishing herself as well, to giving up her resentment and the hopeless war upon her environment.

In these cases, as in many others, we see that the unpleasant neurotic symptom is self-inflicted as a punishment. Self-punishment is expected to expiate guilt but the guilt itself is never recognized and may even be transferred to others. The neurotic's bad conscience leads him to punish himself and others. Should the bad conscience become intolerable, the person afflicted must either destroy himself or transfer the cause of his sufferings to the surrounding world, turning in blind fury on his neighbour. If, however, ethical forces prevent the tormenting conscience from adopting this course there remains another way of silencing the conscience—by transferring the causes of unbalance from the moral life to the periphery of the psychophysical organism.

It is a symptom of our time not only to explain neurotic disturbances psychophysically, but that the effects of these disturbances duly manifest themselves organically. This is due to the fact that the psychophysical system can transmit disturbances in both directions: from body to mind, but also from mind to body. O. Kauders defined this reversible change of gear, rooted in the nervous system, as the 'psycho-physical intermediary level', a term that is philosophically somewhat ambiguous.

The proneness of the organism to somatic illnesses as a way of expressing and symbolizing a psychological crisis has been specially investigated by Victor von Weizsäcker.[4] Countless studies have been published on the role of the vegetative nervous system in originating psychologically determined physical dis-

[4] *Studien zur Pathogenese*, Leipzig 1935.

turbances. Every disease develops according to the psycho-somatic disposition of the patient, which does not mean that every illness is a neurosis! But even a purely 'organic' complaint may herald a profound disturbance of the patient's ego.[5] Certainly there is no purely organic disease just as there is no purely 'psychogenic' illness. Thus the transition between somatic illness and neurosis is a fluctuating one, but for simplicity's sake we might say that neurosis more particularly concerns the psychological side of the personality, and that its somatic effects are merely secondary, and achieved through the process we know as 'conversion'; that is the psychological situation finds a somatic expression but the patient represses the meaning of this expression into his unconscious. What happens, therefore, is that his bad conscience is created by behests and prohibitions which at a certain level cannot be brought into internal agreement with individual development. Every development contains latent conflicts between the requirements of morality and the level actually attained—the level which determines the load the individual ethos can carry. Those claims that cannot be realized produce guilt feelings.

11. *The scapegoat*

The truant conscience, the consciousness of the existential lie is in neurosis repressed into the unconscious; more accurately, this consciousness never was very clear; it was certainly carefully disguised at the moment of origin of the guilt feelings associated with it. The neurotic will not have it that his guilt must be sought in relative values which have turned into absolutes and looks for superficial explanations ('symptomatic pangs of conscience'); he misplaces his deception. Indeed, even these superficial explanations often will be covered up, or even converted into physical symptoms. It is thus not surprising that the self-imposed punishment (paralysis, tic, headache, insomnia, impotence or frigidity, depression, compulsive thinking, inferiority feelings) cannot be effective as it remains at the level of superficial explanation, of which the patient is not fully aware.

The condition we call neurosis, however, occurs only where guilt has not been accepted—where it has been suppressed, and

[5] Cf. the concept of 'organ psychosis' in Heinrich Meng; *Psyche und Hormon*, Bern, Hans Huber, 1944.

gives rise only to a diffuse, or even misplaced guilt feeling. It has been argued that neurosis is not necessarily connected with guilt. Thus, for instance, B. F. Mitzka comments on the present author's conception of neurosis as follows:

> Although it cannot be denied that a purely materialist attitude may in certain circumstances foster neurosis or jeopardize its cure, yet the above thesis can hardly apply to all forms of neurosis—indeed, not to any one specific form.
> Conversely, even the worst affliction of conscience need not lead to neurosis. It would be fatal if pastors or psychotherapists always assumed guilt in the patient.[6]

Of course the pretended 'guilt' of the neurotic is not meant to be the real guilt factor of neurosis. On the contrary, neurotic guilt feelings (inferiority feelings, self-reproach, scrupulosity) are often only a camouflage for the misplaced diagnosis. That even the worst affliction of conscience need not lead to neurosis is no argument against the presence of a bad conscience in neurosis. Even Koch's bacillus does not have the effect of causing T.B. in every carrier. Not every guilt leads to neurosis but that only which is not admitted and yet feared. Often the neurotic will accuse himself of unimportant matters and refuse to recognize his real guilt. That is the guilt of pride, of *superbia*, and this consists in the neurotic's identification with his ideal image, and in the repression into his unconscious of all impulses not in accord with that image. He will not accept responsibility for the repressed impulses. The desire for perfection and moral purity may also be connected with this superbia. The desire may be outwardly transcendental, but relies for satisfaction upon inadequate means. This shows that theologians may also overlook the connection between guilt and neurosis, as in the argument quoted above.

The objection that neurosis need not presuppose objective guilt is thus misplaced, for the simple reason that neurotic guilt feelings relate to a scapegoat, which may in fact be an imaginary guilt. Yet guilt feelings exist, and have psychologically disturbing effects. But their cause is not found where the neurotic seeks it. It is thus hardly surprising that it cannot be found by following the neurotic in his search. The argument against the con-

[6] *Das neue Buch*, Vienna 1946, 14, p.4

nection between guilt and neurosis is itself a typically neurotic argument. It leads logically to a naturalistic psychotherapy which regards guilt feeling as neurotic.

Obviously, a precisely known and circumscribed guilt recognized as such belongs to the moral theologian's or lawyer's domain. But compulsive guilt feeling, born from self-glorification and from the repression of bad conscience, belongs to the realm of the psychologist, whose business it is to investigate unconscious processes. It need not be emphasized that both realms cut across each other, and that psychology has an ancillary part to play within the framework of what Dr Niedermeyer called 'universalistic anthropology'. Meanwhile, however, it would be desirable if pastors and lawyers could familiarize themselves with the complex processes within the unconscious. Indeed, a psychologist who takes his work seriously cannot but conclude from his own experience that subjective and 'mistakenly placed' guilt feelings ultimately cause us to ask whether the individual has not arrived at them through an inability to distinguish between appearance and reality, between relative and absolute factors. This leads us far beyond the confines of psychology. It is indeed the question of our responsibility towards the truth. Even an apparent guilt feeling is possible only where objective value scales have been replaced by subjective feelings.

During the fighting at the time of the liberation of Vienna in 1945, many cases of rape occurred which yield interesting material for the study of neurotic guilt. We have had occasion to investigate these cases in which rape was or was not followed by neurosis. Obviously experiences of this kind set up a more or less deep psychological reaction in any normal woman. The real problem is, however, whether, if a neurosis appears after the rape, its origin can be sought in the fact of sexual violation alone, without delving into deeper and concealed causes. Not surprisingly in all the cases observed by us, in which neurosis did break out, violation was used as a scapegoat for latent neurotic guilt feelings. We are by no means trying to make light of the consequences of the sexual shock. It was found, however, that where there were no repressed or camouflaged guilt feelings, even women of the utmost moral integrity after a passing condition akin to shock, were able fairly soon to overcome the experience. Wherever neurosis occurred careful analysis invariably brought to light the presence of latent guilt feelings which had been located falsely and ascribed to the rape.

Case 1: Miss T. F. presents a picture akin to melancholia, with suicidal tendencies, but with certain features strongly reminiscent of hysteria. This condition has been brought on by the rape. Analysis shows that she had no unconscious desire to be raped; yet she feels guilty, but she locates her own guilt falsely. Because of her overwhelming father fixation, she had never been able to have a woman's normal life, but found her purpose in existence in looking after an old uncle, who died shortly after the liberation of Vienna. This pregenital libidinous fixation was also characterized by meanness in matters of money. She was always afraid of being disinherited by her old uncle if she married. At the age of nineteen she had a love affair, which soon ended. She was frigid in this relationship, but there was an illegitimate child. Lately, at the age of thirty-one, she had been unable to make up her mind between two suitors. The rape showed her, so to speak, the uselessness of her wrongly understood sense of duty: she had missed normal life and normal feminine development, only to be forced into coitus. Moreover, unconsciously, she associated the rape with her father, whose genitals she said she had seen when she was five.

Case 2: Mrs K., thirty-three years old, was raped by two men. She experienced orgasm and felt guilty towards her husband, a prisoner of war whom she had not seen for four years. She repressed the memory of the orgasm, and presented a hysteroid picture, with amnesia and paramnesia. Analysis showed that she believed guilt to be located in the orgasm itself; with her own husband she was often frigid, this was connected with certain youthful experiences, carefully concealed in her conscience.

Case 3: Mrs L. L., twenty-six years old, showed a reactive depression, which came on directly after the event. Psychological exploration showed, however, that she had to a certain extent invited the rape by her incautious behaviour, and that she was thus concealing an unconscious desire to experience coitus in this way. Mrs L. L. had always been frigid, More thoroughgoing analysis showed a homosexual component (fixation of her mother), which led the patient to play her 'feminine role' under compulsion. But compulsion did not enable her to solve her inner conflicts. The latent guilt feeling became active and found a scapegoat in the act of rape.

Case 4: Miss N. N., nineteen years old, also showed a reactive depression with certain features reminiscent of hysteria. The patient had been a virgin, and had been much preoccupied with her virginity, since she was engaged to a man towards whom her feelings were clearly ambivalent. The preservation of her virginity was supposed to compensate for her lack of love, as well as for the fact that she was secretly attached to another man. Her violent defloration deprived her of this excuse.

It is easy to note in these and other cases that the sexual shock is said to be the cause of a previously controlled but not apparent neurosis. The purpose is obvious, lessening as it does the moral responsibility for the guilt feelings that were already present.

Case 5: Mrs J. N., twenty-one years old, divorced, has had psychotherapeutic treatment for two years, after almost destroying herself at the age of twenty by sexual and alcoholic excess. Her family circumstances were as unfavourable as possible; she had been violated by a relative at the age of seven, and from her sixteenth year onwards had given herself up to the most unbridled sexuality, which left her frigid and emotionally completely unsatisfied. Her neglected, still infantile mind suffered intensely under her way of life. She longed for the right road, without being able to find it. The initial psychotherapeutic difficulties were considerable, and only after about a year was there a change in her personality and a clear improvement. The biggest difficulty was to get her to recognize clearly her own responsibility. At last, Mrs J. N. learnt, as she herself put it 'to stop always looking for the blame in other people'. At this stage came the rape, which, moreover, took place under particularly disagreeable circumstances: she was compelled to submit at the point of a gun by three men. The first reaction was very violent, and almost reached genuine despair. Mind-wandering, inability to concentrate, tics and other symptons seemed to point to a relapse into the morbid condition that had preceded treatment. This reaction, however, was very brief, and entirely disappeared, to be replaced by an almost unbroken improvement, as soon as the patient came to realize that this time she was to blame for her ordeal. The guilt feelings she had experienced were partly left over from older, not yet fully expiated guilt feelings, and also to a certain extent, produced by the pride she took in her improvement.

Cases 1 to 4 illustrate the old thesis that, even though a neurosis may erupt as the result of an actual cause, it is likely to have been present for a considerable time. The neurosis is certainly reactive, but in a retarded manner. More interesting, however, is the clear presence, in all four cases, of a scapegoat complex. Case 5 shows that the conscious overcoming of the temptation to look for a scapegoat is also a safeguard against neurosis. We have, on the other hand, also had occasion to examine other victims of rape who did not become neurotic. Evidence of their terrible experience was present in all of them but, unless at the time of the offence they had had repressed guilt feelings, they were preserved from a neurotic scapegoat complex. One rather tense young woman said after her ordeal: 'It has made me more humble, and that was the positive meaning of what happened.' This woman hit the nail on the head. The neurotic locates his guilt falsely from a lack of humility. Pride will not admit any guilt, but will find it more convenient even to invent a false guilt.

We have, then, reached the following conclusion concerning the phenomenology of neurosis: the neurotic punishes himself for a guilt which he has carefully repressed into his unconscious, and in order to be able to explain his guilt feelings, he searches for a scapegoat. As long ago as 1922 Paul Häberlin described 'unexpiated guilt' in children seeking a 'scapegoat' to 'discharge itself' on.[7] More recently, H. Baruk has used the term 'scapegoat mechanism' to render psychologically understandable the history of certain psychoses.[8] The word seems quite adequate to describe the wrong locating of guilt which lies at the root of neurosis, but by 'scapegoat complex' we do not primarily mean a projection of unexpiated guilt on to the surrounding world, but the covering up process in general, which may involve finding a scapegoat within oneself; it leads necessarily to a seeming self-accusation, and then to aggressiveness.

12. The relative as absolute value

The misplacement of guilt feelings, and their simultaneous punishment, implies a wrong evaluation either of the cause of guilt or of the punisher. There must have been an over valuation either of the existential significance of the repressed desires and

---

[7] Paul Häberlin, *Eltern und Kinder*, Basel, Kober.
[8] H. Baruk, *Psychiatrie morale expérimentale, individuelle et sociale*, Paris, Presses Universitaires de France, 1945.

urges, of the 'id', or of the punisher, the 'superego'. Guilt and expiation can exist only on the basis of a general capacity for moral judgment; but the moral judgment is here carried out by means of false evaluations.

Anyone who believes in an order governing the world and human existence will again and again have to realize that the repression of guilt feelings and the ensuing illness caused by a bad conscience are made possible by the very fact that this order is not clearly recognized by the person affected. In analysing repressed guilt feeling it is often sufficient to go back to the unconscious cause, after which psychological development can again function normally. The theoretical question, however, remains—unfortunately. In some cases it will result in the practical question: how was it possible for this game of hide-and-seek with the conscience to come about and which side of our spirit is ultimately right, that which refuses to admit the guilt, or that which suffers under it?

Significantly enough, this problem is already present, potentially, in the first success claimed by the psychoanalytic method. This case was published, if somewhat unsatisfactorily phrased, by Breuer and Freud, and became the point of departure for all later attempts at treating diseases of the conscience by means of depth-psychology. The case concerned the hysterically-conditioned physical disturbances affecting an unusually talented and cultured young woman. It became famous in the history of psychoanalysis; it is of particular significance here. The girl fell ill while nursing her father. Breuer induced his patient, in the course of hypnosis, to express in words whatever affective phantasy possessed her at the time. While not under hypnosis the girl was quite unable to give any indication of how her symptoms had arisen; she saw no connection between them and any impressions received during her life. Under hypnosis she discovered the missing connection. It turned out that all her symptoms were symbolic translations (conversions) of thoughts and impulses which she had had to suppress while nursing her father.

This case history reveals the very problem of the stricken conscience: the girl fell ill because she had, while nursing her dearly-loved father, suppressed certain thoughts; these thoughts, we later find, were tantamount to wishing her father's death.

The girl realized, in fact, that her father's illness represented, both for him and her, a trial beyond their strength. For one instant she therefore wished her father's death. But she rejected this fleeting thought; or rather—and this is the difficulty—she did not reject it, but immediately repressed it because it seemed to her too monstrous to fit in with the ideal image she had of herself. She simply could not have a wish like that! Her filial duties and her own unselfishness had become absolutes. They were of course laudable qualities and well worth aiming at, but she regarded them in an absolute sense. She overlooked the fact that even the most noble human thoughts and feelings are but relative values, and perfection an ideal after which man strives without ever attaining it. How many similar disorders of the conscience arise from the fact that somebody represses his own baseness, or even what he considers to be his baseness, and fancies himself, at that moment, an angelic being! This hitherto rarely recognized process was aptly called 'angelism'.[9] 'Angelism' is, however, as Baudouin himself noticed, a rarefied form of narcissism; that is, of the lowest level of self-love. The self is being enlarged. It is identified with some ideal image, a worthwhile goal is regarded as already attained, and all relative and refractory elements in the personality are sacrificed to it. This is why it is dangerous to treat 'angelism' from a purely spiritual point of view. Man must be able above all to admit his imperfection, to recognize the stage he has actually attained in the interplay and conflict of his urges, for he is capable of having high ideals, and sacrificing everything to them, even truth and love.

Pascal said that he who wants to play the angel, ends by becoming a monster, and in *The Brothers Karamazov* hell is filled with those men who knew what truth and justice are. Dostoievsky's remark is a contribution to the study of conscience in so far as awareness of truth and justice is all that is required to establish guilt if these high values are being misused for the sake of an idol, which is the inflated ego. Instead of taking its appropriate place in a universal system of values, the ego becomes the hub of the world. But if our individuality is regarded as the highest value this will inevitably result in a philosophy domin-

[9] Charles Baudouin, 'Angélisme et faux dépassements' in *Trouble et Lumière*, op. cit., pp. 139–152.

ated by private feelings. Through the inflation of the ego relative values are given an absolute status. That is the very heresy of life.

By heresy we understand the overvaluation of partial truths, which inevitably implies the degradation of absolute to relative values. Our general view of the world is thereby affected, and quite literally 'deranged' by heresy. Even in the theological sense of the word heresy can never be understood in merely rational terms. The first centuries of the history of the Church were marked by dogmatic quarrels, which appear as quite superfluous hair-splitting to our modern rational understanding. Our attitude, however, is not just evidence of greater tolerance; but rather of a process in which truth has become relative. The quarrels about the Incarnation touched upon the very core of human life and human redemption. Both neurosis and modern depth psychology are concerned with this very doctrine of the Incarnation. In its widest sense modern anthropology lacks a comprehensive and universally adequate conception of the spirit-body problem, as we hope to show in Part II of this book.

Just as truth is manifestly true on all levels of being, error too has its causes outside the range of our terms. But it may have positive aspects; for, while truth is one, error is a splinter of truth, a partial truth. It has metaphysical, ethical and biological aspects. Just as heresy in religion extends beyond its religious significance to all aspects of life, the 'life heresy' implicit in neurosis is not just an aberration as it were of 'hygiene' but also of ethics and metaphysics.

All errors, aberrations, delusions and exaggerations can, by the way, be regarded in their relationship to the hierarchy of values, as 'life heresies'. Causal explanations of an error, a mistake, an exaggerated idea (for example through insufficient knowledge or unconscious desires or constitutional weakness) are only partly correct: they never reach the meaning of what has happened. The inner criteria according to which we determine the existence of error or delusion in a given situation cannot, as we have seen in Chapter I, be purely psychological or psychiatric. It is very relevant to ask: 'How is psychiatry to know what value should be assigned to an idea?'[10] A careful examination of the emotional

[10] Alex von Müralt, *Wahsinniger oder Prophet?* Europa-Verlag, Zurich, 1946, p. 110.

assumptions on which the error is based would also be needed. We have noticed, for instance, how far 'oligophrenic'—that is, 'feeble-minded'—answers to Rorschach tests suggest an emotionally conditioned blindness with regard to the test situation as a whole and a disconnected, arbitrary selection of a small part of this situation.[11] Error confers absolute value on finite things by overlooking the overall connection and judging according to the fraction it can see; it recedes from wholeness, and is totalitarian in its attitude. The same is true of ignorance and mental sloth.[12] Fear, sudden fright or other affect responses which suddenly enlarge the sense of self-preservation may also induce a similar restriction of mental vision and lead to fallacious reactions. In all these cases we witness overemphasis of the part at the expense of the whole, a fall from the transcendent hierarchy, ultimately a darkening of the divine transparence. Schizophrenia, with its total relinquishment of reality, is only the most consistent attempt to turn everything into immanence and total heresy.

The absolute value given by the neurotic to his own emotional criteria represents a form of presumption, which, though almost always concealed, is quite easy to ascertain. The significance of this over-valuation, after all, is the neurotic's refusal to recognize an order experienced to be transcendent, replacing it by an exaggeration of his own personality. He refuses to recognize either the reality that is repressed, or the conditioned and relative character of the repressing factor within himself. He cannot quite silence his conscience, the voice of the transcendent order, but he refuses to listen to it. The importance of the 'id' and the independence of the 'superego' (to use Freud's terminology) are exaggerated and elevated into autonomous criteria.

The *hubris* which underlies this exaggerated feeling can be found in every case where relative values have been neurotically or psychopathically elevated to absolute ones. The cases given in sections 10 and 11 abundantly support this statement. Further light may perhaps be shed by the following two additional examples.

[11] *Wiener Zeitschrift für praktische Psychologie* I, 1949, pp. 17 and ff.
[12] Cf. the intelligent little book *Über die Dummheit*, Annie Kraus, Frankfurt a/M., Josef Knecht, 1948.

Miss A. T. suffers from endogenous depression (melancholia) with strong 'psychogenic overtones'. The psychological background of this psychosis is not only striking, but most illuminating as regards the origin of neurotic momenta. Since in her morbid condition she had lost all joy in living, she tried to bring on a joyful experience by force. She hoped to experience joy (despite the fact that she was otherwise a severely virtuous person) in giving herself, without love, to a soldier from the Occupation Forces. She also explained that she was trying to see whether she was still capable of experiencing pleasure. Not surprisingly, her melancholy did not improve in the slightest. Moreover, she felt she had entirely lost her honour; her disappointment and the feeling of having lost her honour led her to a very serious, though unsuccessful, suicidal attempt: she threw herself out of a fourth floor window. Subsequent psychological exploration showed that the immediate motivation for suicide was rooted in the intolerable consciousness of having lost her honour. The patient, a secretly aggressive melancholic, had made of the concept of honour a genuine idolatry. Her moral austerity was, for her, an effective though unconscious reason for fancying herself better than other women, and for silently judging and despising all others. Virtue became a means of self-glorification.

An undergraduate, A. A., seeks psychotherapy because of persistent masturbation. His religious views do not allow him to satisfy his sexual desires naturally. Analysis, of course, discovers a profoundly infantile attitude. But here we only wish to call attention to the following factors: A. A. uses rigoristic religious convictions to conceal his shyness towards the opposite sex (by which of course, we do not mean that this religious conviction was nothing but hypocrisy). A. A. sums up his attitude to life in one sentence: 'If I do not overcome my masturbation, then it means that I am not a man and that life has no meaning.' We can see here how the need to prove himself a man has replaced all other values, and how A. A., in fighting his little demon of masturbation, has overlooked the bigger devils of pride and loneliness.

13. *The heretical view of life: Greed for experience*

We have seen how deeply even the most remote aspects of the personal attitude towards the world are affected by the neurotic life heresy: neurosis may be not only a totalitarian attitude to life, but also a totalitarian attitude to death.

It is not our aim to rewrite the phenomenology of neurosis. Everything has been said already concerning the ambiguity and deceitfulness of neurosis, but at the same time little account has been taken of the neurotic's frame of reference. A very few phenomenological traits provide sufficient evidence of how profoundly the tendency of assigning absolute values to what is only relative can penetrate the neurotic's whole view of life.

In absolutising his own emotions and perceptions, the neurotic is in the first instance prone to a specific greed for experience. In a world where the frame of reference has been disturbed, feeling is not only being experienced as absolute: it becomes the central criterion. Its conclusive force is therefore tremendous; only by constant experience can the neurotic prove to himself that he is alive at all. For him life has no value on the basis of a transcendent frame of reference: its value can be measured only by what is experienced. But it is of little value if it has to be reaffirmed by every fresh experience. Thus the neurotic is led, paradoxically, by the very immanence of his greed for life, to an evil 'transcendence': he is compelled to look for corroboration of the value of life outside, in objects, and placed in a position of intolerable dependence on the things of this world. We are all only too ready to recognize our wants, but the neurotic is particularly sensitive in this respect. Every psychotherapist is familiar with the neurotic's exaggerated idea of his own importance—which is only a kind of magnifying glass showing in an exaggerated manner faults common to mankind. This is what leads the neurotic into the danger of suicide: experience is an uncertain, treacherous value, which soon loses its savour and demands fresh experience. Just as the meaning of life can only be grasped in relation to a scale of fixed values, it is further and further obscured if the frame of reference becomes immanent making the individual depend on some evil pseudo-transcendence. Feeling, in the widest sense of the word, pleasure, in constant need of fresh stimulation, is the basic life value. Victor E. Frankl has summarised this loss of the meaning in life due to greed for experience in these words: 'We have no right to ask about the meaning of life—life itself raises the question. It is we who are being questioned.'[13]

[13] *Trotzdem ja zum Leben sagen*, Wien, Deuticke, 1946, p. 19.

The neurotic greed for experience is a regressive form of what was once a positive desire to live. Pierre Janet rightly regarded neurosis as a rigid, life-inhibiting repetition of a process in itself necessary to life. The greed for experience was originally greed for life of someone threatened in his or her development. This circumstance is the very condemnation of all *a priori* talk about the inadequacy of the greed for experience, and, as we shall see, necessitates an accurate psychological analysis of the neurotic's life-history. The neurotic desire for experience is the result of the disintegration of two attitudes. The first is the desire to make up for not being loved enough, the second for wanting to prolong the pleasurable condition of being loved. The former desire is particularly noticeable in cases where there has been an unhappy childhood coupled with symptoms of neglect, which give rise to an unquenchable yearning for love, however deeply disguised this may be. The desire to prolong the experience of being loved appears more particularly in spoiled children, or in those victimised by selfish parental love. In this latter case greed for experience is a desire to continue to experience the paradise of childhood. This infantile process of prolonging childhood itself is fostered by civilizations in which traumatic experiences are made much of and a sense of responsibility is being undermined. Fear of ageing is the typical neurosis, not only of modern women, but of the modern world as a whole. It is interesting to note in this connection that the analysis of deep-seated disturbances of sleep has shown that they are rooted in an unconscious wish not to miss anything. There is a Russian proverb which says that breathing deeply will not help a dying person. Similarly, the wish for more experience and more possession is useless when life has no meaning any longer.

The phenomenology of neurosis provides sufficient evidence that it is his greed for experience that makes the neurotic insensible to ordinary experience, and that the pleasure principle actually leads him to dislike life itself. In this connection we should like to quote a patient's statement (C. D., a lawyer) written after about a year's psychoanalytical treatment:

As a child, my impatience was constantly being aroused by my parents, who always started preparing me for weeks beforehand

c

for any event which they supposed would give me pleasure. They would whet my appetite a long time in advance; they encouraged me in anticipation. Christmas, for instance; it was talked about for many weeks beforehand, the sort of presents I would receive, and so on. This made me very impatient, and I kept thinking: if only the time would pass! If only it were Christmas now! I could hardly bear to wait. At such times, the present had no meaning whatsoever, it meant only senseless waiting. The same happened before the summer holidays; they were talked about weeks in advance; my impatience was strained. And then, when the moment really came, I was always disappointed, because reality fell short of my feverish expectations. The result was infinite boredom.

In the past, I used to become depressed very easily. I remember when I was ill as a child, it was enough for the sheet to be wrinkled, instead of being nice and smooth, for me to become depressed. Besides, I grew up very largely in a room with walls painted a dark purple; outside the only window, a row of tall lime trees and maples deprived me of sunlight. The window faced north, so that the sun never entered my room at all. Whenever I was ill I had to lie in that room . . .

For some time now I have been much happier than before. I notice the many beautiful things which life presents every day and which, before, I never saw. I am beginning to lose the feeling of numb indifference which used to afflict me very often. I used to find it difficult to enjoy anything; now I enjoy the smallest things as would a child. I am generally cheerful, life's little annoyances no longer bother me.

By making of experience an end in itself the natural perception of what is experienced is being dulled and the meaninglessness of life constantly reaffirmed. Those who are afflicted in this way are compelled to fly from their own threatening emptiness. Neurotic pseudo-activities are also well known: the frantic pursuit of a career, social position, pleasures and adventures may reach the proportions of genuine neurosis. It is immaterial whether or not the individual superego provides this neurotic escape with more or less valid excuses; escape into work may be just as fatal for the development of the personality as escape into frivolity. It is perhaps better at least to be aware that we are drugging ourselves. What is really frightening are the totalitarian systems men will invent to cover up the meaninglessness of their lives.

A defectively cured schizophrenic thinks about the meaning of life, and reaches the conclusion that there is only one universally binding law. This law is neither love nor religion, for many people are filled with hate and have no religion. The law is simply that he must rise in the social scale. The draughtsman must become a chief in his department, the budding doctor a university lecturer, the director a director-general; this is the meaning of life, to this everything should be sacrificed, including one's private life.

We have here purposely shown the view of life taken by a psychotic (admittedly a 'socially-cured' psychotic!); for in that terrifying world, reminiscent of Orwell's *Nineteen Eighty-four*, not mere schizophrenics will be able to recognize themselves. Yet we have already noted that neurosis is closely connected with a repressed bad conscience. The greed for experience drives the neurotic to escape from himself; but this escape is only possible if false values are substituted for real values, and the flight from himself becomes a flight from the absolute—a 'flight from God', as Max Picard suggested. The fleeing patient places and explains his guilt incorrectly. He will always find scapegoats for the necessity of flight, and they will by no means always be imaginary ones. Social conditions may really force us to 'elbow our way through'. Life may really be very cruel. We may really be unlucky. In all these circumstances, which are indeed partial truths, the neurotic will always be able to get rational confirmation. But his basic attitude will always be 'wanting to have'.

'Wanting to have'—if possible without paying. One of the most fundamental human attitudes, which is particularly crudely revealed in neurosis, consists in wanting irreconcilable things and being forced to witness the ensuing conflict. Wanting to have more also means wanting to give up less. If one is nevertheless forced to give up something, as it were to pay for smuggled goods, there still remains a last way out: escape into illness. This extreme among deceptive solutions, revealed through severe organic neuroses, already exists even in the symptons of every neurosis. Favourite pseudo-solutions in the spiritual sphere are bitterness and resentment.

For all its aggressive tendencies, the characteristic feature of neurosis is the desire for powerlessness. Not wanting to give anything up also means not wanting to decide, wanting to have X as well as Y. This ambivalence is supposed to enable the neurotic both to behave 'morally' and to enjoy the forbidden fruit, to taste the delights of the 'id' while at the same time paying due worship to the 'superego'. This process is possible only by means of the ability to repress. Stekel reports the case of a young woman and her stepson, who in their waking hours led strictly respectable lives, but for months are said to have had sexual intercourse while asleep; they were both moral and incestuous. However, such dramatic examples are probably rare in actual medical practice. Neurosis can resort to more delicate 'devices' (Adler): for every neurosis operates with continual self-excuses, carefully concealing the actual reasons that underlie behaviour. The oddest thing is that neurotic guilt feelings are sometimes attributed to astonishingly grave causes, in order to enable the neurotic to commit smaller (real or imaginary) sins in peace. Self-accusations may be used as evidence to one's own conscience that one is severe with oneself, that is moral.

At this point we can barely touch upon the phenomenon of neurotic pseudo-knowledge. We have already (Section 3) referred to the neurotic condition of error. What is involved in this case is not an accidental error of judgment, but an unconscious arrangement to find excuses. Neurotic pseudo-knowledge leads to false self-knowledge. A single example will suffice. The pseudo-scientific denial of unconscious life is based simply on what we have described as 'psycho-phobia', a term first coined, we believe, by Dr V. E. Seiler-Vogt. Thus fear of uncomfortable knowledge leads to more comfortable pseudo-knowledge; though of course true knowledge may also be used to serve the purposes of error. There is a peculiar kind of pride, rooted in false humility, which is capable of justifying admitted lapses. If a man says to himself, and even confesses to others: 'I really am a swine!', this pessimistic knowledge can be misused for neurotic purposes. Moreover, it has often been shown that rational admissions made in the course of psychoanalysis ('I am a classical case of the Oedipus-situation', or 'I am a text-book example of Adlerian over-compensation') can be used for purposes of resistance; for how can so humble a person be reproached with anything? In the same way, many German films of the post-war years made a point of showing the megalomania and absurdity of former German ideals, as if to prove to their foreign and domestic audiences the basic decency of a people capable of so much self-deprecation. Dostoievsky describes a woman who visits the *stàrets* Zossima, because she secretly hopes he will praise her for her honesty when she tells him that her love for mankind is tinged with pride (*The Brothers Karamazov*, I, Book 2, Chap. IV).

By juggling with what cannot be reconciled and upsetting the scale of values, the neurotic also produces pseudo-duties which enable him to evade his real duties. He manages to introduce irreconcilable advantages into the hierarchy of duties, and even to confirm the moral position. The neurosis of 'being busy', mentioned above, fits very well into this category of pseudo-duties. Psychotherapy has shown frequently that neurotics may regard fixations on their mothers not as lacking in independence, but as a filial duty. Scores of neurotics fail in their jobs and families because of pretended filial duties, which of course does not mean that there are no genuine obligations towards parents. Insoluble situations arise because of immature commitments to several partners. A network of contradictory obligations is created in which the neurotic is caught. The types of the neurotic Don Juan or the fast girl with a perpetual bad conscience are often anything but enviable, each new commitment bringing in its train fresh self-reproaches and repressions.

Sometimes its very pretentiousness makes a neurotic pseudo-duty even more difficult to detect. We know well enough how it is possible for coldness of heart or fear of life to be disguised as noble endeavours and exalted vocations. Man is able to make great sacrifices for the sake of his neurotic devices. A stern view of life may be effective camouflage for one's own inadequacy. A man who is proving to his own satisfaction that he is fulfilling a difficult duty is apt not to notice that it serves him to experience his own 'angelism'.

The neurotic compulsively tries to avoid having to pay for his greed for experience and to derive advantage from irreconcilable situations. But his unrealistic defection from the hierarchy of values turns the neurosis into a bad bargain.

14. *The heretical view of life: objectivization*

Neurotic greed for experience is thus born of the defection

from the hierarchy of values: subjective feeling. and certain objects in the outside world which are presumed to be capable of nourishing that feeling, are wrenched out of their transcendental frame of reference and changed into absolutes. The unity and breadth of the world picture are lost. The neurotic world is a world of object. The neurotic's concern is to place his own person (regarded as object) in such a relation to the other objects that these will foster and confirm the supremacy of individual feeling.

The neurotic attitude always evinces certain paranoid traits, just as paranoid traits are also in some measure characteristic of the spirit of our age. The neurotic is trying, by devious and concealed means, to fight for his right to happiness, or self-affirmation, or whatever it may be. Neurosis is indeed an aberration, arising out of self-separation and isolation. It always offends against charity, because the neurotic sets up his own point of view, and not his neighbour's at the centre of his scheme of life.

In this way he cuts himself off from life, seeing it as something external to himself, as an object. He projects his own split on to the world of things: 'Life has treated me unfairly', or 'People (or perhaps men, or women) have never been fair to me'. As in paranoia, the bad conscience is in some sense projected outwards, and the neurotic is thus led to assume that he really has been unlucky, that he really is a victim of fate.

But since neurosis is in conflict with reality, it cannot, as we have said before, but prove a bad bargain. Neurotic illusion necessarily leads to disillusion; and disillusion makes the neurotic still more lonely and still more frightened of the objective world. This isolation and the resulting fear are made possible by the emphasis of the individual personality and of the relative objects. In the asthenic-aggressive type the disillusion leads to such an increase in aggressivity that he may engage in a war of annihilation with the world at large. The asthenic-passive type dare not give vent to his aggressivity and takes refuge in childishly unhappy reactions.

> A suicide F. Qu. puts an end to his life because it has dealt unfairly with him; at the same time, he wants his death to be a punishment for the doctors, whom he makes responsible for his self-destruction.

Miss S. A., a twenty-one-year-old Jewess, suffers from severe attacks of hysteria. During the very first hour of treatment, she vehemently declares (without being asked) that she does not believe in God, because he has allowed the horrors perpetrated by the Nazis upon the Jewish people. She spontaneously reports a peculiar phobia: she is afraid of passing a church: the spire might fall down and crush her under the debris. Analysis almost immediately brings to light the sexual symbolism underlying this fear: the spire symbolizes her father's penis. She was deeply attached to her father, though the attachment has turned to hatred and contempt, because he has disappointed her. It is clear, therefore, that the patient has projected her disappointments with her father outwards on to God. But this is but the external aspect of her case history, the neurosis also has other aspects which give symbolic meaning to the metaphysical core of the problem. The religious factor not only symbolizes the sexual—the sexual also symbolizes the religious. The case is an apt illustration of our belief, to which we shall return later, that causal analysis must in fact be completed by an existential synthesis. The little problem of the relationship between a daughter and her father has become a much bigger problem involving the relationship between a religious person and her Creator. Moreover, it is interesting to note that Christian churches should play a part in the sexual fantasies of a Jewess; it was impossible to clear this problem up, since Miss S. A. did not continue the treatment. However the generally childish attitude of the patient is worth mentioning here; she had prolonged her infantile disappointments into her later view of the world and had built them up into a system of anxiety and separation.

Neurotic fears can be explained in all cases by the loneliness of the individual cut off from God and the world, who reveals himself as helpless and weak and seeks affirmations from outside. Thus the neurotic attachment to the father-image is a separation from the objects of the adult world: it has a weakening effect because it represents a case of arrested development. Materialist psychoanalysis has insufficiently explained the fact that the attachment to the 'Father in Heaven' has a strengthening effect and frees from anxiety.

Fear of life presupposes a wrong objectivization of life. Life is seen from the outside and turned into an object. It is expected to yield only caresses, never blows. This attitude pervades the whole of neurotic infantilism. The neurotic does not want to be grown-up, to grow old, to die, but to enjoy all the advantages of life. This, by the way, also leads to the fear of decision. Wanting to enjoy all advantages likewise means wanting to lose nothing, wanting to have your cake and eat it. The fear of decision is a fear of taking risks, a fear of insecurity. The neurotic wants to be insured against all chances; but the more we insure ourselves, the less we are secure.

In all these cases, fear is 'misplaced', it is projected from the greed for experience into the world of objects. That is why objects acquire such an uncanny importance for the neurotic: the neurotic's world is a world of objects, a world reduced to objects. The neurotic relationship to objects emerges from the notes of a patient C. D., from which we quoted on page 45. During his analysis he wrote:

> My father is a very small-minded man. He is very attached to things. He thinks that things are there not for use but simply to be owned. He has always been pedantically concerned not to damage his things, and he influenced me in the same sense. He often forbade me to use his things, e.g., his bicycle, which I would have loved to. (I had none of my own). With other things, which I was not forbidden to use, he impressed upon me very strongly that I should use them with the utmost care and always replace them after use where I had found them. He also instilled in me severe principles of thrift. Money seemed to exist purely for the purpose of being saved, never to be spent. That is how my inhibitions started. I did not even dare to use the things I was allowed to use for fear of damaging them. So I refrained from using them. If I was given a little money, or earned it by doing odd jobs, I did not dare to buy sweets with it, as I would have liked to do; instead, I saved the money. Not because I risked punishment, in this particular case, but just because the possibility of buying sweets simply did not arise for me; otherwise I would have felt guilty. If the soles of my shoes began to wear out, I could not go on wearing the shoes without feeling guilty. I had to take them to the cobbler's.
>
> My father also cuts out all kinds of newspaper articles, which seem quite unimportant to me, in order to keep them. In fact, he always wants to keep everything, and cannot bear to throw away anything that has served its purpose.
>
> In other matters too, he is always getting stuck in unimportant details. He cannot distinguish between what is, and what is not,

essential. He has never in fact had large sums of (his own) money at his disposal, but he would certainly not have known what to do with them. He would always either just put the money away or invest it in something completely safe. On the other hand, he is extremely tenacious in his purposes, and indeed tends to over-estimate his own capacities, or to set up unattainable goals for his family without thinking twice about it (sending me to boarding school, owning his house). He sets no value at all on a well-appointed home or on a balanced life; these things do not seem worth struggling for. He is unable to recognize and seize the right moment for an undertaking; instead, he keeps hesitating (as in the matter of owning his house, which he has been trying to do for years, without success).

His precision was so exaggerated that pedantry is hardly the word for it. When we planned our garden, all the soil had to be passed through a sieve, so that there should not be a single stone. Later, I often had to weed the garden. I was not allowed to use a tool, which would have enabled me to finish the job quickly; I had to pull out each little weed neatly by hand, so that the roots came with it. And heaven help me if I left the tiniest green blade standing! That would have caused father's wrath. Nobody cared how long I took over the job; the point was that everything should be scrupulously neat and clean. I was miserable at this work, for I was too restless to be as pedantic about it as father would have wished. He is extremely pedantic, although he never aims at any achievement worth mentioning. Our garden looks just like that, too. Every speck of ground is used as rationally as could be, but you can't sit down on the grass, because there is no grass.

*   *   *   *   *

Sometime ago, I tried to repair an old oil-stove; it had not been used for eleven years. Nobody seemed to want the thing; my mother did not plan to use it for cooking or any other domestic purpose, my father had no use for it. I had. As I was busy about the stove, my father came over, looked at what I was doing for about a minute and then began to tell me sharply to leave the stove alone, I might ruin it (despite the fact that it did not work anyway). When I did not fall in with his urgently expressed wishes, he was visibly pained. The possibility of my spoiling something, the fact that something was going on contrary to his wishes, were plainly enough to make him suffer.

A few months later, the patient writes of his own former atti-tude to things:

I was attached to the objects in daily use in just the same way as my father. Above all, I always wanted to hoard up new objects instead of using them. If I had a new exercise book, I never wanted to write in it, because that in itself seemed to me to diminish its value. Once the first few pages were filled, the exercise book had lost all value for me. When I was thirteen, a younger cousin came on a visit. He wanted to play bowls with my chessmen and a rubber ball. I was horrid to him, and wouldn't allow it, because I was afraid it might damage the paint of my chessmen. In the same way, I never wanted to lend a book of mine, for fear it could be damaged. Why, I myself never really wanted to open a new book, for fear of soiling it. On the other hand, I was often too cowardly to say no when I was asked to lend something. Then I would be tormented with fear about the thing I had lent.

Nicholas Berdyaev attached particular importance to the metaphysical significance of 'evil objectivity', making an object out of everything. But this central problem of both individual and collective neurosis can be viewed and explored only from the point of view of values; for natural science, which as we all know pursues 'objectivity' (cf. p. 11), is concerned only with objects. To explain 'objectivization' in neurosis by means of neurotic over-valued ideas is to be guilty of tautology. In fact the tautology is already contained in the term 'over-valuation'—what scale of values enables us to 'over- or under-value' anything?

We are for ever finding, in neurosis, that individuals and the external world are reduced to objects. Emphasis of experience is nourished by this process, because experience is no longer embedded in a frame of reference, but is regarded as object proof for one's own object existence.

Psychotherapists of different schools have observed and described in detail how for instance love relationships suffer when the partner and the relationship itself come to be regarded as mere objects. The union of lovers (what L. Binswänger calls the 'us-ness') is lost as soon as the partner becomes 'another', a stranger, an object. For instance, sexual feelings are turned into absolutes, serving as the outward affirmation of the already impaired 'us-ness'. But the laws governing objectivization are inexorable: sexuality also becomes an 'object' and, like any other thing, needs its specific prescription. But the prescriptions for 'objectivised sexuality' are anything but easy and certain. Most cases of sexual insecurity, sexual dependence, male impotence and female frigidity can well be explained, phenomenologically, in terms of such an isolation of the enlarged self from the world of alien and dangerous objects. Psychotherapeutic improvement also takes place only after a careful analysis of the causal chain, but also after a thorough change of attitude. 'Tactical' advice may in such cases be useful, but in certain circumstances it may be dangerous, further complicating the prescription.

The world cannot be reduced to objects without our own individuality becoming equally reduced. Each traumatising experience, each setback, humiliation and neglect operating in the birth of a neurosis, have at one time revealed to the defenceless self in fragility and weakness. The human person has come to regard itself as a thing, the toy of circumstance, and has accordingly forfeited courage, love, trust and dignity. In his bitterness and disappointment, the threatening world that has reduced him to an object is experienced also as a hostile thing. He thus suffers a loss of reality by withdrawing his energies from communion with the world and casting them upon the defence of his thing-like individuality.

It is instructive to consider the phenomenology of neurosis from the point of view of objectivization. Neuroses are, as Max Picard puts it, 'a disconnected world': they consist of unrelated bits and pieces which resist all attempts to be made subservient to the enlarged individual. What is strange inspires fear. Not only sexual complexes, as indicated above, but even the most inoffensive elements in our surroundings may become threatening objects in this way. A kind of 'motor neurosis' can easily be observed which derives from exaggerated reflex action, that is separation of the self from its surroundings (inability to swim or to dance, being clumsy and so on). Embittered, dissatisfied people often become manually very clumsy—women break dishes, for instance. These mishaps do not arise merely from an unconscious desire for symbolic destruction, but also from a generalised hostility to objects. The mishap is always in some sense an indication of an extreme 'thing-ness', an absence of love being an enemy. It is probably not merely fanciful to maintain that certain objects (watches, alarm-clocks, stoves, tools) like dogs, obey only their master and resist others. There is a case for expanding the psychopathology of incapacities, as well as of errors, although the essential work in this field has already been done by Freud.

It is, incidentally, one of the central symptoms of neurosis, that the unrelated and hypertrophied individual cannot inwardly recognize any Providence, and being of little faith wishes to be secure against all the world and against himself. In the neurotic world where everything has become an object, man himself is the central 'object', which in his fright he worships like an idol.

15 *The false God*

We may now summarise the heretical view of life in neurosis, that is, its *negative* aspect, as follows: Neurotic guilt, which the neurotic has repressed and for which he seeks a scapegoat (cf. p. 33) consists in the fact that he has forsaken the hierarchy of values and allowed his own feelings to become absolute law. The absolute character conferred on partial truths is the neurotic's life heresy. Every heresy endangers the total structure of human relationships to the absolute; it presupposes the existence of an absolute, but transfers its characteristics to relative and partial truths. Heresy is therefore a defection from the absolute towards idolatry; but at the same time it also bears witness to the absolute, even if the evidence has not been fully deciphered or realised. This is what happens in neurosis, and it is not surprising to find that the same phenomenon is described by Wilfred Daim as the 'idol' (op. cit., Part III) and by Viktor E. Frankl as the 'unconscious God',[14] though the 'unknown God' might be a more suitable description. The pessimism implicit in the first term in some sense fits the negative aspect of neurosis, with which we are at present concerned, whereas the latter term is more appropriate to its positive aspect, to which we shall soon turn.

It is evident that, when, in connection with neurosis, we speak of a defection from God we do not necessarily mean nationally founded atheism, but rather a dimly felt conflict of conscience between 'recognizing God' and 'recognizing the idol' (Daim, op. cit., p. 146). Rational orthodoxy can perfectly well coexist with existential heresy, which after all is simply the conferring of absolute character on the relative; and not merely rational orthodoxy alone, but even orthodoxy latent in the emotions.

[14] *Der Unbewusste Gott*, Vienna, Amandus-Edition, 1948.

This is only one more instance of the disconnected character of the neurotic world. The neurotic punishes himself for his defection from the hierarchy of values; the most rational of neurotics —compulsive neurotics—are themselves able to recognize the absolutised character of their feelings fairly clearly, but without being able to draw the necessary conclusions, and existentially to retrace their steps.

Mrs G. H., a fifty-year-old compulsive neurotic, who has suffered from diverse phobias ever since she can remember, writes, after undergoing lobotomy, at the beginning of her post-operative analytic treatment:

All human communities, even the wildest and most primitive, have some kind of religion. Probably because man, powerless in the face of all external forces, needs something to cling to from which he can derive strength and consolation.

My greatest weakness is a probably innate tendency to inordinate pedantry. My memories of this urge go back to my earliest childhood experiences. Already at that time I lived in constant fear of not being able to perform a task, to my own and my mother's satisfaction. When I was ten, this fear had already reached the stage of hours of compulsive activities, which later disappeared and were replaced by others. This fear was constantly fed by 'conscientious' teachers, who were forever telling me that my greatest efforts were inadequate. Such corrections were a mental torture to me, which at the age of six used to drive me into screaming fits of terror.

Thus my fear that even my utmost efforts would never earn satisfaction gradually became a sense of *my own* powerlessness in the face of outside forces, of which I spoke at the beginning.

And, just as every people builds up its own hierarchy of gods, whose favour it curries by constant sacrifices and whom it implores when great descisions are at stake, I too have built up a hierarchy of idols, from whom I hoped for deliverance from my perpetual fear and for the fulfilment of my deepest yearning.

This unbridled longing is simply for a happy, easy enjoyment of life, such as I could only attain if I completed my work to my own satisfaction. But I have never been able to obtain this satisfaction: my pendantry has always stood in the way. Therefore the sacrifices I made to my idols had to be increased constantly. The smallest comfort that might have made my life pleasanter had to be sacrificed. I have read of a Mexican tribe who, in times of great drought, when man and beast are nearly going mad for lack of water, crucify a specially selected member of the tribe so that the gods may send rain. I, too, crucify myself several times a day, for my body suffers more and more from my compulsive actions.

My idols literally form a hierarchy; the highest most dreadful divinity is all the dirt that may be spread from a lavatory. Then comes the dirt from the ground, which all animals use to receive their excrement. The third divinity inhabits all doors and other objects which may gather dirt and pass it on to me or my husband.

But I also have *clean* divinities (as the Buddhists have gods of destruction and of preservation).

The highest of these is the cleanliness of everything I have washed myself, according to all my pedantic rules; for instance, freshly laundered clothes, my own body, my hair, etc. After that there is every possible degree of cleanliness, but these often shift with the varying conditions of my neurosis.

In speaking of the lavatory as 'the highest divinity', this compulsive neurotic starkly describes the absurdity of her existential defection from the hierarchy of values. But she is still mistaken in the way in which she places her heresy; for the defection began with her having set her own self at the centre of the universe, defending it symbolically against the threatening dangers of moral disintegration and contamination. The compulsion to wash is as it were only a symbolic liturgy for the need to have to wash herself inwardly clean. Only a lengthy causal analysis can uncover the origin of this symbol. Yet what is important for us here is above all the fallacious synthesis, the false relation to false gods, which after all constitutes the absurdity and senselessness of neurosis. The fact that Mrs. G. H.'s rational recognition of her compulsive idols for what they were does not free her from them, is shown by the fact that her views on God also still show clearly neurotic characteristics.

What I think about God.
I have two different conceptions of God.
The first is that of my childhood, the one that develops in everyone through religious instruction. According to this, God is a loving father, whom one can trustfully ask for anything that is in one's heart.
But I was afraid of him too, because he was supposed to punish

all lack of faith as a sin. Since as a child I already had all kinds of doubts about the teachings of the Catholic Church, I never even dared to think about any problem. From the time I was six, I lived in constant fear about the health and life of my mother, and of other members of the family; I had to pray about it every day, often for hours, so I needed God's help and could not afford to risk being on bad terms with him.

During the dreadful bombing nights I went on praying, because when they can no longer expect any help from man, weak people turn again to God. The faith of children is indeed strong.

It is strange that since my mother died and the war came to an end, I have stopped praying. That shows that I always prayed only out of *fear*. And ever since I have changed my views about God. My present views are based on an essay by a former president of the New York Academy of Science.

I now see in God a supreme technical intelligence and supreme wisdom. There is a large amount of purely scientific proofs of his existence. The life of every creature on this earth depends on an infinite number of laws, which all have to be mutually complementary. The smallest change in *any one* of these laws would bring about the death of all living creatures. It seems to me as good as impossible that all this should be organized purely by *accident*.

I believe in the immortality of matter and in eternity, and when I think of the wonders of genes and chromosomes, it also seems possible to believe in the immortality of our souls. I am convinced that 'there are more things in heaven and earth . . .', for science is only at its beginnings and there are so many miracles. The universe, all birth and growth and a thousand other concepts are all miracles, which neither science nor philosophy can fathom.

Whether God is beneficent, I am not sure. Force prevails everywhere in life, and wherever there is life there is cruelty and suffering. Yet, since all the higher animals, and man in particular, have also been endowed by creation with the gift of goodness, it seems possible that God may be good after all, since he could not confer upon us an attribute he did not possess.

We human beings are still unspeakably smaller, when compared with God, than say, the infusoria in a water drop are compared with man. What we wish for in our earthly life cannot possibly coincide with the unfathomable decisions of God. I cannot imagine, therefore, that human prayer might alter God's decisions. I have often, in the course of my life, prayed for the life of someone I loved. Some of those people lived, others died. I always prayed with the same devotion, but God paid no regard to my wishes, because *His* decisions, which I cannot fathom, happened to be different. On the other hand, I believe that for every believer prayer represents an enormous source of strength and can give infinite consolation.

In the Our Father, we pray: *Thy* will be done on earth is it is in heaven . . .

This peculiar theology certainly accounts for the incapacity to combine contradictorily absolutised conceptions in a living synthesis. Yet erring though this conscience may be, it is still a conscience. We shall see that herein lies the possibility of liberation from neurosis. If neurosis only had negative aspects, which in this world of limited being is neither possible nor imaginable, it would obviously be incurable. But neurosis is not merely a lie, it is also in some way the sensitive conscience's patent of nobility. Unfortunately, this fact too is misused by neurotics themselves, who use their conflicts of conscience to build themselves up into some kind of intellectual *élite*.

In the following pages we shall attempt a phenomenological investigation of the positive aspect of neurosis, by which therapeutic efforts find in the psychological make-up of the neurotic, something to work on and even a certain measure of support.

Chapter Three

THE POSITIVE ASPECT OF NEUROSIS:
NOTIONS OF THE ABSOLUTE

16. *The neurotic dialectic*

THE picture of the neurotic attitude to life which we have
sketched so far has no outlet for pessimism. It is, however,
a one-sided and unfair picture; and not because the darker
tones have been laid on too liberally—on the contrary, the rapid
description which we attempted in the previous chapter cannot
possibly indicate all the shadows of the neurotic heresy. Yet if
we stopped at this point, our truthful description of neurosis
would amount to an absolutised half truth. We would have described neurosis with neurotic means, singling out but the negative aspect of a very complicated state of affairs. Such a description would be unjust. This is not to say that the moral criterion
is inadequate for the description of neurosis; far from it. On the
contrary, we hope to show that neurotic realities cannot be correctly appreciated unless they are related to metaphysical values
lying beyond the realm of biology. Moral 'neutrality' in judging
a phenomenon which is itself caused by a defection from the
concept of value, is an impossibility. In Chapter I we have
attempted to show that the problem of neurosis remains insoluble
save on metaphysical and moral premises, and in Chapter II we
hope to have shown that the characteristic of neurosis is, precisely, to replace absolute values by relative ones.

We are not concerned with providing our neurotic with some
moral judgments which he cannot understand. We are concerned
with the meaning of neurosis, not with its therapy. Whether, and
how far, moral judgments are to be admitted in the treatment of
a concrete case, remains a problem of method, even technique.

61

Yet it is clear by now that, as long as the neurotic remains blind to certain ethical values, because he has repressed them, it would also be premature to discuss these with him.

It is not a question of showing what moral judgment we should pronounce on a neurotic, but rather that the moral judgment of neurosis itself must not be one-sided. If we were to see only the heretical component in the life-heresy'—the existential lie, the mistaken decision, the enlargement of the individual self, presumption, greed for experience, cowardly machinations, pseudo-knowledge and pseudo-obligations—we would ourselves remain attached to the negative aspects and our knowledge would be not only partial, but in conflict with reality and tainted with error. For truth will not suffer itself to be divided. In order to do justice to a complicated psychological phenomenon, some measure of systematic division is unavoidable, but the part knowledge thus gained must be balanced and supplemented. If we are to overcome totalitarian systems of thought and attain what Albert Niedermeyer terms a 'universalist anthropology', we must be prepared to allow for a living synthesis of apparently contradictory, partial truths. Individual totalitarianism and social totalitarianism mirror each other; individual neurosis heightens collective neurosis, which in turn fosters individual neurosis. Neurosis is in some sense the superstition of our age, and is particularly characteristic of its spiritual make-up. The very fact that neurotics tend to seek the causes of their mental disturbance in the body cannot be considered apart from the prevailing faith in determinism. Similarly, when the neurotic uses the concept of 'inferiority-feelings' in order to give a causal explanation of his fear in the struggle for existence, this cannot be understood except in the light of the dissolution of our outdated social order. Again it is in some sense due to idealist philosophy that experience for its own sake, rather than objective order, is regarded as giving meaning to life. And without the fact of boundless individualism the preponderant position psychology has assumed in the present century cannot be understood. Without the prevailing vulgar materialism psychology could not have considered itself to be a discipline of natural science. Conversely, it cannot be explained without the neurotic rejection of the hierarchy of values, without relative truths being regarded as absolute ones that it is precisely the doctrine of neurosis that remains attached to such absolutising. On the one hand, naturalist psychology diagnosed neurosis as an 'illness' exclusively conditioned from below (the 'nothing but' explanation, Chapter I, 5); on the other hand, there seems to be some inkling of the negative metaphysical aspect of neurosis, and accordingly the whole phenomenon of neurosis is then dismissed from above as inferiority, simulation, weakness and badness. Many doctors are a party to this undignified treatment which is the reverse of materialism; if in an alleged 'illness' not even any organic causes can be found, it is made nothing of and regarded as inferior. There is an unconscious tendency to consider physical disturbances alone as really worth being noticed. Equally one-sided though apparently more differentiated is the view of neurosis of those philosophers and psychologists who attend only to that aspect which is at odds with reality. It has even become the fashion now to see the meaning of neurosis only in the false decision involved. If we intended to follow this fashion, we might have ended this book at the previous chapter. This attitude, which is particularly prevalent in existentialist heroism and stoicism, is a neurotic extravagance. It is a kind of inverted pharisaism, which requires free decision in circumstances in which, due to human inadequacy, it is as yet not familiar with this pharisaism from the phenomenology of the type of neurosis which overlooks its own conditioned character and believes itself to be free, that is neurotic 'angelism' (Charles Baudouin, cf. p. 40).

It is interesting to note, by the way, that such one-sided judgments of the phenomenon of neurosis are generally peculiar to people who have no living contact. The widespread vulgar contempt for neurotics always indicates that there is fear of coming into closer contact with such phenomena, since evidently there is lack of self-confidence. But those grand systems concerning 'decision' and 'freedom' have come about less through contacts with men afflicted by neurosis than through theorising. This is rather more prone to encourage 'angel complexes' than the actual day to day effort to liberate men from them! We may doubt the vocation of any psychotherapist who has never felt ashamed in his own consulting room, and has never experienced something akin to the gospel injunction 'Judge not that ye be not judged'

(Matthew 7:11), or 'Whosoever shall say, Thou fool, shall be in danger of hell fire' (cf. Matthew 5:22).

We have so far been concerned only with one, the *negative* aspect of neurosis. It was essential to recognize this negative aspect clearly, since it led us to our thesis that any conception of neurosis that is not value-conscious will be likely to fail. We now turn to the positive aspect of neurosis. Only that which is positive can be used and developed. It is not intended to give the impression that the author would, like a clever, unscrupulous lawyer, pass all of a sudden from the prosecution to the defence. Above all, it is not a question of accusing or of whitewashing the neurotic; rather it is the ambiguous nature of neurosis which becomes a sort of crucible where the dialectical ambiguity of human life is almost hopelessly intertwined. It can safely be said that every psychological content in neurosis is ambivalent and bears eloquent witness to the ambiguity of human motives. In speaking of the positive aspect of neurosis, we shall have to remember that 'aspect' must not be understood in the noncommittal sense of an uninvolved observer, who can pass at will from the pessimistic to the optimistic point of view. The term is intended to mean, rather, that neurosis has a deeply upsetting function in human destinies and also imposes upon them the obligation to new and positive action. Neurosis is both a betrayal of what we are called to be in life and a confirmation of that calling. It should therefore be clear that it is not for psychotherapy to conjure up the neurotic's calling, but to clarify and encourage it. Psychotherapy will be able to do this only if neurosis itself offers certain facts to go by for its liberating activity.

17. *The voice of the conscience*

If initially it is agreed to define conscience as an innate faculty to designate some matters as good and others as evil, this faculty must, in order to function properly, refer to certain models which education provides. All these models, together in so far as they have proved effective, constitute the Freudian 'superego'. But to equate the superego with conscience is to confuse the exercise of a faculty with the faculty itself. It is a fallacy, a typically 'nothing-but' explanation, which at most can tell us about its author's view of the world. A tyrannical superego, or conversely an excessively lax super-I, merely mean that the capacity to consider something good or evil was due, in the former case, to exaggerated social requirements, or, in the latter, to inadequate models. The superego is the sometimes excellent, sometimes inadequate product of the personal conscience and of the requirements of society. The superego is the concrete, practically effective conscience, but this pragmatic conscience can be evaluated only from the standpoint of a hierarchy of values.

The neurotic punishes himself for faults of which he is not even aware, or else for those which he uses as scapegoats for other, repressed faults. The most striking feature of neurosis is its painfulness, the torment it implies: the neurotic suffers so much from it that he must seek help. The neurotic torment constitutes the symptoms of neurosis. Pain and fever are also the symptoms of illness (sometimes even of neurosis); they are useful signals of a struggle for health. The neurotic signals also indicate that the neurotic is struggling, not with an exogenous disease, but with the 'disease of the bad conscience'; he is fighting for his conscience. The 'health' he has to defend is not merely his physical well-being, but the integrity of his own personality, his peace of conscience. Biological law, C. von Monakow's 'synderesis', implacably punishes every offence against right living. This punishment takes the form of pain signals, which constitute both a barrier for the transgression and an exhortation to recovery. Neurotic torment is evidently concerned with a higher level of integrity; the spiritual justification of life itself. The neurotic symptom represents punishment and exhortation in a conflict situation of conscience. But we have seen that neurosis is a pseudo-solution. No repression can reconcile the irreconcilable; no symbolic action can make the intolerable tolerable. Neurosis is indeed a 'disease of the bad conscience', though often transposed to the somatic level. This is where the positive aspect of neurotic symptoms is revealed, that aspect which, like an expiation, punishes the neurotic for his irreconcilable desires and exhorts him to find a solution. Whenever there is a neurotic symptom there is also striving towards solution and liberation. Neurosis is a pseudo-solution, but it already contains a hint of the final, true solution.

Of course, self-torment, neurotic self-punishment is imposed in order to conjure up an apparent solution of the conflict by means of appeasing the gods, as Polycrates appeased them, but this is unthinkable without guilt feelings; it is born, in fact, out of a sense of sin, out of the torment of a sensitive conscience. The neurotic symptom is closely connected with the problems of offence and untruth; it must be regarded as, on the one hand, a sign of offence that has taken place, but on the other, as a positive exhortation. Neurotic torment is, in fact, an attempt to correct the uncomprehended and unconscious lie at the heart of one's own life. The neurotic dimly feels that he has lost his way, and punishes himself for it; ineffectively, because he does not know where he began to lose it. The neurotic symptom does not, indeed, lead to truth; but it is quite incomprehensible unless we assume that it represents a protest against the existential lie. Even naturalistic depth psychology has recognized this, since it regards the neurotic symptom as an abortive attempt at healing.

These reflections lead to the difficult task of considering the affirmative significance, in terms of life and truth, not only of the superficial symptoms of neurosis, but also of the neurotic mental attitude. Neurosis is a significant vital process, which has a profound existential effect on one's whole outlook. Consideration of this mental attitude is made much more difficult, both by the endless complexity of the process to be observed and by the specific ambiguity by which all motives are affected. We need hardly stress again that it is a simplification merely to differentiate between positive and negative aspects of neurosis. Each neurotic phenomenon must be regarded as being at the same time positive and negative; for there occurs the struggle between good and evil, yea and nay, truth and lie in each neurotic phenomenon. The tragic destiny of existence, weary of its own limitations and for ever trying to bridge the paradox of wanting to participate simultaneously in being and non-being, is reflected in neurosis. A pseudo-solution is, indeed, an attempt at a solution which concerns the very problem of existence. A vital function in every pattern of life must thus be conceded to neurosis. It is an attempt to realise the pattern, though it wavers always between betrayal and fidelity.

18. *The attempt at a solution*

Pierre Janet regards neurosis as a fixed and useless repetition of certain defence mechanisms in a situation in which the sunken mental level, *niveau mental*, frantically tries to meet the raised demands of the surrounding world. This conception of neurosis has certainly not been essentially invalidated by the advances in our knowledge of the subject. We may even accept the pessimistic theory of the sunken level. Doubtless constitutional factors likewise affect the origin and development of neurosis. One person may well be unharmed by troubles that might destroy another. Yet the question also arises whether Janet did not, in working out his theory, use an arbitrary criterion, and whether his apparently quantitative theory of the sunken level is not based on value judgments as unsure as the naturalist theory of the psychic norm (cf. pp. 14 and ff.). For who has laid down that the individual must be able to meet the demands made by his surroundings? Life can become so thoroughly unbearable for people, particularly for small children (since the end roots of neurosis are always to be sought in early childhood) that they simply have to resort to defence mechanisms, to a convulsive *defence* in Janet's sense. The deepest injury and constant threat of their existence, may present them with demands to which their average ('normal') reactions are simply inadequate.

Certainly neurotic defence mechanisms are neither sufficient nor appropriate. Yet they are based on a real experience. 'The burnt child dreads the fire.' Janet's repetition of defence mechanisms is only a special case of Freud's 'repetitive compulsion': both phenomena are closely related to the development of conditioned reflexes in Pavolv's sense. These, however, offer some security for the acquisition, simplification and stereotyped retention of activities learnt by practice, and thus play a distinctively positive role in individual development. It is therefore odd to find the Freudian school assigning this progressive function of the organism to the 'death urge'; repetitive compulsion primarily serves to facilitate life processes by making use of conventional patterns. Life would not be possible if one were exclusively faced with new tasks.

The circumstance that neurosis begins with an attempt to

master a desperate situation proves that—if we assume that desperate situation—neurosis constitutes a valuable, vital function which furthers development. All schools of depth psychology, incidentally, have stressed the compensatory function of neurosis. Obviously there is something to compensate if something is lacking in the development. We have, in discussion, met with the argument that there could be no question of a positive human function in neurosis, because modern research has established the existence of neurosis also in animals. It is a fact that the Russian school of psychology, starting from Pavlov's brilliant experiments, has produced experimental neuroses in animals. After the animals had been trained in certain series of conditioned reflexes, the stimuli used were so arranged as to call for contradictory reactions. The animals showed all the signs of vegetative neurosis, and also such unmistakable psychological reactions as depression and irritability. Severe neurosis can, by the way, also be ascertained in animals without such complicated experiments. Cruel treatment, impatient training, selfish pampering, constant interference give rise to neuroses in animals as much as in human beings. But in the very case of the animals, the sinking of the psychic level is not immediately evident. What is evident is a threat to existence, which causes the animal to panic and which it tries to counter by means of defence mechanisms. As regards the positive meaning of neurosis, however, this affects the total psychological structure of the individual concerned, whether animal or human. All human emotions can also be observed in a rudimentary form in animals. This fact in no way entitles us to resort to a 'nothing but' solution (cf. pp. 3 and ff.) because there is certainly some connection but no identity between more and less developed creatures. Neurosis affects the whole man, as it affects the whole animal. The significance of neurosis in man must therefore be a human one. The significance of human neurosis cannot, admittedly, be purely metaphysical, since man is not a pure spirit; but neither can it be purely biological. Human neurosis (and with this we end our consideration of animal neurosis) has a significance which permeates the biological, the psycho-physical and the spiritual levels, and which must be acknowledged on all these levels.

Neurosis is, as we have sufficiently shown, a pseudo-solution.

But it is a pseudo-solution precisely because the available elements were, as yet, inadequate for a real solution. It is a tentative defence measure; it is therefore of vital importance, but it awaits better solutions.

Neurosis is characterized by greed for experience, it constantly attempts to re-establish the condition of pleasure. Freud has clearly shown the part played by neurotic fixation in pleasurable stages of existence. These stages are normally outgrown in the course of development. But if the process of outgrowing them is made particularly difficult, the individual will fall back upon accustomed pleasurable conditions. For instance, a child for whom the transition from the oral to the anal phase is made particularly difficult, will develop a tendency to meet the difficulties of transition by overemphasising the phase he is accustomed to. This is where the views of Freud and Adler coincide: a factual inferiority in a certain situation (the inferiority need not be, but may be, innate) gives rise to overcompensation. This overcompensation, which confers absolute value on the relative, is profoundly significant, and should never be regarded as purely negative. In the same way, a child returning to boarding school may at the moment of parting show the hysterical symptoms of illness so frequent in children; he is therefore not just inferior. His despair is indeed not wholly adapted to the harsh reality; but the emotions which resist being sent away also have positive significance, and any skilful educator will be able to understand and use this significance. The positive significance of the neurotic defence mechanism becomes increasingly clearer as the claims presented by reality become more severe, indeed more cruel. A child that is constantly and grievously ill-treated, or one that, through being spoilt was not prepared to respond to the normal requirements of life, will defend his integrity still more significantly in his neurotic reactions.

Miss L. G., forty years old, seeks medical help on account of dysmenorrhoea, depression and repeated tonsillitis. After removing her tonsils, however, the physician attending her directs her towards a psychoanalyst. Miss L. G. claims to be *virgo intacta* and declares that men are a worthless lot. However, it gradually becomes clear that even Miss L. G. has, in the course of her life, entertained softer feelings towards men (her transference to the analyst also takes on considerable proportions). But, she says, she has always been unlucky; either she did not explain her feelings in time, or she fell in love with a hesitant man, or even with a priest, etc . . . Eventually it appears that the patient has never been able to overcome an exaggerated attachment to her mother; the mother surrounded her with anxious care, had her taught privately, and would not let her become properly independent. Moreover, the mother allowed her daughter to assume a more or less masculine role in the family: Miss L. G. had to rescue the family's tottering finances and, in her own words, she had to be 'the man in the family'. She now remembers that these periods of great strain and effort were always accompanied by an interruption in her menstrual periods. She also remembers that for a time she must have suffered from morbid fear of objects likely to explode, gasometers, boilers, etc. . . . According to her own statement these memories are accompanied by 'explosions', the patient reveals a veritable storm of emotion; besides, she menstruates heavily and has diarrhoea. But now the long forgotten childhood experiences begin to emerge; of these we need only say that her training in habits of cleanliness had probably been upset by her excessively orderly and impatient mother. The memory of one long forgotten scene gives rise to violent emotion in the usually well controlled patient: she was once severely scolded by her mother when she had diarrhoea, whereupon a lasting constipation set in.

C. D., twenty-four years old, a doctor at law, seeks psychotherapy on account of a speech defect for which no organic cause can be found. Objectively, he does in fact suffer from a slight associative aphasia (stammering), or rather from the initial stammer (E. Fröschels), characterised by a clonus in the rhythm of speech and which appears in the transition from occasional speech disturbances (associative ataxia) to the fixing of the attention on speech. The patient feels that he speaks too slowly (in actual fact he relates his anamnesis at breakneck speed). Already at the age of twelve he had the impression of being unable to express his thoughts quickly enough. Now he wants to become a barrister, but fears that he will be unable to carry out his plan because of his speech defect. The picture of his childhood development emerges only gradually. At the age of twelve he had an intestinal disease which necessitated a certain delicacy in matters of food; he had always eaten sparingly, preferring to nibble between meals, for which he had often been beaten by his parents. Up to the age of about eleven, the family doctor forbade his being sent to boarding school; but his parents were determined he should go. His mother suffered an injury in the leg, which resulted in an operation on the knee; necessitating the son having to run errands for her. The mother was always 'nervous' and overwhelmed him with advice as to how he should carry out these errands; she also scolded him for every little fault, and constantly threatened that he would grow up a ne'er-do-well, a gypsy, and such like. Since the boy was weak and sickly, and moreover brought up as an only child in a small town, was constantly surrounded by his parents' pedantic care, he was ill-treated and bullied by other children. Then, at the age of eleven, he entered a Nazi military educational institution (Napola), where the greatest stress was laid on physical prowess. It is hardly surprising that the boy always failed in physical training. His insecurity and 'incompetence' led, after four years of martyrdom, to his expulsion from the institution. The boy constantly felt himself to be slow, clumsy and physically inadequate. He had the impression that his reactions were far too slow. He now remembers that at one time, during a conversation with his instructor, presumably about his 'incompetence', the P.T. instructor scolded him for talking too quickly. He now thinks that he tried to compensate for his insecurity in connection with the hated P.T. by facility in speech. About his university studies, Dr. C. D. reports that his mother threatened that if he did not work well he would end up sweeping the streets. While preparing for his finals, his haste and nervousness became such that he had to withdraw. He also reported intense nervousness and fear in driving, typing, swimming and dancing (cf. p. 56).

Dr C. D. is the same patient whose accounts we have already met on pp. 45 and 52.

These extracts from two case histories are probably characteristic of the fate of most neurotics. In both cases, the neurosis appeared as an attempt at a solution, in a situation which made excessively heavy claims on the personalities of those involved. Causal analysis in both cases lays bare fixations at the childhood level: the anal phase in the case of Miss L. G., and presumably the oral phase for C. D. In the course of these very early stages of development, the personality was already overburdened by bodily weakness (gastric and intestinal illness) and, no doubt much more significantly, by an unsympathetic, traumatizing education. Then the already evident weak point became the target of psychical affronts. In both cases the incipient neurotics react by means of already acquired exaggerated defence mechanisms. Of course our point of view is only one of many: neurosis is not only positive achievement, as we have already pointed out. The number of possible, and necessary, viewpoints in the consideration of neurosis is so large that very few case histories manage to strike a correct balance between all of them. Nothing is easier than to draw up a neurotic's case history from two or three angles only, and to disregard other important elements.

Probably the greatest defect of depth psychology is its pretension to judge and evaluate psychological phenomena on the basis of unreliable 'nothing but' criteria. We have considered according to Kurt Schneider that abnormal personalities are personalities that are not average. From among these he distinguishes between psychopathic personalities, who suffer from their deviation from the average, and others whose deviation causes suffering to society. There is no need to embark upon a discussion of the concept of psychopathy as a whole. It is sufficient to note that it contains a value judgment which has neither accuracy nor the clarity of a philosophy of value to recommend it. We shall confine ourselves to the consideration of neurotics. According to Schneider's view of 'abnormality', neurotics would be either simple psychopaths or persons showing 'psychopathic reactions'. Apart from the question of whether their 'psychopathic' peculiarity is inborn or reactive, neurotics would be persons with 'psychopathic reactions' which cause suffering either to themselves or to society. But closer inspection will reveal the cloven hoof by which any naturalistic conception of neurosis is marked. Neurosis is being evaluated. Obviously it is evaluated only negatively. It is without further consideration dismissed as inferior. Why? Because neurosis means suffering. And suffering is said to be equal to inferiority. This is the logical result of making an absolute out of a relative experience. This is the most immediately obvious negative aspect of neurosis itself, and also of a science which purports to treat neurosis. The devil is to be driven out in the name of Beelzebub.

That evil must be fought becomes clear precisely in relation to the hierarchy of values. That suffering and pain also have a positive significance is understandable only from the point of view of a theory of values. Of all modern depth psychologists,

Viktor E. Frankl has certainly been the severest critic of the 'untenable character of the success morality' (the pleasure principle made absolute). 'Lack of success is not equivalent to meaninglessness': to suffer from a condition that ought not to be is an 'essential and significant' part of human life.[1] We have seen that the conscience, even if disguised beyond recognition, is revealed in neurosis. At the origin of neurosis lies suffering 'from a condition that ought not to be', and neurotic self-punishment is an imperfect attempt to put an end to this condition. The neurotic becomes entangled in a net of 'faults and endeavours that ought not to be'. The situation is further complicated by the fact that every failure is at the same time an attempt at improvement, otherwise there would be no neurosis but only an unmistakable bad conscience. If I fail to do my duty towards someone who is close to me, and realize my failure, I am free to satisfy my conscience and to make amends. If, however, due to my defence mechanism, I torment the same person, using his qualities, for instance, or his ingratitude as a scapegoat for my egotism, my dissatisfaction increases and I become more rigid in my defensive attitude. This is already a neurotic reaction. Restlessness, depression and fear will accompany my misguided defence. My failure will also be my punishment; an ineffective punishment that was not clearly recognized.

Neurosis is the soul's desperate attempt to emerge from an intolerable situation by self-help. From this point of view, Alphonse Maeder's work on 'Self-preservation and self-healing' (Zurich, Rascher, 1949) is of great importance. Maeder was the first to point out (before Adler and Jung) the prospective self-activity of dreams; he is also one of the few authors who have described neurosis as a positive attempt to restore equilibrium.

It would, however, be false optimism to assume that self-regulation and self-healing could dispense with crises and reverses. The cleansing process of neurosis is a highly dramatic and difficult development, the meaning of which, however, is provided by the search for a synthesis of life.

Certainly the neurotic is unbearable for himself and for those around him. But do we know enough of the struggle implied in

[1] Viktor E. Frankl, *Ärztliche Seelsorge*, 4th edition, Vienna, Deticke, 1948, passim.

his efforts to heal himself? These efforts are apparently useless: if the neurotic directed his energy to seemingly 'useful' ends, he might do great things. This utilitarian argument has a certain justification. Yet it is no mean achievement to keep on struggling for a solution to the problem of life despite constant setbacks. That is precisely what the neurotic is doing. Like Don Quixote, he is fighting windmills, since he has not clearly recognized his opponent, preferring to see in him a scapegoat. Like the fearless knight, however, he performs feats which may seem ludicrous to a utilitarian world, but which bear witness to the fire raging in his conscience.

19. *The question of vocation*

What, then, is the neurotic struggling for? Why does he take upon himself these strenuous efforts, which constantly threaten to crush him? At first sight his aim may appear purely selfish; after all, we have shown how the neurotic, driven by his greed for experience, comes to absolutise certain highly questionable values. Indeed, his aims are so selfish that they may be reduced to a single one—to defend his existence. The neurotic struggles in order not to succumb. He is a dogged fighter, but not a clear-sighted one. One might therefore be inclined to assign to the neurotic struggle a purely biological function: the defence of a way of life, and the neurotic's way of life is incomplete and heretical. Yet, in accusing the neurotic of making the relative into an absolute, we must remain consistent and admit that the neurotic, in defending his existence, also serves the transcendent purpose of that existence. The meaning of life may, for the neurotic, be clouded and diminished almost beyond recognition; in relation to the hierarchy of values it remains transparent and untouched. Moreover, we have sufficiently seen that neurosis is an unsuccessful attempt to come to terms with conscience. For the neurotic struggle is not purely biological; frequently the neurotic even tries to kill his conscience, which, however, Phoenix-like is reborn, from its own ashes. It is not our business, as Frankl said, to ask the meaning of life: it is life itself that puts the questions. This implies not only the condemnation of the neurotic attitude to life, but also its purgation. The neurotic has a heretical answer for questions life puts to him and yet he 'says yea unto life'. How much more difficult it is for him to say yea to this life which he does not understand! The whole system of false rationalizations is a labyrinth through which the neurotic wanders in search of an unknown exit. Ever unfaithful to the meaning of life, the neurotic yet has inklings of a vocation of which he has become aware in his confused wandering.

Thus our question about the meaning of the neurotic struggle turns into the new question concerning the neurotic's vocation. This question too he himself will answer wrongly. Neurotics often say in the course of psychotherapy: 'I want so little from life, I want no more than the luck that is everybody's due, I want no more than average human happiness. Is that really too much to ask? Why cannot I have enough to make life bearable once in a while?' What can we tell him? That he himself is at fault? That he is asking too much, not by asking for average and normal things, but simply in daring to ask for anything at all? That he has no right to bother life, but that life will make its demands of him? Surely such counter questions cannot solve or answer his own questions? Who can be blind to the fact that the neurotic struggle is a struggle for universal human values? Certainly the meaning of life is not exhausted by happiness, joy or pleasure. A psychology which is cognizant only of these values will remain caught in a net of meaninglessness. But surely a man who defends his share in all human values, including happiness, is in his rights?

And yet the neurotic is mistaken. Not in his desire to make human existence as agreeable as possible, but rather in considering this as his vocation. His vocation might on the contrary be described as a vocation to tragic existence. And it is this vocation that he resists. He refuses to recognize it, as it was recognized, for instance, by Job who was a man of God and yet against him. Those who, at this point, speak of unscientific pathos may be right inasmuch as a science that fails to acknowledge the tragic character of human existence cannot be pathetic. Such a science, however, would be divorced from value; such an anthropology would probably be valueless. As for those who, in the neurotic tragedy, can see only masochism, they are simply confusing tragedy with peculiarity. Certainly the neurotic also has masochistic traits. But he has no primary vocation to masochism.

The masochist does not suffer from his urge towards suffering. Did not Freud himself glimpse in neurosis a negation of perversion? To explain the vocation to tragic existence only as masochism is, precisely, only a hedonistic explanation—a 'nothing but' solution (cf. Section 5). The sado-masochist devaluates and 'desecrates' life (cf. E. Strauss, V. E. v. Gebsattel). He, too, proceeds from a neurotic-heretical picture of the world. Yet his attitude is fundamentally different from the usual neurotic attitude: the neurotic does not give up, he refuses to take part in the desecration of life inasmuch as he suffers from that desecration: he suffers from the restricted, threatened, humiliated aspects of being which reveal themselves to him in finite existence. More than the pervert, therefore, he is concerned with what ougl t to be.

Like a bad actor, the neurotic refers the tragedy of life to his own person. He takes on the ham actor's facial contortions, as if the tragedy of life itself were not enough! He misplaces, as we have seen, the tragic elements. His criterion of tragedy is immature and stereotyped: it is his own emotion. He makes tragedy immanent, like a professional tragedian who walks about with troubled brow and woeful countenance. Yet both the neurotic and the actor are displaying to us general human problems. The neurotic's private problem has universal validity; it is the human problem. 'Am I in this world only to suffer?' The question, posed by a young neurotic in an egocentric and unrelated way, is, if it could be posed transcendentally, the main question of human destiny, and not of human destiny alone, but of theodicy, of the divine destiny, the justification of 'the ways of God to man'. If anyone answers that the neurotic's sufferings are 'imaginary', he is judging from a standpoint that is very remote from the sufferer. 'Imaginary suffering' is either a conceptual monstrosity or a very lofty judgment made after the suffering has been overcome. The same human destiny which is meaningful for the history of mankind as a whole emerges also from the subjective suffering of a neurotic's history. Neurosis makes evil immanent; but the evil itself remains potent and can break through the immanence of the life that has afforded it sustenance.

The neurotic wages a day-to-day struggle against this evil, a struggle in which the evil is neither imaginary nor powerless;

and through this very struggle he will try to provide an answer which may be valid within the framework of his own existence, and which therefore refers to all the values which frame, support and shape human existence. Not every neurotic's history is quite as dramatic as the one we quote below by way of example; but each one poses afresh the problem of evil in human destiny.

The case of Mrs J. N., already briefly discussed on p. 37, sheds an interesting light on the consideration of neurotic evolution as a continuous effort to overcome a threat to existence. We will say at once that this sad case ended disastrously, with the patient's suicide, not least because of the inadequacy of the psycho-analyst, who, after some initial success, was forced by external circumstances to interrupt treatment, without having resolved the patient's enormous transference. It is more agreeable to publish only succesful cases, but they can hardly help us to learn from our costly mistakes. We have, moreover, chosen this case to show that, even where the neurotic is defeated at last—pessimists will say by his psychopathic disposition, but this cheap assumption cannot possibly afford even an approximately adequate explanation of the meaning of events—he is defeated only after superhuman efforts to master his life and his sufferings. We have seen that Mrs J. N., whom we left on p. 37 in a condition of improvement that seemed to justify considerable optimism, had already at the age of nineteen been on the verge of a breakdown. The influences at work in her environment, to which we have already alluded, were not immediately clear and only came to light very gradually, after the patient had overcome her extreme shyness and her very considerable repressions. It then appeared that, under a certain cloak of respectability, her childhood circumstances were about as wretched as one could imagine. Her parents were divorced, and she was deeply attached to both. Ever since she could remember, she had witnessed disagreeable scenes, and her own education was inconsistent to a degree, so that as a child she had never experienced anything between exaggerated tenderness on the one hand and a sense of being abandoned on the other. At the age of four, she passed into the care of a young stepmother, who, without intending to be cruel, tormented the child mercilessly. The little girl had more or less forgotten how to speak, and spent her days cowering under the table or behind the laundry basket. She also suffered from severe disturbances in appetite, which her stepmother now tried to overcome by severity. A stick was placed beside the little girl's knife and fork at table; the stepmother, it is true,

D

did not use it very often, but quite often enough to make meals a mental torture for the terrified child. At this stage she also began to vomit. The same thing happened after every meal: the child vomited what she had eaten and received corporal punishment. It is interesting to note that at the beginning of her treatment the patient, then adult, suffered from severe malnutrition and lack of appetite, which were partially overcome only after she had remembered the following events. Her stepmother simply forbade her to vomit, and so the child often sat for long periods with her own vomit in her mouth. Once there was a major misfortune: the child could no longer keep the nauseating mess in her mouth and spewed it out on the table; now she was forced to lick the tablecloth clean. Before her seventh birthday, she encountered a different ordeal: a cousin of her own mother attempted to approach her sexually, an approach which apparently culminated in defloration. The child fled into a kind of stupor, and during her first school years was regarded as practically feeble-minded, so much so that it was thought necessary to send her to a school for retarded children. In actual fact, Mrs J. N. is of above average intelligence, as was shown by tests; and indeed she did manage to stay at a school for normal children, though only by dint of enormous efforts and not without considerable educational gaps. We must now somewhat abbreviate Mrs J. N.'s. history. It is important to note that at the time of puberty she did not regard herself as 'normal', i.e. like other girls, on account of her sexual experiences in childhood: 'I have never been a girl.' She grew up, one might almost say by a malignant fate, into an exceptionally beautiful woman. It is therefore not surprising that this precocious, beautiful, shy girl did not lack male admirers. She resolved not to yield before her sixteenth birthday. However, this resolution, which is to be regarded as a measure of rational self-protection, also had a negative aspect; for as soon as she was in fact sixteen, she considered herself fully entitled to lead a life which soon degenerated into unbridled sexuality. Since externally she looked and acted like a little lady and, internally was looking for the father who had constantly failed her, her lovers were mostly well over forty. So, very soon she had nothing more to learn in the way of sexual technique, but again and again she felt disappointed, and eventually took to drink. What made her suffer most was the fact that her youth and doll-like appearance led men to treat her rather like a little pampered animal. She thus arrived at a feeling of complete emptiness and spiritual dissatisfaction, until, at the age of nineteen (already divorced, after an ephemeral marriage to a man of forty-seven) she sought medical help in order to justify her refusal to help the German war effort in Austria. The doctor who attended her recommended treatment by depth psychology. Considerations of space here preclude us from going into the difficulties of this treatment; but we have already reported the initial successes attained (p. 37). The patient felt she was awakening to a new life. She gave up her indiscriminate sexuality and drunkeness, took up regular work, and matured psychologically and spiritually to such an extent that, as we have already seen when considering the effects of rape (Section 11), she was even able to recover quickly from this great sexual shock. For external reasons (the psychoanalyst had commitments of very long standing in another town) the treatment was discontinued after three years, which at the time seemed to entail only a slight worsening of the patient's condition. She formed a dubious friendship with a businessman, the true significance of which never became quite clear. Yet, this much can be firmly established, that Mrs J. N. had tried with all her strength not to be sucked again into the whirlpool of her planless and meaningless existence, before putting a violent end to her life, at the age of twenty-four, by taking two tubes of a sleeping-drug.

Anyone inclined to dismiss such a case as hopeless from the start must possess elements of judgement bordering on the prophetic! A young, intelligent, sensitive and beautiful woman has herself used more than twenty years of her life in a continual attempt to regain herself. Throughout her life she was therefore opposed to her critic, the psychoanalyst, with our imaginary critic, and supported her attitude by deeds—both by her neurosis and by her attempt to master the situation. She only gave up hope when her most successful attempt to date also proved a failure.

A not dissimilar case is that of Miss E. F.:

The twenty-year-old patient believes herself to be a Lesbian, because she has had a sexual experience with a woman and none with men. Her parents have held it against her from childhood onwards that she was a girl, and that her birth was in any case unwanted. Her parents, in their conventional lower middle class milieu, certainly showed her no intentional cruelty, yet the child grew up in an atmosphere of continual terror, in which severe beatings were no exception. Hatred of her parents, particularly of her father, determines her whole view of the world. Wolff's symbolization test, to which she was subjected at the beginning

of treatment, yielded revealing results. This test[2] consists in facing
the subject with certain complex-laden concepts which he must
symbolize both by a drawing and by mentioning a colour. The
stimulus word 'father' moved the patient to draw a tombstone
with a cross (in actual fact, however, her father enjoys perfect
health). The stimulus-word 'feminine' was symbolized by bars,
'sexuality' by a serpent, 'future' by a setting sun. The colour red
was used to signify activity, mastery, sexuality and strength; black
to signify death, father, future, inner world, past, present, truth.
Grey: depression, outer world, disagreeable.

Of course, not all neurotic anamneses take quite so dramatic a
form. But wherever we look closely, we discover the constricting
and threatening effect of existence.

The childhood of Dr C. D., who has already been mentioned
(pp. 45, 52 and 70), was comparatively peaceful. He did indeed
complain of his mother's moods, rough children in the streets
and heartless teachers. But only after a year of analysis did he refer
clearly to a more intimate threat, the constant fear that conditioned the atmosphere in his home. He wrote: 'My father has
two basic moods. Either he is very gentle, and sweetness itself; or
he succumbs to latent irritability. In that case his ill-will is immediately apparent in the way he speaks, his words resound with
suppressed anger. When in this mood, he always wants everyone
to agree with him. If my mother ventures to say a few words, his
smouldering rage flares up at once. He speaks very loudly and
excitedly, stopping short of shouting. He never shouts at all, he
does not seem able to. This angry mood probably lasts longer than
the other. When I was small, I was always afraid of my father
when he was in this mood. I was also frightened when it was time
for my father to come home, because of course I never knew in
advance what his mood would be. Mother always yielded to this
mood of my father's, she never dared to contradict him, at least
not in those days, when I was a child. I too used to avoid sticking
my neck out on such occasions, so as not to arouse my father's
anger; for me, of course, there were certain physically disagreeable
results. On the other hand I was continually afraid for my mother,
whenever I knew my father was in a bad temper. Thus I once saw
my parents quarrelling; my father threw my mother, who was ill
at the time, roughly on the bed, so that she cried aloud and wept

[2] Werner Wolff, *Diagrams of the Unconscious*, New York, Grune and
Stratton, 1948, pp. 235–240.

with pain, because the ill-treatment had apparently caused her a very sharp and sudden pain. And in any case mother is very sensitive to pain. I was wretchedly miserable at the time, and thought he was going to kill her. I wept loudly, fell on my knees and began to pray aloud for my mother. I can remember two or three situations of this kind. As a result, I developed a fear of my father, which I may have repressed into my unconscious even as a child. Seeing that even the slightest contradiction unleashed my father's anger, I became a coward, a prey to constant fear. The fact that I was later always frightened of boys of my own age is purely secondary. This behaviour of my father's probably made me hate him from my earliest years, though I repressed this hatred into my unconscious because of my mother's teachings and exhortations to unconditional filial reverence. Only after I left boarding school did my hatred of father become overt.

* * * * *

And only now, when beginning gradually to raise these forgotten events once more into consciousness, I again felt a dislike for my father. On coming home, my spirits always sank, as if automatically, to zero, as soon as I cross my parents' doorstep. And yet, as long as I was not at home, I was generally cheerful. When I was at home and my father spoke in the way I have described, my dislike for him would revive, without my knowing why.

The night after Dr C. D. had written down these suddenly emerging memories, he had the following dream :

I am walking in the Museum Strasse, in front of the Palace of Justice. There is a Communist demonstration. As I am blithely walking along, the idea occurs to me: Look out! you are walking right into the middle of the demonstration, you must get away from here at once! Meanwhile I have almost reached the Palace of Justice. I am frightened and horrified, and leave the street. Towards the left a grassy hill rises from the street, at an angle of about 45 degrees. The grassy slopes are full of graves and holes in which a man could stand with only his head emerging. It looks like war. I run up the hill as if my life were at stake. And in fact my life really is in danger, because the Russian occupation authorities know that I am a witness of what happened in the demonstration, and they want to get rid of me. When I am about two-thirds of the way up the hill I meet a British radio journalist, who is sitting in one of the holes I have described. I indignantly tell him what I have seen in the street, and he immediately records his interview with me over the microphone. As soon as I speak, they begin shooting up at me from the street; and being on the hillside I am an unprotected target. Somebody chides the journalist for not having provided for my safety. In a previous, similar case a machine-gun had been used for protection. . . .

This dream shows the patient's recently recalled recollections of hating his father to be charged with emotions. The father's authority is symbolised by the Palace of Justice (Dr C. D. has studied law and has a position as a servant of the law). He does not want to take part in the demonstrations, but, against his will, he begins by marching with the demonstration. Beset by fear and horror he flees to the hilltop, pursued by self-reproaches. He seeks help from the representative of a power more acceptable to his superego. The British radio journalist takes the place of the psychoanalyst, still regarded as a person of authority who should protect the dreamer from his unfettered instincts and feelings of hatred. But instead of reaching safety, the dreamer has to tell about the fighting. He stands unprotected on the hillside, a target as it were for the now unleashed aggressive elements. Somebody (probably the dreamer, who has not, however, the courage to speak himself) chides the psychoanalyst for not having provided enough protection for his patient's security, and good conscience.

20. *The 'Paradise Archetype' and the longing for a redeemer*

It is quite understandable that the neurotic should seek security in psychoanalysis. He looks for security also in his neurosis which, however, as we have seen, is a defence mechanism. The neurotic defends himself against the threat to his existence in a world where men are freezing, are beaten, and frightened, where children cry. Ivan Karamàzov refuses to accept from God admission to eternal happiness as long as, somewhere, there is a child weeping. The neurotic is such a child. He is the martyred child. Neurotic infantilism, indeed, contains within itself the shadowy side of egotistical childishness as well as the bright side of being childlike. The neurotic has been forced to become like a child by the frustrations in his development. He takes refuge in childhood because he cannot overcome the dominant experience overshadowing his childhood. 'Woe unto him through whom scandal shall come (unto one of the little ones).' The neurotic, then, becomes a child—this has been demonstrated in detail by naturalistic depth psychology—but, of course, in a way which does not correspond to his place in an adult world. Yet childlike desires are not necessarily evil. After all, we are bidden to attain the simplicity and unconcern of children—'Unless ye shall become as little children . . .' (Mt. 18:3). Evidently, the neurotic fulfils this injunction in a way that can, in fact, be described as heretical, by absolutising certain traits in accordance with his greed for experience and his magical attitude to the world. In neurosis certain realms of childhood experience remain unconquered territory and thus become factors of restriction and enslavement. 'I know perfectly well that I am as dependent on people as a baby,' says Miss E. F. (cf. p. 79). For the baby, the total satisfaction of his as yet undifferentiated desires is simply the condition of his existence; his greed for experience is still very close to the urge of living.

The longing for the state of innocence is at the same time a longing for what has been lost and a desire for what is to come. Naturalistic depth psychology acknowledges only the lost factor, to which, moreover, it assigns a merely immanent value by making it a yardstick for life within the womb. The promised paradise must, in the eyes of naturalistic psychology, necessarily become a projection of what has been lost. In the case of neurosis this simplification corresponds to reality in so far as the neurotic contemplates the restoration of the condition of pleasure. Paradise was lost through pride. The neurotic too refuses to accept a certain destiny and his paradise is not, in the first instance, eschatological. It is not a promise of history transcended, but rather a fixation on something that is past. Longing for the condition of paradise is a longing for the plenitude of being. It is however the paradox of neurosis that, instead of this plenitude of being, the neurotic attains only a sorrowful restriction of it. To be appears like not being at all. The neurotic greed for experience is a 'negating' result of the denial of being; but at the same time it is an attempt to overcome the 'negating' force. Freud in his old age became a disappointed forerunner of existentialism. His 'death-wish' which he explained rationally has more than terminological affinities with Kierkegaard's 'sickness unto

death'. The concept of the 'death-wish' is a pessimistic absolutising of the neurotic paradox. But what is primary is not the
wish for death; the life urge is however limited and continually
restricted. Sickness unto death is the struggling creature's answer
to such limitation and constant threat. The total restoration of a
condition of perfect pleasure is imaginable only in complete innocence, for guilt entails punishment and loss of pleasure. The
neurotic repression and false localisation of guilt represent an
attempt to restore that state of innocence, as it originally existed
before the appearance of ethical cognition. The neurotic aims at
a pre-natal state and, in a collective sense, at a pre-natal stage of
consciousness, the condition that existed before the fruit of knowledge was eaten and good and evil were recognized. Neurosis is
thus governed by that archetype which links the collective unconscious with the primary state before original sin; neurosis also
attempts to overcome the tragic divorce between good and evil
by repressing knowledge. Yet the 'paradise archetype' is also a
teleological force. We know that the desire for innocence points
not only to regression but also faith and hope. To aim at innocence may, after all, also imply the assurance that existence will
be abolished, not by being destroyed, but by the redemption of
history; and that a redeemer has promised a Kingdom in which
no longing, faith or hope shall be needed, but immediate knowledge in love.

Freud has shown that neurosis can only be cured when all
neurotic longings and desires are being transferred to the person
of the analyst. In order to overcome his sickness unto death, the
neurotic has to transfer it to a healer. There must be one to
identify himself with the neurotic's history of suffering. Neurosis
searches for a redeemer. The 'Christ archetype' is the central
factor in all psychotherapy, as we shall discuss on p. 162 (Section
30). Naturalistic depth psychology is incapable of proving that
humanity's great drama of the redemption—the Word that has
become flesh, takes upon itself the sins of the world, dies for
the world, descends into hell and rises again—is but a neurotic
projection into myth. To maintain this is in itself to be neurotic,
for it absolutises a preconceived attitude. To any mind not
a priori enslaved by the dogma of naturalism, it will seem at
least equally plausible that the soul's desire for transcendence

and redemption corresponds to a necessity which must be rooted in reality. Otherwise the most important and central functions of the soul would be meaningless. It would be extremely one-sided to consider, say, sex or power complexes as referring to reality, while in the 'paradise archetype' or the 'Christ archetype' they are seen as mere by-products of the former or, at most, the product of subjective forces.

There is another factor which seems to us very important in connection with the 'neurotic vocation'. The plenitude of being is, for the neurotic, a dimly sensed plenitude of his claims to love. The neurotic suffers from a 'love impediment'. He claims love for *himself*, he is in the grasping stage; he is not ready for sacrifice. Yet the hunger for love implies some notion of it. This hunger was instilled in the neurotic by being deprived of love. In the psychoanalytic transference he believes he has found a loving mother or a kind father. Thus, if one were to see in trans-ference only neurotic traits or only subjective projections, one would logically also have to deny father and mother. It would be equally illegitimate to explain the relationship to a heavenly father only in terms of an earthly father, Miss S. A. (cf. p. 51) thought that she hated God because he permitted evil, just as her earthly father had once permitted it. To see in this neurotic fallacy proof that the father in heaven is a projection of the father on earth, or the Son of God a projection of the father's sex organs, is to commit the very same fallacy as the neurotic.

The neurotic's 'call to transcendence' has neurotic traits as has his whole spiritual life. Assigning an immanent character to this call is to emphasise the neurotic traits and to kill the fruit which is ripening despite drought and cold. Especially in the case of the neurotic to assign such an immanent role to his vocation is equivalent to spiritual abortion.

21. *Neurotic problems and psychotherapeutic solutions*

If we try to solve neurotic problems at the same level at which the neurotic poses them, we share in the guilt of neurosis because we would thereby approve of the neurotic scapegoat and of the place where the neurosis occurs.

Speaking quite generally, we might even say that the more superficial the improvement in neurotic suffering, the closer the psychotherapeutic solution is to the neurotic 'placing' of that suffering. It is not by accident that the so-called short treatments in psychotherapy are in danger of remaining on the purely symptomatic level. The name of 'causal therapy' could rightly be applied only to a therapy capable of discovering and removing the deep, dynamic causes of failure, as we shall show in Parts II and III of this book. In any case, we must already at this point express our agreement with Dr A. Kronfeld, who observed that the opposition between causal and symptomatic therapy is in principle abortive because the psychotherapeutic effect is never limited to an isolated symptom, but always influences the personality as a whole. The distinction between causal and symptomatic therapy would accordingly be one of degree; depending on the depth of its effects, every psychological influence constitutes in some sense re-formation and re-education.

Much more important than this somewhat artificial distinction between purely causal and purely symptomatic psychotherapy, is perhaps another distinction, which may be derived from all that we have said about the genuine or imagined calling of the neurotic. If the therapist is gifted and experienced enough, impotence or speech impediments may be corrected surprisingly quickly. Indeed, even in a 'complete' psychoanalysis, the causal link may be subjected to minute scrutiny, which may likewise entail the disappearance of the symptom. But can we be sure that it will not be replaced by another symptom, perhaps less readily apprehensible, but all the more harmful for the personality? The formerly impotent patient will be able to perform the sexual act; the patient formerly suffering from a speech defect will at last be able to speak fluently; apparently the aim has been achieved, and to do more would be superfluous. But this would imply that the patient's calling was just to have sexual intercourse or to speak without impediment. In most cases, however, this is not so. The symptom is, certainly, meaningful in that it can help us to understand the deeper meaning of the neurosis; but its own meaning is not self-exhaustive. Of course, the symptomatic disturbance must be removed, and a therapy not capable of doing so is not a successful therapy. The impotent patient must become potent, the speech-impeded patient must learn to speak fluently. But it is impossible to say in advance whether they will be able to do so only at the end of therapy or even at the beginning; and in the latter case it is quite possible that therapeutic effort will have to continue for months after the disappearance of the symptom.

We have already stressed sufficiently that a psychotherapy which regards the neurotic's problem as immanent, and reduces his scale of values to a relative and utilitarian point of view, cannot cure neurosis; for neurosis is a tragic conflict, which presupposes both intimations of the absolute and infidelity to our calling. At most, this utilitarian type of therapy can achieve an apparent cure, whereby one neurotic symptom, which in the existing state of society was immediately obvious, is replaced by another, more in accord with the neurosis of our age. Thus individual neurosis is replaced by a participation in the collective neurosis. Many psychotherapeutic cures offer frightening examples of the collectively neurotic attitude of the present age. It is obvious that the fostering of collective neurosis at the expense of individual neuroses represents a dangerous, and in itself pseudo-solution, which deepens and makes more insoluble the life-heresies of society.

Neurotic case histories afford innumerable examples of such frustrated, but still vital vocations, which seek to assert themselves in devious ways in neurosis. Here are a few additional cases:

Ch. L., forty-six years old, a shoemaker, seeks psychoanalysis because of total impotence. For several months, the analysis is concerned with the investigation of causal circumstances, which incidentally meets with very little resistance, partly because of the several depth-psychology treatments he had already undergone abroad. Ch. L. was born in a tiny village in a fairly backward part of the Carpathians; he comes of a very pious family of orthodox Jews. He has never known his father, who died a few weeks after the patient's birth. Thus he grew up as the only son of a young widow, and continues to entertain for his mother, now dead, feelings of deep reverence and touching love. When the boy was five, his mother married again. Her second husband, also a Jew, seems to have been a somewhat harsh, dour character. There is no doubt that the patient's stepfather helped to shape important elements in his superego. These traits were not, however, sufficiently integrated into the boy's personality, which had already found a very different model in the person of his beloved mother. He certainly acknowledged his stepfather as the supreme authority, but at the same time regarded him as a hostile power and as a rival. Latent homosexual traits arose through strong identification with his mother and subjection to her male possessor. At the age of fourteen, the boy entered upon his apprenticeship in the neighbouring small town, where he suffered hunger and beatings. Since then, his life has been very restless. The government of his country changed hands a dozen times since the first World War. Ch. L. worked his way up through many hardships, and soon married a girl from a pious Jewish home, who made him very happy. But this happiness was short-lived. His wife was murdered before his eyes, and he himself barely escaped death in several concentration camps. After the second World War he went abroad, without quite knowing why, since by his acount the new regime offered no dangers to him as a small artisan. Meanwhile, he also formed several relationships with other women, with increasing disturbances in his potency. During the course of his wanderings through Central and Eastern Europe, he sought the help of a number of psychotherapists and psychoanalysts; all these treatments, however, lasted for too brief a time to afford him relief. When he began a new psychoanalysis in Vienna, he had already decided to emigrate to America; but, despite the psychoanalyst's objections, he wanted to make use of the waiting period for his psychoanalysis. In Vienna he worked at his trade in a workshop, but lived in a displaced persons' camp where life was, by all accounts, fairly wild. The patient, a very likable, friendly man, felt, lonely, worked hard, and took part in the dubious entertainments afforded by the promiscuity of camp life. He remained totally impotent, which seemed to worry him quite desperately. His one idea in life seemed to be to get rid of this impediment; he was unable to think about anything else, and tried again and again, always without success, to overcome his sexual inhibitions with the women internees and with prostitutes from the Viennese working-class districts.

In the fifth month of psychoanalysis the patient was encouraged to paint; after some unexpected resistance, he handed in a few sketches representing himself, surrounded by shoes, by a seven-branched candlestick, a Torah script, Stars of David and rather unidentifiable household animals. So far his verbal associations had never concerned themselves with either his religion or his people. On the basis of verbal associations alone, there might have been no religious or national problems at all. To the patient's own astonishment, the drawings produced a change in him. It is worth noting that his sexual troubles were not reflected in his drawings at all. The shoes symbolize his work. The domestic animals remind him of his village, and suddenly an intense longing overcame him of which hitherto he had not been conscious. What was completely new, however, was the collection of liturgical objects and the national emblem. The patient himself believed these to be chance doodles, yet at the very next session he reported a dream which continued the same theme: he saw himself in the synagogue, dressed in liturgical garments, which, however, to his dismay, he had put on the wrong way round. He was afraid he would be asked to leave the synagogue, but was able to adjust his prayer-garments in time. The analysis of the dream afforded no evidence of the pressure of sexual symbolism. From this time onwards, his long muzzled and disavowed Judaism broke through with the force of an avalanche. The triple concept work-home-Judaism was revealed as the mightiest complex of this persecuted, lonely and apparently rootless person—indeed, as his calling. Especially effective and urgent was the problem of piety. As with all orthodox Jews, religious and national feelings were inseparable for Ch. L. Denial of the former was equivalent to suppression of the latter. The conversations with Ch L. during the psychoanalytic sessions were extremely instructive, and indeed moving. The example of Ch. L. may in some measure obviate in advance the suspicion that psychoanalysis which is not purely naturalistic should take on overtones of propaganda. On the contrary, this Jewish patient felt his Christian analyst to be a witness who *in no sense* tried to foist his own convictions on him. Conversely, the situation was a new and difficult one for the psychoanalyst, who sensed that the connections between faith, law and morality were quite different in the Old Testament from the attitudes he was used to which were steeped in Christian tradition. On the other hand, any attempt to dismiss Ch. L.'s religious and national problems out of hand as the results of a mother-fixation and a severe superego would have been inadmissible, if only because the patient himself had, in his own neurotic attitude to life, regarded these very real factors as purely immanent. Ch. L.'s trouble was precisely that he assigned a relative character to central spiritual problems, and an absolute one to sexual symptons. What he was repressing was not so much instinctual experience as the voice of his own conscience. It must also be said that the eventual revelation of his spiritual concerns plunged him into a depression the like of which he had never before experienced, and which led him to think of suicide. Only later did the symptom begin to show signs of improvement; but he was now less concerned with proving this. It did, however, enable him to form an intimate friendship with a woman. If we present this case as an illustration of the positive aspects of neurosis, we do so because this particular neurosis gives a very clear picture of the protest of the spiritual person against unfaithfulness and neglect of a dimly sensed vocation. Of course the effects of Ch. L.'s mother-fixation and superego were discernible in his homesickness and in the revival of his piety. However, the fact that vocation, among other things, makes use of the psychophysical personality and of its whole instinctual development can in no sense be regarded as proof that vocation is a mere inessential superstructure of this instinctual development.

A 'symptomatic' treatment in this case would have been any process, such as hypnosis, which would simply have erased the characteristic symptom of impotence, without bothering too much to find out how it arose. But a complete causal analysis might also, in such cases, deserve the name of 'symptomatic' treatment, inasmuch as it would fix its attention on the symptom itself, the causes of which it would then trace back and investigate down to the earliest stages of development. The question of vocation could, according to the psychoanalytical model, also be reduced to elementary instinct structures, simply because these structures do in fact influence and change the development of human vocation. Even final considerations may be simple logical reversals of the principle of causation. Such analyses are, in practice, indispensable to psychotherapy; but one should remember that they are simplifications which cannot lead to an understanding of the spiritual whole and which, if they are generalised, may degenerate into the 'nothing but' solutions described in Chapter I. The Jungian school is the least open to criticism as regards over-simplification; yet it is not wholly free from it, in so far as it tends to a solipsist relativism as regards the frame of value-references. For Jung and his disciples, vocations are in the last resort only 'symbols and mutations' of the libido working within the individual.

If we wanted to insist on maintaining the distinction between 'causal' and 'symptomatic' cure or treatment, since it has already become part of depth psychology, we should have to regard the symptom, however obvious and painful it may be, as a change-able sign of 'life heresy'. This alone has a decisive significance. Naturally, the choice of the symptom is in itself by no means unimportant. Yet in the last resort there is only one neurosis, which is 'life heresy'. Clinical distinctions are generally based on symptom images. The choice of symptom has in itself a sym-bolic significance, and is conditioned by the stage of regression to infantile levels. The physical constitution, too, and innate or acquired organic inferiority are decisive in the selection of the symptom and in the extent of the regression. But until the 'heretical' attitude to life has been overcome, we are in reality moving on the surface of the neurotic phenomena. The symp-toms are a kind of ritual or incantation of fate, which are subor-dinate to the heretical creed, but are capable of changes and transformations. It is due to this multiplicity of layers that the criteria which therapists use for the relief or cure of neurosis are handled with such uncertainty.

After a few weeks' psychotherapy, Dr C. D. (cf. pp. 45, 52, 70 and 80) was fortunately rid of the symptom of his speech impediment. We can easily imagine that Dr C. D., instead of being directed towards psychoanalysis, might have sought treatment at some logopaedic outpatients' clinic (for example, a laryngological clinic) and might have been released as 'cured' after a few weeks. His attitude to life, however, would in the main have remained un-changed; the same sympton, or another, might perhaps have reappeared fairly soon; or, which would have been worse, he might have shown almost no symptons at all, but a largely intro-verted psychoneurotic condition.

Other cases, of a type familiar to every experienced psycho-analyst, might also serve as warnings not to localise neurotic problems elsewhere than in the 'life heresy'.

Mr I. C., fifty-three years old, French, residing in post-war Vienna on account of his important business interests in Central Europe. Mr. I. C. had, about fifteen years previously, in Shanghai, successfully undergone a disintoxication cure for alcoholism. He now seeks medical help because of nicotine and caffeine addiction. He smokes up to fifty cigarettes daily, and drinks enormous quantities of black coffee. The new process of disintoxication is apparently successful. It is not accompanied by any psychotherapy, since Mr I. C. confidently believes that he knows exactly where the trouble lies; his harassing, exhausting business life tempts him to make use of stimulants. A few months after the cure, however, he begins to suffer from severe insomnia, and his consumption of tobacco and coffee once more increases, though without exceeding that of many active men (twenty cigarettes and a few cups of coffee daily). The neurologist who treats him now energetically recommends psychotherapy, despite his patient's obvious reluctance. Unfortunately, the time available is very short, since Mr I. C. has to go on a long trip to South Africa. He is an extraordinarily calm, affable and pleasant man. Robust, lively and exhilaratingly active, his intelligence and experience enable him to grasp new situations effortlessly and manage them with consummate skill. His activities and plans are on the scale of those modern *conquistadores* who, in our century, are to be found in the realm of economics. Short-term therapy, unfortunately all too hastily performed, points to strong oral fixations. What is very interesting, on the other hand, is the patient's own mental balance sheet, which he eventually draws up despite strong resistances. Spurred on by his enormous ambitions, Mr I. C. had, before the outbreak of the second World War, resolved to acquire estates in Kenya, where he intended to lead a sort of feudal existence, with such features as the exploitation of untapped natural resources, hunting parties and . . . a harem. During the war, however, he 'backed the wrong horse'; his armament contracts have not enabled him to realize his dream. He had thought he would be able to reach his goal by the age of fifty; but now, at the age of fifty-three, he had to 'start all over again'—an expression which should not be taken to mean that he was in any sense a poor man. The analysis of his wish fantasies afforded him some surprise: he realized for the first time that his old dream, however grandiose in structure, rests in the last instance on the repression of higher spiritual claims. Analysis leads him through a short, but exceptionally severe, depression. After the depression he once again loses his specific symptoms (although he does not give up smoking or moderate coffee-drinking); he is, moreover, in his own words 'reconciled to life', has become less hard and lost some of his overtense activity, and spontaneously declares that psychotherapy has shown him that 'man does not live by bread alone', probably quite unaware that he is quoting Christ.

The positive aspect of neurosis, then, can be seen in the breakthrough of the buried vocation by means of the symptom. For instance, in cases of hysteria close observation will show that the neurotic symptoms are grouped around the problem of love; though, naturally, in a way which, as we have already indicated, depreciates the problem of love and is centred on the greed for experience. The examples we have cited in Section II all point to the fact that the neurotics concerned take the problems of love relationships and purity with great seriousness. The examples of compulsion neurosis, too, indicate that the compulsive neurotic experiences his (misapprehended and deranged) relation to sacred things very deeply. The compulsive neurotic is said to live in a 'magic' world. This is true in so far as neurosis represents a regression to pre-conscious stages of thought, which are characterised by a flourishing animism. Yet the 'black magic' of compulsion neurosis is but the shadow side, the unredeemed accompaniment of a 'white magic' to which modern man, and naturalistic depth psychology, have lost all connections. We may wonder whether naturalistic depth psychology is not just such a scientific system of 'black magic'. Such would be the collective compulsion neurosis, just as other modern pseudo religions are also distinctly reminiscent of magic. As is well known, Freud tried to prove that religion is a collective compulsion neurosis. His argument is a typical instance of the wrong generalization of data taken from pathology. If religion is a compulsion neurosis, it has been with mankind from its beginnings; and even where it has been replaced by other views of life, it is surprising to note the reappearance of religion behind the mask of natural science or sociology, then leading with still greater certainty to anthropological phenomena. Where there is no faith, superstition flourishes; of course not only in a primitive, overt fashion, but all too often disguised as science.

From our point of view, *superstition* is as yet a positive aspect of a capacity for faith. This is true even more for the compulsion neurotic than for the complacent scientist, for the neurotic suffers from the problems thrown up by his neurosis. The neurotic is a person with problems. A person may be said to have more problems the more he is exposed to inward tensions. Of course the existence of inward tensions relates to the effectiveness of 'autonomous complexes'. The complexes work on the conscious self, and their multiplication diminishes its freedom and self-determination. Yet the inner struggles of a person beset by problems are not necessarily unfruitful. They may bring him victory and enrichment, and in a way they protect him from drying up spiritually. Self-satisfaction can also become a dangerous illusion, as for instance when at the beginning of this century the unimpeded progress of human development was widely believed in.

Every human action and endeavour partake of both good and evil. Good and evil do not coexist statically, but are dynamically at work in each ambiguous and finite motivation of human actions. Man is characterised by a continuous dialogue, a continuous conflict within himself. All human principles and feelings are transitory and relative, uncertain and ambivalent, for on the one hand they relate to the hierarchy of values and, on the other, to the immediate reality of existence; and can thus be considered only dialectically.

The very fact that the neurotic is dissatisfied with his experience, and dimly feels that all sensation foreshadows illusion and limitation, that all existence is finite and all pleasure poisoned, all this enables us to discover the positive aspect of neurosis. The rise of neurosis is a testimony that being cannot be rooted in sensation alone. Satiety of feeling affords no peace to the neurotic, and the dissection of experiences through depth psychology can be meaningful only if the relative character of these experiences can be recognized. Otherwise it only confirms the neurotic greed for experience through an illusory greed for knowledge, 'total knowledge' as Jaspers calls it.

Yet despite its greed for experience and sensation, neurosis is haunted by a sense of what ought to be; for the neurotic is dissatisfied with his greed for experience, his pseudo absolute values and his idealised image of himself. He feels that his fears and disappointments could be assuaged by some absolute, which the dismal attempts to absolutise old fixations cannot attain. Thus his greed for experience itself ensures the experience in every core of his nature that no earthly love will ever wholly satisfy him, that there is no treasure 'safe from thieves' nor any home in 'this world' to make him happy.

Psychotherapeutic solutions can build only upon the positive aspects of neurosis; further consideration shows this to be a self-evident truth, almost a tautology. If neurosis were only 'bad' (but nothing is only bad in this world) there would be no means of coming to grips with it. The ideal psychotherapeutic solution would be one that uses everything that is positive in neurosis as a stepping stone to improvements. We are, perhaps, still far removed from this universal type of psychotherapy. Yet we ought, to the best of our ability, to seek for ways and means to achieve it. It was said earlier that we consider superstition itself as an indication of the capacity for faith. By the same token, we would gratefully borrow and carefully use all the positive elements contained in the superstitious systems of the old masters of depth psychology.

Part II

The Method

Chapter One

THE FUNCTION OF PSYCHOTHERAPY

22. *Orientation towards the absolute*

THE method of treating neuroses discovered by Freud was both a means of therapy and an instrument of research. A method based exclusively on *a priori* assumptions would always, however clever and logical it appeared, remain an unknown quantity until it could point to practical results. Freud discovered a new world, and explored it step by step. He mapped new regions of the soul but, in so doing, based himself on assumptions which corresponded to the general cosmology of his time; his achievement could be compared to the increased field of vision of the old geographers, who extended what they believed to be the surface of the earth but remained faithful to the Ptolemaic view of the world. But at some stage the widening field of vision requires a radical transformation of the whole world picture. The time came when the extensions and supplements in the East and West began to touch and interpenetrate each other, and required a radical re-evaluation of geographical conceptions and a new system of cosmology. At that moment the earth was perceived to be round. A similar development is taking place in the evolution of depth psychology. The map of the psyche is indebted to Freud for its most important constituents. He was the first to draw the outlines of the continents of the soul. Yet as the geography of the soul became more accurately and extensively known, it became increasingly clear that Freud's two-dimensional cosmology, or psychology, would have to be replaced by another in order to account for the facts discovered by Freud himself.

The genius of Freud's intuition and his most accurate research were responsible for this turning-point, which would certainly not have found the approval of the master himself, who remained attached to the old view of the world. The regrettable misunderstanding between Freud and Jung, so humiliating for the cause of science, already pointed to the inner contradiction between the true scope of the discoveries of depth psychology and their inadequate and restrictive systematization. It would be tempting, incidentally, to continue the metaphor in order to suggest that Jung's psychology also constitutes a necessary stage in spiritual cosmology: its immanent psychologism with its solipsist overtones does, indeed, replace Freud's flat-earth model by a round one, but without abandoning the geocentrical conception, which requires correction by an overall frame of reference.

What are the features of Freud's map of the psyche? Besides the conscious mental life there are vast realms of unconscious or pre-conscious mental activity. The latter has been governed originally by the law of pleasure; however, in the course of development, certain mental energies are diverted away from the original purpose of pleasure, into social functions. If this diversion is prevented from taking place by endogenous or exogenous difficulties, the asocial claims of pleasure are repressed from consciousness into the unconscious, where, unrecognized, they influence and disturb conscious behaviour. The dynamics of the psyche are largely determined by the polarity between pleasure and displeasure. Adaptation to social models, however, can and should become a new, progressive and differentiated source of pleasure. The whole psychic picture is essentially characterised by this polarity, and is therefore in some sense flat and two dimensional. In the teaching of Jung, the outlines of the mental continents, conscious and unconscious, are clearly recognizable, but the whole picture becomes rounded; the dynamic factors in the psyche are no longer simple pleasure-tropisms, but the vital concepts of God, the world and man, hidden within the specific psychic structure of the human race. Whether these concepts relate to any transcendent reality is a question which, to answer Jung's psychology, would not claim to be competent.

We have shown in some detail that it appears essential that a science of the human psyche should study man within his specifically human frame of reference. Both Freud and Jung's cartography is essentially correct; but it is equally essential to ascertain whether the outlines they have drawn appear on a flat surface, on a motionless sphere, or else on a sphere circling around a life-giving centre of energy like the earth around the sun. This is not a foolproof metaphor, but as far as the 'cosmology of the soul' is concerned there are these obvious and similar questions. We hope we have shown that the problem of neurosis is essentially the problem of human relationships with the absolute. Everyone is free to accept or reject such an absolute order, but not free to reject the essential core of the problem of neurosis in advance as non-existent.

Neurosis is what it is because it cannot agree with the absolute character it has itself assigned to relative values. In its negative aspect, therefore, neurosis appears as a metaphysical lie inherent in the neurotic's life. In its positive aspect, it represents an attempt to unmask this very lie, in order to re-establish orthodoxy of life, a true relationship to the hierarchy of values. Neurosis is simply devoid of all purpose or meaning unless it is at one and the same time a flight from the absolute and a yearning for the absolute. In the same way a psychotherapy which began by annihilating the problem it approaches would miss its own purpose and meaning. If neurosis is concerned with the absolute, psychotherapy must be concerned likewise.

It may be argued against this view that the very notion of coming to grips with the absolute is itself simply neurotic, as Freud affirmed in *The Future of an Illusion*. But here we are confronted by the vicious circle of 'nothing but' science: if defection from the absolute makes us ill, the absolute itself must be regarded as an illusion. Since, however, the absolute also makes itself felt in other ways than the illness of the bad conscience, the notion of illusion is applied to all relationships with the absolute.

As has already been indicated, Jung attempted to break this two-dimensional circle. Jung deserves credit for having shown that the most powerful formative forces of the soul manifest themselves in primitive images, which are common to all men (and not only to unfortunate neurotics!) namely archetypes. These are in no sense 'illusory', but are genuine functional capacities of the soul which must be studied seriously; they have a general character, being the most important focal points of mental morphology. It is the archetypes that make the human soul what it is: if they did not exist, its ability to function, indeed to live, would be essentially different. Of course the archetypes may be buried deep and, so to speak, atrophied in their specific function. Modern man in particular presents a disastrous atrophy of the archetypes, as also of the instincts. It is no accident that the archetypes are correlates of the instincts[1] on the specifically human level. They are not figments of the imagination, or some purposeless game played by nature, but life-preserving 'organs' which enable the soul to function. However, mental life would certainly be such a purposeless game if the archetypes reflected only projections emanating from the *solus ipse*, like the water reflecting Narcissus' own image. For Jung, archetypes are, quite rightly, means to emerge from narcissism; their significance is not merely social but even cosmic, since the instincts and (on the specifically human level) the archetypes assure our capacity for contact, our relationship to the world at large, which is vital for our body and soul.

Jung's complex psychology falters perceptibly only where the 'divine archetype' is concerned. In this context Jung can hardly find enough figures of speech to ensure that we stay at a safe distance from any relationship that might exist between this central archetype, which is after all the most important and objective truth. This looks like blatant contradiction or obvious prejudice. Yet every psychologist should be prepared to see the psychological conclusions to be drawn from this attitude; great psychologists cannot forbid our entering into their own psychology. Jung is absolutely obsessed with the problem of the divine archetype at the primal core of the 'self'. We are indebted to him for taking upon himself the cross of this obsession; but we cannot help noticing that he shies away from the final solution of the problem he has himself posed, and which, in psychology, is the problem of problems—so much so, indeed, that we could almost subscribe to Daim's words: 'We can but choose: either the life of the soul is meaningless, or there is psychological proof of God's existence.'[2]

[1] Cf. C. G. Jung, *Über psychische Energetik und das Wesen der Träume*, Zurich 1948, p. 276.
[2] Daim, op. cit.

23. *Restoring the hierarchy of values*

Neurosis is not merely a disturbance in equilibrium, but also an active attempt to establish a better equilibrium. It is a well-formulated problem in which the elements of the solution are already contained in the formulation itself. Neurosis arises from the repression of an instinctive claim which, though disavowed, is at work in us. Its repression means that the repressing self on the one hand identifies itself with an ideal image but, on the other hand, is unable to integrate this instinctive claim into the personality. The process of repression points both the hypertrophy of sensation (the instinctive claim, as it were, slipping through) and to the hypertrophy of the superego (angelism, angel-complex). Both the repressing agency and what is repressed are, as it were, seen in a distorting mirror. The neurotic recognizes the scale of values, but not as it really is; he distorts it. He recognizes, at least implicitly, his responsibility towards values, but circumvents it by a false emphasis of his guilt and by passing responsibility to a scapegoat.

Neurosis as an object of psychotherapy will therefore, in practice, determine the latter's method. But before dealing with psychotherapeutic method we must briefly discuss the question of the basic attitude taken by psychotherapy, as determined by its object. The attitude of psychotherapy differs fundamentally from any impersonal therapeutic attitude. The patient is not thereby regarded as an object in which certain signs (symptoms) could be detected and treated. The psychotherapist, without giving up his freedom, has to identify himself as far as possible with the patient under analysis. Doubtless this is one of the reasons why every analyst student is required to give an analysis lesson.

The psychotherapeutic attitude consists of two elements. One of them derives from the scientific, inductive attitude common to all therapy. Psychotherapy is a natural science in so far as it takes into account certain experiences, certain so-called 'laws' governing the workings of the psyche, which it systematises and treats. In this sense psychotherapy may also be regarded as causal and deterministic, since the methods of natural science can perforce ascertain only causal and determinate relations, linked with immediate experience, rather as a thermometer is linked with subjective sensations of heat and cold. Indeed, psychic laws correspond but coincidentally with living reality (cf. pp. 11 and ff.).

The second element in the psychotherapeutic attitude consists in the intuitive approach of practical psychology, by which we mean not so much applied psychology or psycho-technics as a direct sharing of the patient's experience and suffering, through identification. From this point of view, the patient is always regarded as a subject by the psychotherapist. In psychotherapy there is an encounter of two equal subjects in a realm of common interest. This aspect of psychotherapy is far less a matter of natural science than of an understanding and appreciative attitude, and as such requires values in order to shape and save the living subject.

However, as we have indicated in Part I of this book, this second aspect has come to be neglected, or even completely displaced by an over-emphasis upon the first. In the course of centuries psychotherapy has been separated gradually from magical medicine as well as from pastoral direction; but it was not until the end of the nineteenth and the beginning of the twentieth century that it claimed to be a branch of natural science. This new viewpoint was responsible for great achievements, but also for the dangerous and fallacious over-emphasis of causal and deterministic findings. Thus psychotherapy as a mere natural science has turned partial values into absolute ones. Many of its practical achievements are due to the circumstance that this over-emphasis occurred in accordance with the spirit of the times, and transformed individual into collective neurosis, for that happened best to fit in with the *zeitgeist*. In any case the two aspects of psychotherapy became intermixed, or perhaps the second came to be atrophied.

If psychotherapy were prepared to distinguish the two aspects and to respect both, no further misunderstandings would be possible. Psychology is first and foremost a natural science, as was even held by Aristotle and St Thomas Aquinas. Yet the conclusions drawn from the observations of nature ought to allow themselves to be fitted easily into a general view of life. There should be no dilemma such as the alternative between 'Psychoanalysis *or* Christianity'.

The psychic elements repressed in neurosis must first be recognized and referred to their proper proportions. In the same way, the repressing agency must be recognized and re-evaluated in free discussion. Guiltless scapegoats, including those within one's own psyche, must no longer be burdened with guilt. Guilt must rather be recognized where it really exists.

These conditions for achieving a new equilibrium are not just intelligence tests but testimonials of experience. Neuroses originate in the realm of experience and must be resolved in that realm by retracing their passage into a living view of the universe of man. Relative and absolute values can be properly assessed only when the sense of a hierarchy of values has once more become a living experience.

24. *The one-sided solutions of classical psychotherapy*

We have already criticised the systematic aspect of depth psychology. Now that we have embarked upon the problems of neurosis we have to recognize that psychotherapeutic solutions, as advocated by depth psychology, are themselves half-truths, relative answers masquerading as absolute ones.

There are two scientific attitudes and two ways of thinking about these problems which tend to *over-emphasise* their partial knowledge. These attitudes are basically as old as philosophy itself. The first is the *determinist* attitude. It is not necessarily materialist, it may also be pantheist, pietist, or magic. The second attitude might be defined as excessive indeterminism. It, too, may claim kinship with stoicism, idealism or pietism; or it may be considered, as it has been in recent years, an 'existentialist' attitude. It is not our intention to provoke a fresh outbreak of this old theological and philosophical conflict; instead we should like to show that present-day psychology, which embodies each of these tendencies, could, with the aid of an integral perspective, find a way to make both tendencies complement each other.

Over-emphasis of a way of thinking based on *partial results* is a characteristic feature of that totalitarianism which is manifest today in many spheres, in politics as in the sciences. The image of man has been removed from a petrified system of theology and metaphysics and has become *autonomous*. Man came to be regarded as a self-sufficient being. The secularised thinking also severed all essential connections with transcendent reality. But man without his transcendent links is no longer man. Man is essentially part of an order which is more than himself. Secularised thinking has taken a part to be the whole, since man himself is only part of an order. It is not difficult to see that the determinist concept of man, man as the creature of his instincts, has given absolute emphasis to a partial truth.

We have already criticised the biological 'nothing but' solution. In practice, however, depth psychology could not remain pure natural science. Its very nature made it inevitable that its own crisis would follow along the lines of the spiritual crisis of the times. It is a natural science inasmuch as psychological phenomena, in particular those of neurosis, are systematized and classified by it. Yet, willy-nilly, it ceases to be a natural science as soon as it begins to change a living personality and to guide it towards new ends. When that happens psychotherapy becomes a system of ethics, or its substitute. Every practical psychology, medical psychology and psychotherapy, education, therapeutic education and psychological advice, needs to be related to the hierarchy of values. If the personality is shipwrecked in the service of false values it ought to be the task of education, of the physician, psychotherapist or psychologist, to lead it to genuine values. This raises the old quarrel about the relation between normative and descriptive science. In depth psychology the line between 'objective' scientific knowledge and 'subjective' metaphysical or philosophical interpretation should be drawn particularly strictly. Every attempt to justify depth psychology as a substitute for ethics derived from natural science is bound to be caught in a neurotic vicious circle. Depth psychology as a natural science has great achievements to its credit; but as long as the ethos of depth psychology is but over-emphasis of natural science, one superstition has merely been replaced by another. Upon the data of natural science diagnosed in neurotics, Freud constructed an anthropology, Adler a sociology and Jung a mythology and near theogony.

The influence of depth psychology on the spirit of our times must not, however, be underrated. Whether we are Christians or unbelievers, physicians or patients, priests or laymen, psychologists or those who consult us, we still have to deal with the problems of depth psychology and its answers. Depth psychology owes its development to neurosis, and has indeed been chiefly nourished by neurosis. It reflects, as we have already said, the superstition of its age. The superstition, however, represents the special features of the *zeitgeist* on an abnormal plane. The Swiss writer on mental hygiene, Heinrich Meng, suggested that 'the main task of mental hygiene is to awaken the understanding of the ordinary man, so as to enable him to recognize and correct his superstitious view of the world'.[3]

It was a misapprehension from the start to attempt a purely biological evaluation of neurosis. This, however, is not the place to investigate some of the revolutions in modern medicine. We may just recall that, for example, Binswänger considers mental illness to be an expression of the patient's life history, and that von Weizsäcker regards every illness, whatever its nature, as the result of physical and mental disturbances. The necessity of such considerations in the study of neurosis is quite evident. Depth psychology, and more particularly its practical branch, psychotherapy, needs clean scientific method. But it needs this method for ethical purposes, because it is concerned with the psyche and its salvation. While ethics has an extremely clear concept of mental health, natural science, as every psychologist should admit, has no concept at all of mental health, clear or otherwise.

If a vague interpretation of 'mental health' is attempted, not much more can be said than that it is rooted as much in values as in biology. Even Freud's very exact causal-deterministic psychoanalysis is forever straying from biology into metaphysics. It cannot help doing so, because, although materialistic, it is still concerned with the mind-soul and its salvation. Psychoanalysis has also recognized that the neurotic symptom is already an attempt at a cure, and should therefore be evaluated positively, which adds to the paradox of 'mental health'. The so-called 'final', 'teleological' schools of depth psychology—Alfred Adler's Individual Psychology and C. G. Jung's Complex Psychology—went further still in their positive evaluation of the neurotic symptom, and recognized that a biological 'inferiority' may include a possibility of progress in the existential sense. At the same time depth

[3] Heinrich Meng, *Seelischer Gesundheitsschutz*, Basel 1939, p. 152.

psychology, if we exclude a few cautious remarks of Jung's, fails to recognize that a so-called neurotic conflict may in fact be so fruitful and rich in values that a psychotherapy which aims at 'freeing' the patient from such a conflict, without projecting it on to a higher level, would perforce entail an impoverishment of the personality. What, one wonders, would psychotherapy have made of St Augustine's unrest, of Pascal's anguish, or of Kierkegaard's depression? But if we acknowledge that apparently neurotic phenomena may contain higher values, we must assign to metaphysical significance a position of preponderance with regard to the findings of depth psychology. Yet depth psychology continues to assume, even in this case, that its tried scientific method can be a substitute for ethics. Biological research, however, is quite incapable of investigating the metaphysical principle of the psyche. What it can grasp is but the biological derivative, which could be called 'animality'. It is Freud and Jung's 'libido', Adler's 'urge towards self-assertion', Jung's 'psychic energy' and Janet's *niveau mental*.

There is a tendency to confuse 'mental health' with the pleasure principle. The free unimpeded play of the libido is regarded as the hallmark of health, though Adler introduced the added social element; a full and harmonious development of psychic energy at peace with itself and with society. Thus the concept of 'mental health' becomes a new value-concept, not an ethical but a hedonistic-social one, inadequate for biological investigations.

It is quite true that there are different degrees of mental healing, and the highest of them leaves room for genuine transcendence; but this possibility lies outside psychotherapy. On the other hand, psychotherapy, because of its this-worldly attitude, often tends to 'reduce' or 'analyse away' the existential conflict, including the positive aspect inseparable from the neurotic pseudo solution. This means that psychotherapy sometimes cannot find any solution for the genuine existential problem which lies behind neurosis.

A discipline which attributes the search for truth to a morbid feeling of insufficiency is, quite obviously, as short-sighted as the attempt to explain the experience of God as a product of sexuality. Such attempts are based on *partial truths*; a partial truth usurps the place of a greater truth, and the result is a demonstration of the self-deception of our time, so prone to exalt what is relative into absolutes. In this connection we should like to say explicitly that we have no quarrel with the causal chain of psychological events, as has, for instance, been so acutely revealed in psychoanalysis. But the human spirit is all this and is yet something else as well; therefore 'all this' should not be regarded as absolute. Yet psychoanalysis alone is not responsible for this superstition.

Incidentally, a search for values, a striving towards an objective set of moral values, is becoming increasingly evident in psychotherapy. The growth of personality does in fact require extra-psychological ends; and if one is going to search at all, it is felt more or less consciously that these ends must not produce near pseudo-values, or the search would hardly be worth undertaking. Thus psychotherapy is feeling its way towards absolute values. It is going through the same development as its patients, trying to transcend its desire for self-assertion into a desire for truth. It no longer feels at home in solipsist psychologism and seeks an approach to the hierarchy of true values. Through its transference the neurotic image has distorted the face of psychotherapy. The time has come for it to grow out of this childish phase and to develop further. Psychotherapy, just as much as the neurotic, is in need of truth.

As the desire for truth leads to genuine fulfilment, and to genuine freedom and power, all absolutising of what is relative separates from truth, and leads to loneliness. Man was never so poor and weak as when he wanted to be God. Evil is apart. However, neurosis was given to mankind for a warning. Lucifer is alone, but presumably he is no neurotic and the neurotic, certainly, is far from being Lucifer! Neurosis is self-deception; but, through the voluntarily imposed punishment of the symptom (placating destiny) it is also a timid effort in the direction of truth, a yearning for communion. It is no accident that we have found the neurotic symptom to be an abortive attempt at liberation. Liberation can come about only through adherence to true values. The life heresy must be unmasked and, if possible, should not be replaced by restrictive half truths. Even if the neurotic's conscience can consent to relative values being turned into

E

absolutes, the therapist must refrain from making new absolutes of other relative values. The attitude of some psychotherapists to the philosophy of values is a chilling example of false prophecy, even when it is combined with the expert's seductive modesty ('Perhaps we had better stick to psychology').

The attempt to heal sick minds must not itself become a bad example of the repression of true values.

It is the paradoxical, indeed, scandalizing, factor of depth psychology that man is completely divorced from his knowledge of himself, and becomes completely autonomous. He loses his connection with true objectivity. And the result is fear of being cast down into what Max Picard has called our 'disjointed' world, in which man, himself a particle and composed of a jumble of particles, struggles against an equally jumbled universe. This is nowadays called existential anxiety. Man thus uprooted is ever searching for stability and values. But as an autonomous being in a disjointed world he can but select his own experience as the sole criterion, burning it into an absolute. This fallacy causes him never to be able to transcend himself: love, humility and God become dead letters for him. His own experience is the absolute, in a many-coloured stream of unrelated sensation, so that he is tempted to want to have pleasant experiences only and to dread what is unpleasant as such. Thus the pleasure principle is exalted into the highest of all. This disjointedness, and absolutising of subjective feeling, are bound to lead to hypertrophy of feeling, and feeling is itself regarded as the only sure criterion. The fall of Man, his being cast into this 'world of sorrow' (Heidegger), results in self-centredness and anxiety. His is the Promethean attempt: 'Ye shall be like God'. This hypertrophy of self may conceal itself even in an ideal (an absolutised goal) or in wisdom itself (absolutised knowledge). We are dealing here with an extremely significant and serious problem, which is the central problem of all psychotherapy. Depth psychology, in evaluating human development, tries to make use of criteria which lie within the individual; it cannot, therefore, reach beyond the individual. Thus the aim of autonomous depth psychology is but one-sided: the fulfilment of the individual self. The perfecting and fulfilment of the self is, of course, a noble aim; but, as long as it is not bound up with objective values, it cannot transcend the individual frame. A value-bound fulfilment of the ego is, however, unthinkable without renunciation, that is without the real subjection of one's own egotistic values to the values of love. 'He that shall lose his life for me shall find it' (Mt 10:39). It is impossible to enter the kingdom of truth, goodness and beauty without first having renounced the aesthetic end in itself, such as sensation for its own sake, or the pleasure principle. But it is just as necessary to have renounced all rationalist ends in themselves, such as pride of knowledge. All relative and finite values, however noble in themselves, as soon as they become absolute are presuppositions for the hypertrophy of the self.

Kierkegaard has shown what happens when values, noble in themselves, but still centred upon the self, are turned into absolutes: Ahasuerus the perpetual seeker, Don Juan everlastingly a prey to his sensations, Faustus constantly striving for knowledge —they have separated themselves from objective values, and are pursuing absolutised selfish ends, without ever being able to find genuine fulfilment.

Yet psychologists are also children of their age. The disease of the bad conscience has marked not only the multitude of neurotics—those typical contemporaries—it is, quite simply, the disease of modern civilization. Anxiety too, as it appears today, collectively and individually, is but a symptom of this disease; it is caused by the impossibility of doing away with the bad conscience that rules the world of the hypertrophied self. When what is relative is regarded as absolute and the world of values is turned upside down, the whole world of man must of necessity become disjointed too. The hypertrophied ego must, since it recognizes only its own laws, paradoxically lead to the lowering of man's dignity, indeed to its destruction; just as one of its offshoots, the totalitarian state, must, despite the fact that it disposes of every means of destruction (or rather, because of it), succumb to a psychosis of terror. This, indeed, is the oddest aspect of our problem: the more inflated the self becomes, so the conscience worsens; the more totalitarian the state, the greater the fear; the more autonomous mankind, the more absurd and despairing its creed.

25. *The one-sided solutions of existentialist psychotherapy*

As a reaction against the inadequacy of biological psycho-therapy, a new method has emerged, particularly after the second World War. Following various schools of existentialist philosophy, it seeks to treat the neurotic as a free subject.

These new paths had already been paved by the extreme psychology of consciousness, which equated all mental activity with consciousness, so that its opponents compared it to the caricature of a man with a gigantic thinker's head on a tiny body. In answer it might have been said that the great pioneers of depth psychology themselves, in paying attention exclusively to the unconscious and regarding man's consciousness as unimportant, were also caricaturing man, but this time by standing him on his head. The errors of the extreme psychology of consciousness, which has very few supporters nowadays, may be explained by the discovery that consciousness appeared to be the foundation of human autonomy: *Cogito ergo sum:* I think, therefore I am. But who is 'I'? Thought alone is worth considering. This kind of megalomania does, indeed, lead to disappointment, to dissatisfaction, to fear, to neurosis. But man owes it to his enlightened autonomy, so runs the argument, to repress these inadequacies. Therefore anything that lies outside the proof of self by means of *cogito*—whether God or devil or the id (yes, indeed, the Freudian id!)—is superstition, unworthy of representatives of the psychology of the consciousness school.

But the psychotherapeutic achievements of the classical psychology of consciousness school were nil. On the other hand, it is by no means equally obvious that those modern trends in psychology which present man as a being deciding existentially and in freedom are equally inadequate. For the over-emphasis on freedom is likewise a result of secularization and autonomism. Man now appears as a little god, who believes he creates himself, and whose idolatry is constantly fed by 'freedom' and 'responsibility'. Victor von Weizsäcker has aptly remarked that 'Freud could have originated only in the Christian era—indeed, only in an age of Protestantism. Freud regards man as he is as being out of order.'[4]

[4] *Schweizer Rundschau*, 1948, p. 726.

We may say with equal justification that existentialism could arise only out of a profound crisis of faith. Existentialism regards man, indeed, as being out of order, but as representing at the same time the criterion for order.

Since primitive materialism was unsatisfying a new psychology emerged in connection with the general crisis, which explicitly recognized the reality of the spirit. This new psychology no longer regarded man as a machine, consisting of association, wires and a consciousness engine. Rather, it proposed to approach man *concretely*: in his freedom, his life plan, his mental and spiritual resolve—in brief, in his *existence*. The new psychology was daughter to a new philosophy: existentialism. Its significance in psychology was quite revolutionary. Certainly, like all revolutions, existentialist philosophy too was but a symptom, a symptom both of disease and of the struggle for recovery. Existentialism as such a time-conditioned factor is now quite inseparable from the crisis of the secularised approach to life.

For the existentialists also, man is self-sufficient; and for the most consistent among them he is the creator of his own existence. Thus their approach is accompanied by a veritable inflation of concepts such as freedom, responsibility and decision. If the psychoanalysts during the period between the wars defined man as the product of his instincts, he is now defined as the product of his own decision. For Jean-Paul Sartre man exists only in so far as he 'realizes' himself. It is not mere rhetoric when Sartre declares that man is 'the invention of man'. There is no such thing as human nature, man is what he creates himself to be.'[5] And Simone de Beauvoir begins the second volume of her extremely interesting book on *The Second Sex* with the apodictic remark: 'Women are not born; they are made.'[6] The only conclusion that can be drawn from this approach is that man is *fully* responsible; 'he is condemned to freedom'.[7] This school of existentialism preaches not only the creative act, but also continual re-birth; for the creative act becomes, in the last resort, self-fulfilment.

Yet Sartre's uncompromising position contains within itself

[5] *L'Existentialisme est un Humanisme*, Paris, Nagel, 1946.
[6] *Le Deuxième Sexe*, Gallimard, II, 1949, p. 13.
[7] Sartre, op. cit.

the error that attaches to all artificial absolutes. It is simply not the case that man invents himself! It is not true that man is identical with his own planning. In the first place man brings with him the inertia of the creature, which is precisely the condition of being driven, the 'id'. The human ego is insidiously affected and conditioned by the 'id', the general human instinct; and neurosis shows us what happens to the ego that takes its own plans for unadulterated freedom. In the second place the idea of creating oneself out of nothing is absurd, and amounts to 'angelism'. There is a generally valid plan for mankind, and the conviction that man is part of a plan is certainly closer to the truth than Sartre's excessive indeterminism. In carrying out his planned development, man must take into account both the plan made for him and the determining factors of his own being.

It is, incidentally, worth noting that the extreme existentialist conception of human freedom illustrates unequivocally the denial of transcendental links. Its history shows that existentialist philosophy owes both method and dialectic to Soren Kierkegaard, whom it is somewhat reluctant to acknowledge as an ancestor. But Kierkegaard was not only a passionately convinced Christian, but also a thinker whose ideas cannot be abstracted from Christianity. For Kierkegaard, too, every moment of existence involved a decision, a resolve, an 'either-or': for freedom or for slavery. But the decision implied for him either a decision for the rule of God, the absolute, the 'I am that I am', or for the rule of determinism, that is of spiritual non-being. We see, therefore, that the choice lies in the confession: God or the limitations of one's own being, regardless of whether this occurs in apparent autonomy of the human spirit or of his instinct. Kierkegaard's responsibility and freedom, then, were simply the surrender of the self to the will of the Father, 'Thy will be done'. But in speaking of the freedom and decision of autonomous man, existentialism came to choose 'My will be done'.

It is not here intended to attack existentialist philosophy. Anyone nowadays dealing with psychology, who sees in it more than laboratory experiments, is in his conception of human personality likely to be conditioned by the spirit of the times, because he is concerned with a real situation and with real people. Probably the most significant intellectual trend of our time is this reference to human existence struggling in the world and threatened from all sides. But often it tries to take heaven by storm, and thereby to leap across the gaping emptiness of man in his self-imposed solitude. Even Sartre by choosing the humanist service of mankind moves towards overcoming anxiety. A Christian philosopher like Gabriel Marcel only sees in the encounter with the 'absolute Thou' the possibility of overcoming this anxiety. This is already an unconditional recognition of transcendence, but a transcendence still *centred* on threatened, transitory existence. Karl Jaspers shows the same hesitation when he says 'Transcendence is in need of existence'. Yet man as a centre represents a fallen existence, someone cast down. An existence of this kind cannot, on its own, be otherwise than of a 'fallen state'. It would be an over-simplification, a 'nothing-but' explanation, to try to explain existentialist philosophy itself by means of depth psychology. It is certain, however, that the existentialist philosophies have found a fruitful psychological soil in our times; they have attempted both to express and to overcome the solitude of autonomous man. The philosophers themselves were far from being as 'free' as they imagined and as they 'condemned' man to be free. Existentialism is a symbol of the collective neurosis of our time, and thus has positive and negative aspects.

The positive aspects of a psychotherapy influenced by existentialist thinking are obvious. Existentialist psychotherapy, which includes different trends, has been able to defend freedom and the significance of existence against the mechanistic determinism of classical psychotherapy. But human freedom, and more particularly the freedom of the neurotic, is anything but absolute. Paradoxically, this freedom is tied to determinism, so that it can be conceived only as a progressive liberation. In the same way, the meaning both of neurosis and of existence itself is not immediately and entirely apparent, but has to be progressively understood and analysed.

A person in the grip of an affect is in no condition to understand explanations about his freedom and the meaning of his life. In order to be able to understand them, he must first be freed from his affect. Neurosis is a protracted and insidious affect, the causes of which are not easily discovered. Before the neurotic can think clearly about freedom and significance, he must—and this is anything but easy—have a clear notion of the *unfreedom* and *meaninglessness* of his 'life-heresy'.

It is interesting that existentialist psychotherapy does not go beyond describing the meaning of existence and setting forth a sometimes rather grandiose phenomenology of neurosis. The *methods* to be used are distinctly unclear, and it would certainly be desirable if existentialist psychotherapists descended from their phenomenological clouds and, instead of significant explanations, suggested also a few practical steps.

The criticism which existentialist philosophy and psychotherapy have levelled against classical depth psychology ought, of course, to be taken very seriously. Thus, Jaspers criticises psychoanalysis for being 'a faith': 'Psychoanalysis as a faith is possible only because of fundamental scientific mistakes . . . The understanding of significance is confused with causal explanations . . . What is termed neurosis is not characterised by the comprehensible contents of its phenomena, but by the mechanism of translating from what is mental to the physical level, from significance into a physical process devoid of significance.' 'It is wrong to absolutise any kind of knowledge into total knowledge.'[8]

Equally incisive is the criticism of Freudian psychoanalysis expressed by V. E. Frankl. He very rightly observes that in the psychoanalytical approach 'the will is not supported by a conscious "ought", but rather the conscious will is backed by an unconscious "must" . . . The ends of the self, in psychoanalysis, are really only means to the ends determined by the id. Thus, for psychoanalysis, all motives must appear to be unreal. Man himself becomes totally unreal.'[9] However, reaction upon the 'unconscious must' from an 'ought' yet to be made conscious, has led in practice to existentialist psychotherapy all too often identifying itself with the mere presentation of what ought to be. Yet there have been remarkable changes, and it is something to be

[8] Karl Jaspers, *Vernunft und Widervernunft im gegenwärtigen Philosophieren*, in preparation, R. Piper and Co., Munich; quoted from *Der Monat*, III/26.

[9] *Logos und Existenz in der Psychotherapie*, Wissenschaft und Weltbild, April 1949, p. 2.

thankful for that there is today a psychotherapy, and even a psychiatry, which unequivocally acknowledge spiritual values and present therapy as something both 'originating in the spirit' and 'directed towards the spirit' (Frankl). In the German-speaking countries V. E. Frankl,[10] and in France Henry Baruk,[11] have written persuasively of ways of treating emotional disturbances which go beyond biologism and psychologism and are based upon ethical values. The thinking of both these authors came as a breath of fresh air in the specialised literature of the last few years. The fact that both are believing Jews has more than private significance, because it bears eloquent witness to the forces of spiritual renewal at work in the Old Dispensation. Eminent personalities like Leo Shestov and Simone Weil had, indeed, prepared the ground for this spiritual renewal. The lives and works of these two existentialist thinkers also gave expression to the 'Christ archetype', which is less noticeable in the theoretical considerations of the two previously mentioned psychiatrists. Baruk and Frankl have made remarkable contributions to the realm of psychology which concerns us here.

It can be said generally of the new existentialist and ethical orientations in psychotherapy that their findings are great and admirable. It means above all the inclusion of the spiritual in psychology. Yet nearly all trends of this psychotherapy are marred by an ambiguity which is due to a secularised concept of man—of man who, in the last resort, is regarded as the sole criterion of transcendence. Thus Ludwig Binswänger, for instance, considers the problem to be that human existence as a whole, with all its physical and spiritual modes of being, must share in the penetration of the world of anxiety and finiteness through the infinite and the fullness of love. Yet how often in actual practice does a finite and threatened, self-centred and isolated mode of existence prove quite impenetrable to the fulfilment of love! In existential analysis, then, fear is to be overcome by the human 'us' feeling. Existential analysis is secularised and religiously neutral; it does not go far enough in the acknowledgment of the whole hierarchy of values. 'The basic forms of

[10] *Ärztliche Seelsorge*, 4th edition, Vienna, Deuticke, 1948.
[11] *Psychiatrie morale expérimentale, individuelle et sociale*, Paris, Presses Universitaires de France, 1945.

human existence can be considered only in the light of a neutral or secularised anthropology.'[12]

We are once more faced with the problem of the scale of values, and existential analysis will be found inadequate. Nor is it sufficient to recognize *homo religiosus* theoretically, while remaining 'neutral' in practice. A scale of values that would form part of an objective order cannot be attained in this way, for our contemporary neurosis represents a defection from just these objective values. A depth psychology of this kind must perforce remain attached to the magic circle of its own problems. Depth psychology cannot afford to remain neutral towards either *homo libidinosus or homo religiosus*. If it recognizes only *homo libidinosus* it is only a biology, and not a genuine anthropology. If it disregards *homo libidinosus* it is untrue to the facts. But if it overlooks *homo religiosus*, it becomes divorced from true values and once again falls a prey to deception.

It seems paradoxical that, on the one hand, the principles of existentialist psychotherapy are not quite adequate for a universal anthropology; yet, on the other hand, and conversely, its methods overshoot the mark since, by its own account, it shows the neurotic 'what should be'. With its contempt for the 'id' that is influenced also by anxiety and repression, it hesitates, despite contrary assertions, to analyse the determinate aspect of man. Thus it turns all too easily into mere stoic preaching; but this may, under certain circumstances, foster neurotic repression of, and resistance against, existential truth. Existentialist psychotherapy may then identify itself with the superego, an identification which has anyhow led the neurotic to 'angelistic' delusions.

In principle, existentialist psychotherapy is an instrument of individuation, more or less in Jung's sense of the word. It endeavours to raise into consciousness and responsibility the concrete, living, unique human being, out of his impersonal, collective and undifferentiated existence. The specifically human feature of man is his spirit; and 'logo-therapy', as Frankl calls his psychotherapy, 'based upon the spiritual', is to foster man's acknowledgement of this specific feature. It might appear that

[12] Ludwig Binswänger, Preface to *Grundformen und Erkenntnis menschlichen Daseins*, Zurich, 1942, p. 18.

such a therapy could never be accused of reducing men to an impersonal mass. But what happens in practice? We are quite prepared to await the publication of descriptions of treatment, and to accept assurances that this type of therapy is not intended to replace but to complement psychoanalysis.

Yet in reviewing the various existentialist schools in psychotherapy, it is difficult to avoid the impression that they had their origin less in practice than in the theorist's study. In practice, it all too often seems to be the case that the 'analysis of existence' (or 'analysis in respect of existence') represents a sort of confrontation of the neurotic's real existence with an imagined *norm* of existence of complete freedom and responsibility. Such a confrontation, however, destroys the core even of existentialist philosophy. The neurotic tragedy is an existentialist tragedy. Freedom and responsibility are effective beyond all abstract norms. No amount of stoic or existentialist preaching can help a man who is struggling for more freedom, but is deprived of freedom by forces unknown to him. To argue as Jaspers does against didactic analysis in the name of freedom has an air of helplessness.

The neurotic's 'angelism' forces him to identify his ego with a superego taken over from outside; this means he simply bypasses the steps of his 'id-development'. It is therefore not much use presenting him with a new set of external norms, since in the analytical development he has in fact often to retrace the very steps he has bypassed. This leads to difficult situations which may involve the psychotherapist in many scruples, and often perplex the moralist. Freudian psychoanalysts have been accused of advising their patients to give free rein frequently to their difficulties. This may have been so in a number of instances, because many psychoanalysts regarded relative values as absolute. Freud and Jung, however, have been quite unequivocally against psychoanalytical unrestraint. Yet it was Jung who rightly said: 'The mere suppression of the shadow is as little of a remedy as beheading is a cure for headache.'[13] 'The shadow' is, according to Jung, a powerful archetype, which keeps alive within us everything that is repressed and rejected, including urges. Coming to terms with the shadow is a difficult problem. The neurotic solves

[13] *Psychologie und Religion*, p. 138.

it inadequately, by trying not to recognize his shadow. The shadow is not only the mere id; it is rather a synthesis of all those forces which appear to us, consciously or unconsciously, as immoral or dangerous. As long as man fails to acknowledge his own immoral and dangerous forces, he will remain on the defensive towards them. But the acknowledgement of the shadow is seldom a smooth and easy process, and it cannot be done at all by merely meditating about responsibility.

Moreover, any analysis may necessarily lead to certain periods of unrestrained living. It must be remembered that the neurotic has quite simply missed certain necessary steps in his emotional development. An unimpeded integration of these by-passed stages of development is very rare indeed. As we have said, psychotherapeutic development may entail conflicts of conscience for the therapist himself.

The compulsive neurosis briefly described on p. 31 was eventually cured; but not because the patient immediately renounced her instinctive desires. Mrs O. Z.'s second marriage ended in divorce by her own wish, and she married a third time. In this case, the patient was incapable of the lofty renunciation we observed in the subsequent case of Miss L. K. (pp. 31 and 32).

Dr V. W., a physician, has very largely remained at the anal-sadistic phase. Psychotherapy leads him through a period of stubborn defence, and he only gradually arrives at the formation of the Oedipus complex. He now has a stereotyped dream, of sexual intercourse with his own mother. At the same time, the thirty-six-year-old patient begins to masturbate frequently. After a few weeks, this phase was overcome; but before this happened, every attempt to make Dr V. W. prematurely aware of his responsibility met with dangerous aggressiveness.

Dr N. O., also a physician, seeks a cure for his impotence; the symptom is quickly relieved. But now there follows a period of unbridled sexuality, which can be brought under control only very gradually, even though the patient, a religious man, is himself unhappy about his undisciplined behaviour.

It is not always possible, then, to keep the moral law effectively before the patient's eyes. Certainly truth is one and indivisible, and allows of no compromise, but man must experience its progressive discovery and eventual adaption in his own heart, in his flesh and blood. Only very few are privileged by grace to possess this living truth from the beginning.

A psychotherapy which is to give up the absolutions of relative values must allow all values to be recognized clearly, both the most unimportant and relative ones and those which are highest and most indispensable, and allow them to be experienced without compulsion. Every attempt in psychotherapy to disregard either biological foundations or transcendental heights, and to develop a neutral and rationalist depth psychology—even one that acknowledges the existence of the spiritual—is doomed to failure and rendered valueless through the fatality of half-truth.

Chapter Two

PSYCHOLOGICAL ANALYSIS
AND EXISTENTIAL SYNTHESIS

26. *Aspects of a personalist psychotherapy*

IT is our view that the psychotherapeutic method ought to do justice both to man's conditioned, unfree, determinate aspects and to the 'individual', free and responsible principle within him. The method of a universal psychotherapy cannot, therefore, be simply based on biology and natural science; it cannot even be purely psychological, if by psyche we understand, as contemporary usage will have it, something more closely akin to psycho-pathology than to the Aristotelian-Thomist soul; but neither can such a method be merely 'logo-therapeutic', a method 'rooted in, and directed towards, the spirit'. It ought to include the whole human person; and might be described as personalist. It proposes to subject the development so far attained of the human person to a searching analysis, and, at the same time, to pave the way towards the perfection of his or her individual vocation.

A personalist psychotherapy, then, should be both 'universal' and 'integral', that is it should be based both on determined factors and on human values.

It is noticeable that all the disciplines that deal with man are increasingly concentrating upon the human person; this should have been a natural process, but it is actually taking place slowly and reluctantly. The reluctance is due to man having been considered by natural science as being devoid of, and outside, transcendental links. His spiritual life, and his freedom as the proper sphere of that life, could not, as we have seen, be known by the means of natural science. While a trend towards the personalist approach is now apparent in many anthropological disciplines, psychology is particularly backward. So far, its specialized literature hardly contains a single concise presentation of the personalist approach, nor has this approach found expression in handbooks or introductory treatises.[1]

A similar situation also exists, for instance, in medicine. We owe a great deal to the so-called psychosomatic school in medicine; but it is far from being a complete and exhaustive way of looking at a sick person. A promising school similar in tendency to A. Niedermeyer's 'universalist medicine' seems to be the *Médecine de la Personne*, whose advocate, Paul Tournier, has written about psychosomatic medicine:

> The 'soma' and the 'psyche' are phenomenological concepts. They are accessible to scientific investigation, and their mutual relationship is the essential subject of psychosomatic medicine. The realm of the spirit, on the other hand, can only be sensed intuitively or experienced through an inner encounter with God. Once one has recognized its existence, it follows that, contrary to what is still widely supposed today, a complete medicine, that deals with the whole of man, cannot be purely scientific; this also means that the physician, in dealing with the factors productive of health or disease, must take into account not only the physical and psychological ones, but also the existence of certain spiritual factors, which are, however, inaccessible to science. Psychosomatic medicine, however, has so far remained a purely scientific school of thought. Its work has meant a great deal to us, in that it has given us a better synthesized image of man. Nonetheless, it is concerned exclusively with the exploration of that part of man which is accessible to science and subject to the principle of causation: the mechanistic part. What seemed to us to become particularly clear in the course of our talks and discussions, is simply that a physician who begins by refusing to leave objective scientific ground is, by the same token, incapacitated from seeing the specifically human element in man and from practising a genuinely complete medicine.[2]

[1] Among the exceptions are Emmanuel Mounier, *Traité du Caractère*, Paris, Editions du Seuil, 1947; also Charles Baudouin, *De l'Instinct à l'Esprit*, Bruges-Paris, Desclée de Brouwer, 1950.

[2] Tournier, *Die neue Sendung des Arztes*, Tyrolia, Innsbruck-Vienna, 1950, pp. 22–23.

There are those who make fun of 'universalistic' or 'personalist medicine', accusing it of trying to pray its patients back to health; whereas in fact Niedermeyer, Tournier and others have protested often enough against any supra-naturalism or pietism. 'You may obey God by prescribing medicine; and you may disobey him by praying.'[3] Tournier goes on to say that every illness requires two diagnoses; from the point of view of natural science, which is concerned with causes, and from the point of view of the human person a 'spiritual' diagnosis of the significance of the illness, which seeks to ascertain 'what God is trying to say through the phenomena of disease', and how the personal task thus set within the plan of creation may be fulfilled.

These findings of medicine can also be applied to psychotherapy; not because neurosis is an 'illness' like any other, but, on the contrary, because every illness seen from this angle has a part to play in the plan of human life, and neurosis is precisely an attempt to carry out this plan somehow or other. As regards method, it cannot be emphasised sufficiently that any absolutising is to be guarded against and that it ought to cover all aspects of human existence simultaneously. The division between the biological, ethical and religious spheres is, then, an artificial division, to be justified only heuristically. A personalistic psychotherapy may *never* be either purely nosological or causal or purely spiritual. The levels or steps we may distinguish here are simply concrete descriptions of different aspects of a single process. Analysis and synthesis are the two poles of every psychotherapy. Psychotherapy always tries to lay bare the concealed causes of suffering, and at the same time to help the patient to experience the existential meaning of his going astray and the new direction his life must henceforth take. What varies is but the ratio between these two elements and their self-evident connection in any given case. Danger arises if the synthesis is forced on the patient without uncovering the neurotic condition; or if the analyst's apparent objectivity has already given the synthesis a fatal twist in a certain direction, as happens in some so-called 'neutral' analyses. The first and most obvious feature of psychotherapy is its causal-analytic aspect. The neurotic's unfree actions have to be connected by way of experience with earlier stages of

[3] Tournier, op. cit.

his life history, which stages normally should no longer have been active. In other words, fixations have to be uncovered and allowed an outlet. What one sees in neurosis are not the normal stages, say, of early childhood development in their healthy and necessary aspects, but protracted and disturbing after-effects of stages that have not been overcome. The stages in themselves were healthy and necessary; what is morbid and abnormal is the fixation on stages already overtaken. To regard the stages of development as 'morbid' in themselves is possible only in the light of a false perspective, which projects back from the pathological fixation on to the particular object of fixation. Classical psychoanalysis has often been guilty of this false perspective. Freud regarded the infant as 'polymorphically perverse', because in him are active all the forces which may later, through pathological fixation, lead to specific abnormalities. Of course, the infant is in no sense 'perverse'; he is pervertible. The adult who has not overcome the claims of the infantile stage is perverse. In other words, the same desire must be differently evaluated in the infant and in the adult. Or: what is valuable for the infant may be just the reverse for the adult.

This development shows a progressive attachment to values of life-history, the essential element being the widening of values. The same contents acquire different values; which is not to say that all values are relative! On lower levels, the height of valuation is proportionately lower than on higher levels. The symbol of the absolute is different on the primitive level than the highest. If, on the higher level, we should recoil upon a lower level, this would be tantamount to absolutising what is relative.

On the other hand, the widening of values taking place in the process of transcending the various stages of development means a progressive liberation from the compulsory false absolutes of the lower levels. Life within the womb, the digestive tract, the mother's breast, the developing defiance-ego—these are some higher values in primitive stages of development. The child, in order to subsist, is bound to regard these primitive values as absolute; but, in order to develop, it must also progressively free itself from these compulsory absolutes. A fixation on primitive stages is therefore a genuine regression to primitive compulsory mechanisms. This regression is due to different constitutional, biological and sociological influences. Background and education seem to play the most important part. The regression is accordingly determined to a large extent by outside forces; but at the same time it poses the problem of our evaluation of, and our relation to, freedom. In order to remove the determinate regression as far as this is possible, it is necessary to penetrate to the stage in question, and experience, relive and rearrange the loosened forces. Analysis has to penetrate to the 'specific childhood situation' and cannot be content with generalities and preaching. Yet at the same time psychological abnormality is a false synthesis of human existence. The removal of this abnormality therefore creates a new existential situation and a new synthesis and is, in the last resort, once more a spiritual problem. If the rearrangement of the personality merely ends in new relative values being set up as absolutes, the synthesis remains incomplete and the neurosis has simply changed its form. The reduction of all spiritual life to material factors, or a self-righteous 'angelism' without recognition of shadow aspects, or the unresolved transference of the patient's fixations on to the analyst —these and many other methodological errors produce the kind of abortive synthesis we have described. Analysis and synthesis can thus be seen at work even in the apparently purely causal-analytic aspect of psychotherapy. Yet in this aspect the main emphasis is on the analytic process, since the concern is not so much with rational synthesis as with absolutes and processes of liberation as they are experienced by the patient. Just as there can be no false absolute without an experience of fixation, the new synthesis must also be rooted in insight into the regression, by way of experience, which means that strict analysis is indispensable.

It is obvious that analysis and synthesis lead to an ethical transformation of the personality; indeed, one might even regard this transformation as a second aspect of psychotherapy. In neurosis, we meet not only the fixation on infantile instincts, but also the identification with an infantile superego, which has taken the place of the free conscience. If the instinct fixations were not at the same time rejected by the superego there would be no neurosis, but a free outlet for the claims of instinct, which would result in perversion or crime; which constitute as it were the reverse of neurosis. In neurosis, however, the ego obeys the prohibitions of the superego, and at the same time tries to satisfy the claims of the id obliquely and in disguised forms. The result is the repression of the id's claims and the deceptive belief that the ego is identical with the superego ('angelism'): we have already spoken in some detail of this neurotic pride.

It should not be forgotten that classical psychoanalysis regards individual development as a progressive freeing of the libido from the ego, that is a leaving behind of the original narcissistic attitude for the sake of new objects. The meaning of psychotherapy, particularly for Freud, lies in the liberation of the neurotic from his narcissistic fetters so as to enable him to become capable of love. In this sense, however, the conversion to a capacity for love is, on the ethical plane, equivalent to a conversion to humility. Neurotic arrogance, as we have seen, is the remnant of a narcissistic occupation of the ego by the libido. Neurotic greed for experience is, after successful psychotherapy, replaced by new duties and new joys. Neurotic pseudo-knowledge and pseudo-duties are replaced by a new scale of duties.

What is needed is not, however, an atheist system of moral imperatives but a conscious acknowledgement of the system of relationships within which man is placed. That synthesis may be regarded as complete the purpose of which it would be to lead the individual through life as economically as possible. A system of moral imperatives which is concerned merely to attain social relations without friction is, as has been shown in Part I, also a false absolute—a collective instead of an individual neurosis. Man's essential nature is to be centred on transcendent values. It is an error in perspective to regard the ethical level as a mere superstructure of the biological; but it would be an equally partial synthesis to dismiss religious values as fundamentally superfluous, or perhaps even neurotic, complications of the primary urge.

Existential synthesis means making man progressively responsible; that is why it meets with continual resistance. We have seen that the overcoming of neurosis poses a guilt problem, for there can be no responsibility for errors without the possibility of guilt. But how can one be guilty of unconscious fixations? How can one make somebody responsible for developmental disturbances which have arisen in earliest childhood or perhaps even at the moment of birth? Daim (op. cit., p. 253) remarks that psychotherapy is combating the natural results of collective guilt, that is of original sin. Unconsciousness and untruth are characteristic of fallen nature. All neurotic behaviour, too, conditioned by original ignorance, carries within itself the consequences of the universal offence. Having eaten the fruit of the Tree of Knowledge, we are obliged to consciousness. Thus the state of our responsibility is ambiguous, and its paradoxical character is incomprehensible on purely naturalistic premisses, just as by the same token Christ's words are incomprehensible: 'Father, forgive them, for they know not what they do.' We need to be forgiven for what we do not know, for *being unfree*. We have sufficiently analysed the meaning of the neurosis that seeks to avoid this paradox (pp. 64 and ff.). Thus neurosis is an exhortation to humility, towards which existential synthesis must consciously strive: for, in spite of his responsibility, man is still dependent on a chain of causes, and every step he takes has its inescapable consequences. This is why a phenomenological treatment of neurosis without causal analysis is ineffective. Anyone who fails to understand his unfree condition thinks himself like unto the angels, but remains fettered.

However, the religious significance of a personalist psychotherapy obviously does not lie in psychotherapy usurping the province of spiritual direction. On the contrary, it is a feature of the neurosis of our time that psychotherapy is required to be a substitute for religious direction. The religious significance of psychotherapy lies in finding the existential synthesis (after the 'life-heresy' of neurosis) in a 'life-orthodoxy'. Existential synthesis can only indirectly attain certain values which are important to every religious faith. Thus the main task of existential synthesis is to turn former egotistically absolute values into relative ones. Harold Schultz-Hencke has observed that the neurotic greed for experience cannot be brought to agree with genuinely *lived* Christian virtues: 'The dynamic factors at the back of neurosis are the spheres of emotional experience that find expression in the urge to self-assertion, the possessive urge and the sexual urge. This triad, however, will yet provoke astonishment and scepticism. A very remarkable indication of its accuracy may perhaps be seen in the fact that the monastic vows are: poverty, chastity and obedience.'[4]

The object of all psychotherapy is, briefly expressed, the acknowledgement of a transcendent hierarchy of values which should become, according to individual possibilities, a truth expressed in terms of one's own life. This acknowledgement certainly involves a decision, a free decision essential to human existence. This existential synthesis, however, can be free and effective only if it results from an accurate investigation of psychological possibilities; that is after a psychological analysis in the widest sense of the word. Existential synthesis, moreover, is not just abstract freedom, a self-activating scheme of life. If we speak of freedom, choice, decision, plan, responsibility or the spirit without an adequate investigation of the un-free part of human nature—and sometimes these terms in themselves are believed to contain a new method of cure—we are continually in danger of reinforcing man still further in his defenceless autonomy, and in the last resort to congratulate him for his aberration.

27. *Life-orthodoxy as a truth to be lived*

There can be only one salvation from the neurotic existential anxiety, from the disjointed nature of feeling: the hierarchy of objective values. Objective not in the sense of the intra-individually proven findings of science, but in the sense of a truth lived through existence. A truth can be known without necessarily being possessed. It does not become operative in one until one has *made* it one's own truth, and admitting that there can be no turning back, that all one's behaviour is governed by this acknowledged truth. That is why V. E. Frankl rightly warns against forcing a recognized truth upon another person, for he in turn must first assimilate the truth and make it *his own*. But as soon as it has become my truth, it ceases to be a mere hypothesis, which can always be pushed aside temporarily. Being my truth, it pervades my belief at all times, even when I am talking about the weather, let alone about psychotherapy and education. Indeed, I often have to remain silent precisely because I must not

[4] Harold Schultz-Hencke, *Über Organneurosen*, in Siebeck, Schultz-Hencke, Weizsäcker: *Über seelische Krankheitsentstehung*, Leipzig 1939, pp. 35–36.

force *my* truth upon the other person; yet even though it may never be touched upon, my truth will still permeate my whole being and still govern my actions. I am unable to turn back; and I can heal and teach only according to my conscience. The whole of education starts from fixed, permanent values; and yet success is so variable. The art, indeed, lies in making these values so accessible to the growing person that education ceases to be a training merely outwardly imposed, and instead becomes an individual decision, a genuine acknowledgement of these values.

While, therefore, we cannot warn sufficiently against theorising and preaching in education, it is also fatally inconsistent to stop just short of the highest values, the very nature of which should give them a central position. Moreover, since, as a number of modern psychotherapists have already recognized, every neurosis represents a spiritual problem that resides in the defection from absolute values, it ought to be admitted that the educational task of psychotherapy, like every other educational task, can be performed only on religious principles. It was no coincidence that psychotherapy was in the hands of priests for thousands of years; nor that in Nazi Germany, for instance, it was demanded that the care of souls should be transferred to psychotherapists. Let there be no misunderstanding; we are living in the present, and its claims will be accepted by all except those hankering after utopias. We do indeed hold that modern psychotherapy should be the province of trained specialists, but since psychotherapy, by its very nature, poses spiritual, and even religious problems, the psychotherapist himself will have a position second to that of the spiritual adviser. The disintegration of man's view of the world and the resulting specialization of knowledge have, unfortunately, meant that not only many spiritual directors but also many physicians are quite helpless when faced with psychotherapeutical problems. In principle, however, since man has but one soul, there can be but one way of healing and directing it. Even medical psychotherapy should ideally serve as a preparation for a change of heart. When nowadays there is sometimes talk of medicine's 'pastoral care' (cf. Frankl), we would accept this only in so far as it meant medicine's aid to pastoral care (cf. Niedermeyer).

We have said that all genuine objective truth must be made

one's own in a subjective, personal sense. This is possible only by
constant decision. But once the objective values have been acknowledged, in the sense that there can be no turning back, there
will also have to be the resolve upon their transcendence. Such
transcendence is possible in terms of Kierkegaard's categories of
existence, the first step being the aesthetic category, based upon
sensation, the second being the ethical category, based upon law.
The third and highest step, is the religious category, with
acknowledgement of a personal God. Each trait of character, each
ordinary failing, each trial, and joy, all knowledge, each temptation, each vice should, in order to be made fruitful, be transcended from the lowest to the highest category.

It may here be recalled what Kierkegaard wrote about his
melancholy. We have deliberately chosen Kierkegaard as our
example, in order to remind even religiously neutral existentialists of the teachings of their great predecessor. Kierkegaard
suffered from a depression which he himself diagnosed as con-
genital. The Danish psychiatrist Hjalmar Helweg also declares
him to have been a depressive type within the manic-depressive
orbit, that is, a melancholic. In our view, however, Kierkegaard's
condition seems to a considerable extent overlaid with 'psycho-
genous' or 'neurotic' characteristics derived from his history,
more particularly from his uncongenial upbringing. But whatever the scientific diagnosis, a terminology derived from psychiatry and depth psychology will convey nothing of the richness of the whole picture; for Kierkegaard himself saw his depression as a trial and an expiation, to be understood only in the
sombre light of original sin and of his own personal sinfulness.
He also wrote a profound study of melancholy, or of the anxiety
connected with it, which he regarded as attached to every finite
existence in this world of care. In some cases, however, it reveals
itself with particular force; and this, according to Kierkegaard,
may take three different forms. First, there is an *aesthetic* melancholy, which is the portion of the man of immediate sensation,
the pleasure-seeker; he is nourished by fear that his sensations
might deceive him and his pleasures might prove to be limited.
Nero, for instance, would be a typical melancholy aesthete
swollen to monstrous proportions. In the second place, there is
an ethical melancholy, stemming from an awareness of the finite

and equivocal nature of this world, and from the straitened and threatened character of our existence in it. Thirdly, there is a religious melancholy, the longing for our eternal home, the awareness of the human ambiguity between sin and grace. Indeed, depression and anxiety must perforce spring from the acknowledgement of Christian values, since the animal instincts are inevitably subjected to painful tensions, in the case of those professing Christian beliefs. Kierkegaard struggled all his life to transcend his own melancholy from a lower to a higher level, and was constantly tormented by the possibility of failure in each case, at each moment of existence, at each 'either-or'.

Certainly religious people will always be reproached for the discrepancy between their convictions and their conduct. We do not wish to find excuses for those who, having once recognized a truth as their own, do not live by it. But to live in and by the truth is an end which we spend a lifetime struggling to attain. Until we have attained it, part of the truth will be like a dead letter; but this in itself is valuable. What matters is no longer to regard our own sensations as absolutes, but to have recognized the objective criteria and to use them for our further painful endeavours. There is, of course, nothing wonderful in then acknowledging one's conviction; it is, indeed, a frightening decision to make. Thus there arises a constant tension through the discrepancy between convictions and actions; but this tension itself may reveal a form of progress incomprehensible to a psychotherapy that is based on the pleasure-principle. For the positive element in this conflict lies in the fact that the religious patient has, once and for all, recognized objective criteria, and thus sees his goal, in objective truth. By 'analysing away' a psychological conflict, the deeper problem which lies behind it may in certain circumstances be overlooked and thus remain unsolved.

In the case of the believer who lives as yet neither in nor by his truth, the realization will cause tension, and tension causes a bad conscience. But the bad conscience in this case is not being repressed into the unconscious; the believer is for ever being faced with the harsh demand: you must choose and decide between two courses. On the other hand, neurosis develops in the case of one who has lost values and lives in the superstition of feelings. Such a person is dimly aware that he has not made the right decision, and suffers from it; but he has no criteria to help him to decide rightly. Or, if he has them, they are dead letters to him; the punishment of his bad conscience, accordingly, remains ineffectual, and is even, according to the laws of the pleasure-principle, repressed into the unconscious where it produces neurotic symptoms.

To become children of God is, for Kierkegaard, the supreme decision of our lives, the either-or of our existence on the way towards being or non-being. But in order to attain this goal, in order to give it concrete reality, I must struggle with myself at every junction of my life. I am always being drawn downwards to non-being, and rising up again through defeat and crucifixion. Every human principle, every feeling is transient and relative, uncertain and ambivalent; progress can be measured only dialectically, in constant struggle with oneself, in an eternal dialogue, sometimes through doubt and vexation.

These very theories, exalted as they may appear superficially, can nonetheless inspire the practice of psychotherapy. For, if we return from these considerations of Kierkegaard to psychotherapy, we find that, in their light, the goals of psychotherapy cannot but be, to use their fashionable and often misunderstood term, 'existentialist'. This means that the objectives of psychotherapeutic effort cannot be separated from the framework of human existence and the living encounter between psychotherapist and patient. The former is not a lecturer trying to impose his view of life from a position of theoretical certainty; on the contrary, he will be able to free his patient from his instinctual servitude and blindness only in so far as he himself has managed to reach a living knowledge of existential values.

In order to gather knowledge and be able to make existential use of it, one must first set one's own house in order, and be thoroughly familiar with the data afforded by one's own constitution and development. This is the first aspect of psychotherapy, extremely important technically, but in the main still a negative aspect, which was given an undue and one-sided emphasis by classical psychotherapy, and particularly by orthodox psychoanalysis. We shall call this aspect psychological analysis. Every psychotherapist should master it fully, otherwise he will remain a perpetual amateur and sorcerer's apprentice. He will, however, be a still more dangerous sorcerer's apprentice if he fails to put to constructive use the material he has collected out of the dirt and rubbish of the human inferno which is the soul, and attain to the constructive aim of psychotherapy, which we define as its existential synthesis. Psychotherapy must always take both aspects into account. Without analysis, without penetration down to the hidden layers of the personality, synthesis will remain a dead letter; but unless an approach is built towards a scale of values, all that has taken place is at best the smooth and theoretically acknowledged play of the libido in man.

Man brings to every situation of his life, to every moment of experience, an infinite number of latent potencies, in which are co-active the consequences of what he has experienced and done. These latent potencies, all of which are thrown on to the scales at every given moment, may on that account awaken the illusion of an absolute freedom, since they consist of unconscious impressions, of stirrings and instinctual desires, which their possessor is either reluctant to admit, or transforms in such a way that they become more and more adapted to his situation. This is the vast realm of the personal unconscious which Freud discovered, and to which his life's work was devoted. C. G. Jung has gone on to discover, at depths that are partly inaccessible to our investigation, archaic structures which determine the feelings and beliefs of the entire human race, but which may also turn against man destructively, if he fails to link up with these sources of his psychic life by simply denying or disregarding them. Some years ago, a new explorer of the unconscious, the Hungarian psychoanalyst Szondi, came on to the scene. He devoted his attention to the hereditary factor in the unconscious, that is to those innate peculiarities of the unconscious which determine the choice—so often regarded as either free or, on the contrary, determined by coincidence—of love, friendship, profession and even illness and mode of death. Szondi's methods of research are still matters of discussion.

One of his principles, however, seems to us unassailable. It applies equally to Szondi's own hereditary factor, Freud's personal unconscious and Jung's collective unconscious. It is his way of defending himself against the charge of being a determinist and at the same time attacking the illusion of absolute freedom. 'The personality', he writes in *Schicksalsanalyse*, 'has however, itself to affirm the one from its hereditary fate potential and deny the other.' In other words, the overall plan is there; but rather like the talents in the parable, of which one brings forth many and the other few. We must learn to read the plan but calculate the talents. We cannot take up another plan, or choose other talents than those that were entrusted to us. This plan also entails our condition of 'being driven'. Man cannot (by natural means) have at his disposal any raw material other than that entrusted to him, at any rate not while he has to make do with natural means. But he is free to use the given material well, passably or badly, to waste it or to use it constructively.

Part III

The Technique

Chapter One

ON THE NEUTRALITY OF THE ANALYST

28. *Is neutrality possible?*

IT is not intended in the following considerations to provide a systematic outline of a complete technique of personalist psychotherapy. Such an outline is not even possible in written form; but neither would it serve our purpose to set out a series of important techniques. Starting from the example of neurosis, and criticizing different remedies that have been suggested, it is our purpose to justify the necessity and feasibility of a universal personalist approach in depth psychology and to chart the path which such an approach should take. We are concerned with the discipline of depth psychology rather than with psychotherapeutic technique as such. Moreover, we share the view of other analytical psychologists, that techniques, that is the practical application of our knowledge of depth psychology, cannot be learned from books but only from personal experience of analysis. This will be dealt with in the chapter on training analysis.

Our concern is rather with the consideration of certain technical problems which may arise in applying the method. This consideration may be useful, in so far as our personalist conception of depth psychology may shed a new light on these problems.

Our investigation of neurosis has shown that it constitutes a false synthesis of existence and cannot therefore be divorced from a much broader outlook on life. This suggests the question whether it is possible to help others to achieve existential orthodoxy of life, while at the same time respecting the freedom of their basic outlook. This question can be reduced to some subsidiary questions, such as whether classical psychoanalysis, emphasising so vehemently as it does its own philosophical neutrality, can guarantee sufficiently that this freedom will be respected; or whether the patient is even influenced by it; whether a psychoanalysis without existential synthesis is possible; whether influencing the patient can always be avoided; whether situations may not arise when a supposedly 'neutral' psychoanalysis communicates a narrow and disguised basic outlook to the patient, thereby damaging the free core of his personality.

Whether patients are 'influenced' by an expert psychoanalysis has been vigorously denied by orthodox Freudians. They have always held that merely to ask such a question showed an insufficient knowledge of the facts. Very rightly, they have always insisted on the necessity of didactic analysis, in order to provide an empirical answer to doubts of this kind. Experience, however, differs somewhat from theory on this point, for the denial of the psychoanalysts is based not so much on experience as on theoretical assumption. In the first place, psychoanalysis has to deny the very possibility of a free personality being influenced by expert analysis, because it also denies 'free will' and believes the purpose of the psychoanalytic process to be in the disentanglement of the hidden causes which strictly determine mental activity. In the second place, and somewhat inconsistently, this materialist school of psychoanalysis would say that the patient's freedom is not in the slightest danger, for psychoanalysis is entirely neutral and simply offers the patient a 'screen', a 'mirror', on to which he can freely project the contents of his psyche. The contradiction between these two answers is, incidentally, more apparent than real: for if human behaviour really could be completely determined, analytical neutrality would be possible, simply because in that case psychological analysis would not differ appreciably from chemical analysis.

It is necessary, as we have emphasised, to analyse accurately the determinate part of human personality and thus to restore to man the conditioned freedom that is his as a partly spiritual being. Freud has demanded such an accurate analysis of the determinate factors in human behaviour, of the factor outside the scope of free will which restrict that very freedom. Anyone who has ever done any serious psychoanalytical work, will realise the presumption implicit in wanting to make man responsible for all his 'decisions'.

However, the theory of the analyst's complete neutrality, of his being the patient's 'mirror' or 'screen', is much exaggerated, because it springs from the materialist dogma that psychological analysis can be determined as completely as chemical analysis. All the tendencies of the psyche, and particularly pathological tendencies and neuroses have, of course, aspects that can be strictly determined. Every event in nature has its natural cause and these causes have to be discovered, but neurosis also has a spiritual and indeed a religious aspect. A phenomenon is not equal to its cause; the whole has a significance beyond the sum of the parts. The effect is not yet contained in the cause, but becomes possible through it. Psychological effects have their own significance, especially since neurosis is concerned with the larger issues of the world and of God. This means that a neutrality which does not differentiate between spiritual problems and biological causes is simply absurd; and, like all absurdities, impossible. On the mental level to be apparently neutral is already to have an attitude, and consequently a decision and an obligation. But this attitude has been disguised, and the decision is therefore repressed and becomes negative. The wish to reduce spiritual problems to their determining causes is indeed to exert a strong influence on the patient and to cause a new repression in him—the repression of the spiritual. It is, incidentally, quite obvious to see how some analysts are able to repress the spiritual development; and there have been cases of patients who, after analysis, had indeed achieved better balance, but had become a kind of automaton, well-balanced and purely functional.

We have already (Part II, Section 25) expressed disagreement with those psychotherapists who talk of 'decision', 'duty' and 'responsibility', but are incapable of penetrating to the unconscious causation of a neurosis. They are trying to strengthen morality and freedom at a time when their patients are as yet incapable of free moral action, simply because their freedom is restricted by unconscious and often non-moral causes. It is our view on the other hand that, whether or not we are aware of it, or like it, all psychoanalysis is inseparable from existential synthesis. This synthesis may constitute an impoverishment, if it is

F

based on the repression of spiritual values, but, if it follows the freeing of spiritual values, it should constitute an enrichment of the person.

This does not mean that we are imposing upon the patient an existential synthesis. Such an imposition occurs only when the analytical process has been neglected. Personalist existential synthesis, as we understand it, is the fruit of analysis. The patient who has built up this synthesis has become more responsible and more conscious. All we want to do is to avoid a neutrality-at-all costs attitude, while at the same time aiming at genuine neutrality with full recognition of what is determinate in man and of his spirit and sense aspects. The theory of the 'mirror' which reduces spiritual problems to their psychological causes, is a preconceived synthesis. But an exact analysis which illuminates the genetic conditioning of our psychological and spiritual development, becomes an illicit synthesis when the whole personality is being referred back to the womb status view. If, on the contrary, the archetypal and irreducible character of certain forces in the human personality is respected, the conscious synthesis will be revealed, together with the analysis of the various psychical contents. Let us remember that Freud himself emphasised the fact that every symbol is 'over-determined', by which presumably he meant that each symbol represents various psychic contents, which also cover various levels of the personality. However, Freud regarded the material level as self-sufficient, and he concentrated his whole attention upon the analytical discovery of determining causes. To the latter circumstance we owe an incomparable analytical method; the former, however, reflects merely a short-sighted, *a priori* point of view. This explains that Freud's own theory of over-determination has borne little fruit. C. G. Jung has shed a rather clearer light on the genuine riches of psychological symbolism; though, as we have seen, he too was misled by considering this symbolism to be immanent. Every symbol can bear quite different interpretations and can, as its name implies, 'sym-bolise' very different aspects of being and numerous dimensions of the soul.

Here are some examples to show the richness of dream symbolism.

A psychologist under didactic analysis dreamed as follows:

He was in a very untidy room. A young woman, a friend of his wife's, remonstrated with him; she told him to tidy up the room a little, and thus to save his wife unnecessary work. But, instead of doing this, he made advances and the dream ended with a sexual act. Analytical interpretation enabled the patient to retrace unconscious desires connected with his mother (here symbolised by the wife's friend). This is a reductive analysis of the classical theme. This aspect of the analysis is necessary in order to understand the patient's ambivalent attitude: his mother—in the dream represented by the wife's friend—attracts and at the same time repels him (remonstrances). *But there are also associations at work.* He declares his wife's friend was quite right, it would really have been more sensible to tidy the room. Here another interpretation begins, just as necessary and spontaneous as the first: the room symbolises the patient's ethical condition, and his attitude towards the young woman likewise corresponds to a real attitude. This attitude is unconscious and perilous, because it offends the ethical values of womanhood and leads the patient to a distorted relationship with women. This is what corresponds to Jung's problem of the 'anima'. It should be said at this point that even this double analysis of the dream is by itself inadequate, for this dream still symbolises other problems of great importance. Here merely two aspects are to be indicated.

A patient dreams constantly of wild bulls. In analysing the dream he first recalls that the bull is a symbol of sexual sensuality. The analysis thus at first follows upon Freudian lines: the sexual urge is connected in his dreams with his mother who—as the patient remembers—was born under Taurus. He also dreams about bullfights in ancient Crete. These bullfights were part of the archaic religious mysteries. Thus the patient realised that this implied an as yet archaic level of his own spiritual development, and that his instinctual attachment must be overcome and transcended. Indeed, he recalls that the bull is not only the symbol of sexuality but also a sacred animal, which was killed and sacrificed in the ancient mystery ceremonial and thereby brought into the economy of healing and salvation. Thus the unconscious reflects a difficult and manifold development, which only an instinctual level will allow to proceed to existential synthesis.

A colleague, who was undergoing didactic analysis, once dreamed he was in a military barracks. It was Christmas, and presents were to be distributed in the basement. In this underground vault he met his sister, and was confounded because he, while himself expecting presents, had prepared nothing for her. But on a table there lay a ring, set with a beautiful pearl. He could give his sister this ring. Thereupon he suddenly found himself out of doors, with his sister and an old woman teacher to whom he owed a great deal. It was a clear night and they were in Egypt. In silence, he gazed upon a wonderful natural spectacle. Although it was night, the sun was shining. Surrounding it above were three smaller suns, and below twelve moons.

It is unfortunately not possible here to give a full interpretation of this dream; for its analysis took many hours. Yet there can be no doubt that it belongs to that category of dreams which C. G. Jung regards as milestones in a person's spiritual development. This dream also marked the first appearance in my colleague's analysis of that mysterious and lofty structure described by Jung, the square and at the same time circular *mandala* (cf. pp. 199 and ff), here composed of suns and moons (Plate I, Drawing No. 1). This significant dream clearly reflects a wholeness being driven and deciding, 'id' *and* spirit, immanence *and* transcendent link. First the dreamer sees himself in the midst of herdlike, undifferentiated existence, symbolised by life in the barracks. Before celebrating Christmas—the feast of re-birth and redemption—he must descend into the deepest underground room of his soul. There he looks for presents for himself and only after disappointment and sorrow is he able to enrich, to use C. G. Jung's expression, his anima. Silent and motionless, accompanied by *anima* and *wisdom*, to the land of occult knowledge, he sees the symbol of *revelation*, which illuminates the night in an unspeakably wonderful way.

This interpretation is not the only possible one. Laboriously, step by step, with much inner resistance and spiritual delusion, it was worked out by the dreamer himself.

One could quote countless examples of dreams and fantasies which represent, at one and the same time, both a return to analytically accessible stages of development and premonitions of a new phase which cannot be reduced in the same way. Indeed, one might almost say that the overwhelming majority of dreams present this ambiguity. But there are also some which contain almost exclusively the repetition of a long past event, just as there are others which are quite clearly 'synthetic', dreams which do not lead back into the determinate past, but produce spiritual considerations. A fine example of the kind of dream that cannot be reduced to its instinctual components is the following amusing dream produced by a young woman of twenty-six.

I was walking along the sea-shore between Epictetus and Epicurus. Epictetus tripped me up and I fell. I was vexed, and told him that he was the last person from whom I would have expected such behaviour. He replied: 'It is not things in themselves which disturb men, but the concepts of things make men unhappy.' I became furious and told him that he bored me. My leg was hurting me, and I didn't consider that a concept. Epicurus laughed and drew me aside. He said: 'You are on the way to becoming a good disciple of mine. Never mind that old bore. Take something of everything life offers you, but never take too much: don't be too greedy, and don't take more from anybody than he can give. You will understand the game of love, and derive only good from it.' I interrupted Epicurus and told him that he might be more amusing than Epictetus, but that he, too, was a meddler and a theoretician.

This dream dramatised the conflict between stoical 'angelism' and facile rationalisations, which the patient underwent at that time. During the same night she had another dream, which is a companion-piece to the first, and shows the way towards a spiritual solution. She had, shortly before, read a traveller's account of the Mount Athos monasteries, which among other things mentioned a learned monk who had given up teaching and intellectual discussion, and spent his time knitting, with endless patience.

An old monk sat beside me, knitting. He asked me to do the same. I didn't want to: I was afraid I should not have the necessary patience. But he was so kind to me that I tried. Each pattern cost me a tremendous effort. But the old monk radiated so much peace and understanding that I went on trying and was content.

This clearly points to a type of synthesis that neither Epictetus nor Epicurus could have foreseen.

Dreams like the last two, however, are very rare; most dreams provide the analysis with the double aspect of a reduction and a prospective synthesis. Here are two further examples, which also occurred in one night and were interpreted immediately upon awakening. Both dreams and interpretation were written down during the night by the dreamer, a psychologist undergoing didactic analysis:

I dreamt that I was lying in bed and that the top sheet was covering my face so that I could not see what was happening in my room. I only knew (or rather, sensed) that my father and mother, united in one single person, were in the next room. This filled me with fear. I also knew the door opened; my fear grew into panic terror. I began to say the Our Father, aloud and clearly. But my fear was greater than the comfort afforded by the prayer and I woke up screaming. Once awake, I realised that my face was *not* covered. I have heart trouble: my hands lie folded over my chest in an attitude reminiscent of prayer. I felt ill. The dream at once began to reveal its meaning. I understood that a certain long-forgotten event, among others, chained me to both my parents. The thought of the next room and of the door continued to fill me with horror, and I was seized by the vague recollection of something at once frightening and sexual. I was surprised that I sought refuge in prayer. At the same time, I have the impression that my inability to pray had something to do with the horrible event in which my parents were involved. After all, God had something in common with my father, and the events in the next room had shaken and disillusioned me. So the dream was fairly clear to me (it concerned the sexual act between his parents—*Author's note*) but not quite. It left behind an impression of bottomless depth, like that of delirium perhaps. Yet I felt there was a certain progress. I was beginning to understand certain things, and I was glad that in spite of everything, I prayed in my dream. I fell asleep again. I dreamt of a royal palace. I saw from the window the changing of the Guard. But I also saw wounded revolutionaries in the palace courtyard. They were rebels, who attempted to overthrow the King and put the Crown Prince in his place. The Crown Prince in the dream was myself and yet he was not at all like me. I saw him and knew quite well he was me, in the guise of the Crown Prince. Thus the interpretation came into the dream itself, since I was present as an eye-witness. I liked the Crown Prince very much. I thought ironically that this was hardly surprising since he was myself. Outside there were shots. But the Crown Prince had no part in the rebellion; after all, the rebels were trying to depose his father. the King. On the contrary the Crown Prince was talking to the

King, their conversation was perhaps a little cool, but not un-friendly. The Crown Prince was like the King. The rebellion was at an end. Court officials and ladies-in-waiting congratulated both of them. I awoke, wrote down the dream, but felt I had for-gotten a good deal. I was definitely ill and felt very cold, yet the dream left me with an agreeable impression. Of course the Crown Prince represented me. Rebellion against my father made no sense. The likeness between father and myself has to be under-stood and my aggressive feeling towards him to be resolved.

The simplicity of these examples is only superficial. They either summarise in a few lines the work of many hours, or they are the product of many months of analytical preparation. Be-sides they are likely to leave certain areas unexplained, and to take no account of inevitable contradictions and numerous doubts. There are also, as we intend to show in greater detail, certain psychological symbols which cannot be explained at all.

But how is it possible that serious, sincere and well-meaning analysts and their patients can but discover foreseeable theoreti-cal interpretations? Some are able to diagnose only symbols of primitive instinct, others see only symbols of existential decision. This leads to mutual suspicion that the analysis has not been sufficiently 'objective', and to justifiable distrust on the part of the layman who is only too ready to imagine that all interpre-tations have been invented by the psychoanalyst. These con-tradictions only demonstrate the shallowness of the extreme theory of analytic 'neutrality'. The reality of the soul is immeas-urably more complex and equivocal than theories largely in-fluenced by one-sided philosophies. Certainly there are analysts who make hasty judgments and impose these upon their patients. That this is done also by specialists can be explained by their belief that they have grasped the meaning of psycho-logical symbols empirically and that, in explaining analogous symbols to their patients, they are gaining time and making progress. This 'activation' of analysis, however, is permissible only if, on the one hand, there can be no doubt about the meaning of the symbol, and, on the other, there is no doubt that the patient understands and accepts the interpretation with a sense of overwhelming proof. Both these conditions, however, in the last resort depend on the analyst's whim, and thus the deliberate 'activation' of analysis is a dangerous undertaking, as we shall show next. At this point, we shall leave the 'active' process aside, and assume that the analyst, in order to safeguard his 'neutrality', is anxious to avoid any interference in his capacity as 'screen' or 'mirror'. How does it happen, in this case, that the analytical process serves apparently to confirm different theories of depth psychology? In the first place, simply through the fact that the suggestion remains undeveloped and will have a purely negative effect. Chains of ideas which lead back to the sources of instinct are, for instance, taken as final and definitive, and the symbol (dream, association or whatever it may be) is passed over as adequately interpreted. Chains of ideas which could lead to existential synthesis are, however, treated differently. They are treated as resistance, or are discussed until perhaps finally they associate with sexual interpretations. The patient soon realizes that, to his analyst, every content of the psyche represents a symbol of sexuality. Unless he has ideas that be given a sexual interpretation, he will feel unhappy. If he can manage to find some link between his ideas and sex, he believes that he can relax. If he has sexual images, he will be unlikely to look for another meaning behind these sexual images. For he has the impression that some such symbol may conceal sexuality, but not a spiritual problem. This distortion of analysis is still more obvious in a type of treatment which from the start neglects the investigation of primary instinct, and only accepts interpretations which confirm the patient in the erroneous conviction that he can actually always make a free decision. This 'existential' analysis is gratifying for the patient's resistance, for it is incapable of penetrating to the hidden causes of a psychic attitude, whatever the existential significance of the attitude might be.

Apparent objectivity, then, may, by omission and generalization, narrow the patient's potentialities and force upon him an artificial balance. Man is not one-dimensional, and it is possible to offend against a higher conception of neutrality by explicitly or tacitly assuming but one dimension. This is all too often the case in the different schools of analytical depth psychology. We shall see how sensitive, indeed how exaggeratedly susceptible, the patient becomes owing to transference towards all his psychoanalyst's views, even if the latter tries to conceal them. The patient may not always consciously recognize and understand the synthesis which, in the course of the analytic process, is assumed or gradually developed on the analyst's part; but he will always sense and eventually absorb it. Partial syntheses may thus invite false totalitarian absolutes. From the point of view of genetic depth psychology, mental achievement and religion are the superstructure of instinct; from the existential point of view, every instinctual move is regarded as taking up a position towards existence, that is towards the metaphysical and religious order. In the first point of view, error and guilt are but regressions and fixations; in the second, every regression and every fixation is a 'life-heresy' and a reduction of being to non-being. An analysis which upholds only one view refuses to recognize the specific characteristics of the human person; instead of being integral, it becomes totalitarian. In this case the analyst is likely to violate the integrity of the human person; he will find his own reflection, like Narcissus in the soul that surrendered to him, and which, by usurping the place of God, he is tempted to refashion in his own image.

29. *Transference, resistance and non-intervention*

The Freudian requirement that the analyst should constitute a 'screen' for the projections of his patient, has, of course, a profound and important justification; but it ought to be understood as an exhortation and a warning against any arbitrariness, rather than as an attainable norm. Indeed it cannot be a norm precisely because the analytical process, so far from being a one-sided projection by the patient on to an abstract analyst, is an exchange between two living personalities. It is a materialist view that this exchange can be reduced to a purely mechanical re-grouping of psychic particles. The analyst has, of course, to remain objective; he must operate neither with absolute nor with religious standards. The patient need not even know his analyst's philosophy of life—though we can hardly object to his legitimate desire to know about it.

Yet the relationship between analyst and patient will always be based upon mutual exchange, thus excluding a static 'non-intervention'. The minimum of preconceived attitudes on the part of the analyst is that he is prepared to help his patient.

Sometimes, indeed, the analyst's faith in the possibility of freeing his patient from his deceptions and inhibitions will have to be stronger and more effective still. On this score, the analyst cannot assume an 'as-if' attitude; for the patient will not put his trust in a mere 'as-if'. And the analyst himself will be able to work only if he never gives up the perhaps quite irrational hope of being able, despite everything, to help a neurotic patient through his skill. The generally accepted belief that psychotherapy remains ineffective in cases of psychosis has, perhaps, been responsible for the failure of many an honest attempt; for if, on the basis of theoretical prejudice, you believe a certain undertaking to be impossible, you will deprive yourself of the strength to risk it.

Strict analytical 'non-intervention' is misguided also on purely technical grounds. There have been many cases like that of the patient on the analyst's couch who uttered scarcely four sentences in the course of a month, after which he never came back. Unless analysis is exalted into a meaningless rite, the analyst's 'non-intervention' that leads to such grotesque situations must be regarded as wrong and neurotic. In the case of such 'difficult' beginnings, it suffices generally to give the patient an explanation of neurosis adapted to his understanding for him to begin to speak, first hesitantly and then with growing confidence.

All such analytic deadlocks are generally ascribed to the patient's resistance. But this is a facile excuse, and the analysts forget that, even if they have undergone their own analysis, they remain human and thus subject to their own resistance. Placing the burden of resistance on the patient alone provides a good excuse for one's own incapacity and totalitarian one-sidedness. The real art would lie in being able to treat the patient, including his resistance. And if resistance against this consciousness is inevitable, as depth psychology in particular has discovered, it must be accepted and ways have to be found to overcome it.

Besides, resistance is not a simple phenomenon; it is not only an evasion of consciousness and a clinging to the neurotic pattern, but it also has positive functions, which must be taken into account in analysis. Like every psychic event, and in particular every event rooted in the unconscious, resistance too is 'over-determined'. Every resistance contains an element which is not directed against the analytical process in its positive aspect, but represents the instinctive defence of the ego against attempts to take it to pieces. Resistance can certainly be fanned by aggressiveness, but other, positive and highly differentiated, psychic functions also play a part in it. For instance, the sense of shame —a factor hardly mentioned in the literature of psychoanalysis, which is not surprising, since a high degree of spiritual shamelessness is, so to speak, part of the analyst's professional ethos. There are some notable examples of patients who have become all too inured to spiritual nakedness. In principle, only neurotic resistance, the refusal to admit reality, has to be analysed and removed; though of course in practice it is difficult to disentangle the different components of resistance.

Strict non-intervention in the analysis of strong resistance is an absurdity. In order to get on, the analysis has to overcome the resistance, but in order to overcome the resistance, it has to get on. As we have said already, a summary of the theories of depth psychology may often prove helpful. The patient can be told that it is quite normal that he has produced no material for analysis, for his neurosis is due to a repression; and he may then be told briefly about the meaning of repression, with examples drawn from his own attitude. In order to prevent such explanations and examples from becoming themselves a prey to repression, it might be as well to get the patient to make a record of the sessions. Generally resistance is not strengthened by drawing attention to its concrete manifestations.

A professional psychologist who began his own school analysis with very strong resistance, wrote in his record of the tenth session: 'Arrived late at the psychoanalyst's; brought no record of the ninth session; annoyance of the analyst and explanation of resistance; this, however, surprisingly strengthened resistance.' (We shall see that the alleged annoyance of the analyst and the alleged strengthening of the resistance are in this case attempts to retain the resistance; but later sections of the same record and later records enable us to form a different picture.) 'I did not want to speak about a particular evening in carnival time because that would have led to sex. Tried to remain in the abstract sphere.' (Instead of speaking of his carnival experiences the patient now barricaded himself behind the secret of the confessional, and then spoke of communication in Jasper's sense, of Heidegger,

Kierkegaard, etc.) 'On reflection I feel that my attitude towards the psychoanalyst is definitely unfair. It would have been better and more sensible to have stuck to the question at hand. Rationalization is an attitude of avoidance and concealment. In analysis it is better not to remove but to disregard it.' The compliment to the psychoanalyst here conceals a lesson to him: he is advised to adopt an attitude of non-intervention. But ten sessions have already been spent by taking up positions of avoidance and concealment. There is no record of the eleventh session. In the record of the twelfth session, however, it was noted: 'The rest of the hour spent in vain attempts to interpret the dream. This is because the analyst tries to hold on to the association by sheer force, and wants to go as deep as possible in the shortest possible time. Perhaps he is frightened of repression. I, on the other hand, try to make clear to him what I mean by spiritual maturity. This presupposes belief in Providence . . . Roots in Chinese and Indian thought . . . In writing record after three days, found interpretation of the dream: Original Sin theme'—here the patient undertakes to analyse his analyst. He projects on to the analyst his own desperate fear of his repressions. He forgets that in the last resort it is all the same to the analyst what the patient represses or does not repress: here resistance feeds upon the projections or transference. It is also forgotten that in the last instance psychoanalysis is an uncovering of repression; instead, he talks all the more about Providence, Chinese and Indian thought, etc. The analyst is even accused of using force. This accusation is based on the analyst's remark that his patient should try to hold down on his own spontaneous associations by sheer force, as one tries to hold a rat back by its tail when it tries to slip back into its hole. In the record of the thirteenth hour, we read: 'The analyst tells me to concentrate strictly on my own analysis and not to bother about his. He says so far there has been no noticeable progress in my analysis, no insight into personal conflicts. The analyst asks me to bring forth concrete interpretations and not form premature philosophical syntheses after the fashion of existential analysts. This spontaneously sets up a relation of authority. At first I felt the ground had been swept away from under my feet and I was free-wheeling in space, like in the Ferris wheel in the amusement park; then suddenly a giant in a fairytale, and I stood beside it like a little child.' (Here the magical fantasies of transference violently burst through resistance; of course these fantasies represent a regression into childhood, but they make the analytic process possible at last and will themselves have to be analysed only later.

For the time being, an avalanche of concrete associations about the patient's childhood breaks through.)

In these excerpts, which reflect the breaking-down of resistance from the tenth to the thirteenth session, we can recognise a psychologist's dexterity in wanting to turn the onesideness of non-intervention to the advantage of his own resistance. If the analyst had not intervened, the patient would probably have spent another twelve hours talking about Kierkegaard, Heidegger, Jaspers, Chinese philosophers and providence. Such a process would in a sense have corresponded to the extreme school of existentialist psychotherapy, which as we have seen (Part II, Section 26), pays insufficient attention to the dynamic factors of the psychophysical level.

The example of this confused struggle shows that the analyst's intervention is always in danger of strengthening resistance, while yet within certain limits being necessary, in order to weaken that very resistance. The example also shows that the measure of intervention can be a very delicate matter, though its danger does not always invalidate its usefulness. As a rule, intervention does not take the form, say, of exerting influence, if by influence we mean the suggestion that the patient projects associations with a certain definite content. In the above example ideas were by no means suggested to the patient: in this case and in others like it, the analyst should merely ceaselessly point out to his patient that he, the patient, cannot express all ideas even though the likely content of the ideas may be irrelevant.

The analyst's intervention becomes still more tricky when he is to draw his patient's attention to the omission of definite psychic contents. In this case, however, he can be very restrained in voicing his own assumptions, however justified they may be. But he can confront his patient with certain facts and draw his attention to obvious tangles of contradiction. That is why it is useful for the patient to keep a record of the sessions and the analyst, too, should note down discreetly his ideas. Take, for instance, the psychologist whom we have just quoted. His resistance was indeed, as we can see, much reduced. From then on, he was less inclined to seek refuge in rationalization and produced an abundant flow of real ideas. However, resistance did not entirely disappear, and the analyst soon noticed that the patient's records of the sessions did less than justice to certain important aspects of the analysis.

Let us for instance, compare the record of the sixteenth session, as written by the analysand two days later (despite a request that he should compile these notes on the same evening), with the analyst's notes taken during the same session. The analyst merely wrote down the changes of theme during the session. The comparison runs as follows (the left-hand column contains the analysand's record, the right-hand column the analyst's notes):

After concentrating for some time I think of an argument with my colleagues. Incidents during this argument: my colleagues refuse to acknowledge my views, enmity as a spontaneous reaction.	Difficulties with superiors and colleagues.
	Spontaneous association: These difficulties are the same as his difficulties with his mother, who, he says, did not take him seriously. He says that in general he takes children more seriously than those who educate them (his profession as a co-determining factor).
Incident with the NCO in the army. He tells me I had better leave thinking to horses, they have a bigger head.	
	Association: the original pattern of this army language points to the mother.
There followed some thoughts about my fiancée.	Next spontaneous association: the fiancée is the opposite of what army language stands for, and therefore also of his mother.

We note that in the patient's record everything connected with his hostile feelings towards his mother was omitted. The error is all the more interesting, because at the end of the sixteenth session the patient himself had said: 'I realise that my attitudes to my work are connected with my upbringing.' This momentary insight, however, was not maintained. In the same way, no trace remains of the effect of his mother fixation on his attitude to the army, his fiancée, etc. It would have been premature to put such detailed explanations to the patient; but it might have been useful to point out to him, without any comment, the incompleteness of his record and the fact that he had forgotten certain categories of ideas.

Another example, which shows how illuminating the comparison between patient's record and analyst's notes can be:

Dr C. D. (cf. pp. 45, 52, 70, 80 and 91) writes in his record: 'When I was small—I think before I reached school age—I used to wish myself back into a woman's belly, because I felt I would be safe there.' The note made by the analyst on this point awakens the strongest resistance when the patient is reminded that he spoke not of 'a woman's belly', but explicitly of 'his mother's belly.'

Sometimes the analyst's intervention can only anticipate aims and results, though of course without forcing the patient to accept any unproven assumptions. The purpose of a psychoanalysis is, after all, to enable the patient to understand his own mental processes; thus it is not necessarily inappropriate to further this understanding by general explanations. This can be done, as we have indicated above, by a discussion of an adapted theory of neurosis.

An analysis is started on account of a young man's homosexual tendencies, which he tries to suppress by force. He is on the verge of despair and thinks of suicide. His physcian advises him to try psychoanalysis, but he has long been discouraged. He is so paralysed by fear and shame that the first few sessions take place in almost complete silence, still further increasing the patient's depression. One day, the analyst gives him a short talk on the Jungian problem of the anima. He speaks of the femininity in men; there are no 100 per cent. masculine men; a man need not be afraid to face his own femininity. Owing to his feminine components a man is often able to actualise important feminine values, such as intuition and gentleness, or to develop certain artistic traits. The important question is: what can he make of his bi-sexual nature? We may hope that psychoanalysis can elucidate and perhaps remove the patient's homosexual tendencies;

and even if this can be done only to a small degree, there still remain two possibilities: either the homosexual traits are allowed to lead to perversion and to conflict with one's own conscience and with society, or they may be integrated more or less into one's own personality; they may be made to bear fruit and may be sublimated.

After this explanation, analysis became possible: resistance did not entirely disappear, but the patient was now able to make use of the analytic method.

This example shows that saving time may imply saving the possibilities of treatment. It is, however, a difficult question of balance, not wanting to over-emphasise the time element. We may here touch in passing, upon the connection between the so-called 'shortened therapy' and resistance. An arbitrary acceleration of the analysis towards a 'shortened therapy' always implies a conscious and active intervention on the part of the analyst. The analyst's active intervention can save time, but it increases the element of uncertainty in the treatment and makes the whole process appreciably more difficult. Such an intervention will fail unless valid means are found to accelerate the psychic 'dissection' of the patient. The patient will, even and especially in accelerated therapy, accept only what he can accept at the level of self-knowledge he has actually reached. There is therefore very little point in apparently 'accelerating' the analysis by sermonizing or philosophical explanations.

At most the goal may be reached more quickly by 'confronting' the patient with his spiritual reality, that is, by making him aware of certain processes not yet fully conscious, but already on the verge of consciousness. Again, it is a matter of offering him, gently and carefully, a practical explanation of neurosis *based on his own example*.

The so-called projection tests may be very useful in this process of acceleration. An analyst who has really mastered the Szondi test, the Rorschach test, or the T.A.T., may present the results in an exactly apportioned measure to his patient in order to accelerate the analysis. These and similar tests catalyse the patient's projections. They are not just assessed averages of his psychological development (as for instance an intelligence test); they are the very means of psychoanalysis.

However, the means of accelerating the analytical process (teaching about neurosis on the basis of the patient's own example, confrontation with one's own spiritual reality, 'dissection' of the psyche, etc., are not to be regarded as ends in themselves; a 'shortened therapy' which becomes a dogma is more likely than an ordinary therapy to remain unproductive or to be harmful. Experience contradicts Stekel's assertion than an analysis that does not reach its objective within a few months will never get there at all. The means of acceleration fail where the patient is not yet ready to accept them, that is, where his resistance is still too great. A vague explanation of the theory of neurosis is useless unless it is experienced in oneself. Indeed, no purely rational insight helps, unless it becomes an 'emotional understanding' (Raoul Schindler), a concrete truth known to experience. Unless, however, the patient is ready also to experience new knowledge, resistance against such concrete knowledge, too, will not be recognized as pathological or mistaken, as is always the case with regard to symptoms that are felt to be painful. Thus, accelerated therapy may achieve symptomatic results, but will not affect resistance against the process of becoming more conscious; but it is this resistance that restricts and cripples personality. The more analysis is open to persuasive interventions, prohibitions, advice and explanation, the greater the risk that it will either remain ineffectual or merely symptomatic, or build up still further the neurotic superego instead of leading on to a progressive increase of awareness in the patient. Systems which turn acceleration into an absolute will always find a hearing, not so much because of the real need for a shorter therapy, as because of emotional resistance to analysis that will lead to consciousness. Such systems, therefore, often represent a regression from Freud's discoveries. In cases where time and means are available to carry out a full-scale psychoanalysis, the analyst's advisory activity is nearly always a sign of his inability really to master the technique of skilful analysis. Conversely, we believe that no psychotherapist is really able to make deliberate use of the accelerated technique unless he is also, and primarily, capable of applying the full-scale analytical process in practice. Of course shortened analytical therapy has become an incontrovertible necessity; but this method is still in its infancy, at least as a method, and its application ought never to be due to the psycho-therapist's inability to use the full analytical method.

Psychoanalysis, then, is an active exchange between patient and analyst. That is why the theory of absolute non-intervention cannot be realised in practice. However, psychoanalysis is not, or should not become, the analyst's one-sided influencing of the patient. In its formal discretion, psychoanalysis is probably the subtlest kind of mutual influencing between two persons. Knowledge of psychoanalytic method—and it can really be known only by submitting oneself experimentally to this method (in didactic analysis)—would lead one to summarise the paradox of the psychoanalytic process in this way: psychoanalytic method is exhaustive and penetrating because it is discreet, restrained, and uncompromisingly truthful. This 'because' as it were condemns every possible form of 'shortcut' therapy, which cannot achieve the same penetration because they do not attain the psychoanalytic restraint. The hardest rule for the budding psychoanalyst is to learn to be silent. The second hardest rule is, when speaking at all, to say only what is most certainly true. Such rules are easy to lay down, but hard to follow. It is not easy to be silent when you are tempted to speak in the interests of someone who is seeking help, when you are convinced that you could so easily help him with your advice. Nor is it easy to be truthful, because the conviction is deep rooted in human fanaticism that the end justifies the means. If only we could achieve somebody's happiness by a slight twist, a tiny blurring of the truth! Yet to remain silent and to speak but the most essential truths is the very opposite of fanaticism: it implies an unconditional respect for the freedom of our fellow-men, for we cannot contribute towards their liberation by the disregard of freedom.

This concern to respect the patient's freedom as far as humanly possible was also one of the reasons (besides the materialistic illusion of an analysis as in a chemical process) why the theory of the analyst's total neutrality could be maintained. This love of freedom is the positive aspect of a one-sided attitude. Basic respect for the human person is anything but neutrality. Neutrality in analysis is impossible on account of the transference. Chemical elements do not transfer any energy to the man who makes the experiment. The patient under analysis transfers to his analyst large amounts of energy-laden ideas, and we shall see that the analyst, because he is also a living person, transfers ideas to the patient. This mutual exchange is as inescapable as the transference itself.

It would be an over-simplification to depict transference as though the patient simply transferred certain ideas to the analyst, as we might project pictures on a wall by means of a magic lantern. In actual fact the patient identifies himself with the analyst. This is no one-sided process; the patient absorbs the analyst's traits. It may be said that he absorbs ideas which the analyst has caused in the patient. But if these ideas were based on nothing more concrete, we would arrive at the absurd conclusion that the patient retracts the very same ideas which he has previously projected, which is simply meaningless. Reality is quite different: in relation to his analyst, the patient develops an extraordinary intuition; he becomes remarkably sensitive. Perhaps much of what he absorbs is based on wrong ideas of former projections; yet the mixture of projected and absorbed traits is a very effective and dynamic one. Indeed, how could the analyst possibly elude his patient? Certainly not just by sitting where the patient cannot see him! No amount of secrecy will ever enable the analyst to appear a blank page to his patient.

We know of a case in which a psychologist who was undergoing didactic analysis wrote to his analyst a business letter and signed it . . . with the analyst's name! This tells us much of the patient's identification with the analyst.

A physician undergoing didactic analysis began imperceptibly to arrange the same magazines in his own waiting room as he had seen them arranged in the analyst's waiting room.

A remark by a woman patient will serve to show the depth of the patient's preoccupation with the analyst's person, inducing in him even conclusions from non-existing signs. This patient suddenly fell silent in the middle of her speech and when asked what was passing through her mind, said hesitantly: 'Do you know, you have beautiful hands? You don't wear a wedding-ring, and yet I wonder whether you are not married after all.' Thus the patient would have been equally concerned with the analyst's presumed married life, whether or not he wore a ring.

The late Professor August Aichhorn told me of a psychoanalysis which caused him many difficulties because the first time the patient consulted him he held her hand in his for perhaps a second too long, to express compassion.

Another analyst was quietly listening to his patient—a physician —as the latter took his leave at the end of a session; at the same time he looked at him, perhaps somewhat absent-mindedly, whereupon the patient shouted in sudden fury: 'You can't get me down with your eyes.'

Other examples could be quoted *ad infinitum*. They can show that on the one hand the patient projects great bursts of tension to the analyst, but that on the other hand, even apparently harmless and insignificant traits and attitudes on the part of the analyst exercise a strong influence on the patient. It is also evident that, paradoxically, resistance knows well how to exploit the process of transference.

It should not be forgotten that the emerging ego of the patient, like that of any other person, is a more or less successful integration of the instinctual claims of the id with the claims of the superego, which indeed arise from some superficial introjection of the patient's standard-setting images. The 'I' thus, in a sense, consists of different layers of identification. Charles Baudouin has shown that analysis removes these identifications successively, thus giving the patient the frightening impression of gradually losing his self altogether. If there is no successful initial integration, for instance in the case of the neurotic—if the libido remains in a floating condition, freed as it will be through the growing relative significance of earlier fixations—the patient will be all the more inclined to fill the vacuum thus created by identifying himself with the analyst.

Thus, when all restricting fixations have been analysed away, and false absolutes revealed as relative, there still remains the fixation on the analyst, making an absolute of transference. All psychoanalytic schools have pointed to the need of analysing transference. An analysis will be completed only when the transference has been resolved. But we must not forget that transference itself has to be analysed with the help of the analyst! Certainly, after his infantile fixations have been removed, the patient is ready to be freed from the very last fixations. Yet even then ultimate liberation becomes possible only through identification with the analyst. At this point it becomes clear that unless the analyst himself has passed the test of didactic analysis and unless—this is particularly important—he has a just conception of the human person, this last liberation of the patient from dependence is fraught with danger. Unless the transference is satisfactorily resolved, there remains the absolute into which unconsciously the analyst himself has been turned. Very often even this condition is an improvement on the original neurotic state, but there are only too many neurotics who have paid for their restoration to mental health by a change for the worse of their personality. If the neurotic remains caught in the relationship of transference, his neurosis may break out afresh, perhaps in a different form, after separation from the analyst. If the analysis of earlier fixations was sufficiently advanced, there is always the possibility that the patient may be unable to free himself from alienating influences on the part of the analyst. If these influences, moreover, are coloured by a distorted philosophy, as often happens in the case of seemingly neutral analysts, the original neurosis will be replaced by another, less noticeable restriction of the personality.

Any eventual growth naturally presupposes the emulation of certain models. Thus the patient too may, after the end of his analysis and after successful resolution of the transference relationship, freely accept certain traits of his analyst's personality and consider them worth acquiring. Ideally this would be a master-disciple relationship, an intellectual friendship that would preserve the free development of both personalities. The resolution of transference has sometimes been naïvely pictured in the sense that analyst and patient have nothing else to give to each other in any circumstances; they were accordingly to part as strangers. That sort of thing leads to stories about analysis coming to an end when the patient's pockets have been emptied. This kind of wit is largely owed to those psychotherapists who have not themselves undergone any training analysis, but when faced with the phenomenon of transference are completely helpless. But fortunately the danger of playing about with this phenomenon in such cases is offset by ignorance of the actual analytic process.

30. *Transference, counter-transference and the 'Christ-archetype'*

In the course of analysis the mental and emotional integrity of the patient is, of course, more deeply affected than that of the analyst; otherwise the analyst would lose all control and court disaster. Yet the analyst's psyche is considerably influenced. As we have seen, it is not only the patient who makes use of resistance and transference to involve the analyst in his own neurotic 'life-heresy'; the analyst himself cannot remain wholly 'neutral'. For analysis ought to be an adventure of existence voluntarily experienced by two partners, with every risk for each. The patient's emotional participation will be far greater than the analyst's; but for the latter, too, every analysis will prove a severe trial.

In the section dealing with the need for training analysis (34) we shall have to return to this burden which is encountered with the patient for the analyst. Apart from its didactic purpose, training analysis is to enable the future psychoanalyst primarily to become as fully conscious as possible of his own complexes, in order to enable him to escape the unobjective fascination which could arise from his contacts with the complexes of his patient. Many complicated and painful relationships are caused because the partners have involved themselves in the same or complementary projections. The danger of such ties is always present in psychoanalysis; it will be lessened only in proportion to the analyst's awareness and understanding of his own mental and emotional forces.

It must not be assumed that every tie that has been formed unconsciously and is also due to the complexes of the analyst is bound to lead necessarily to dramatic events or catastrophes. Certainly it *may* lead to catastrophes. More often, however, it remains unnoticed, and thus exerts an unrecognized influence on the course of therapy. It may be a favourable influence; but it is more likely to be negative, and then the analysis will be dissipated.

It is quite certain, however, that the analyst also has to create a certain counter-transference in order to help his patient. Without some degree of identification with his fellow-men he would not be able to make any contact with them. And what is more, the analytic vocation may itself have originated in a powerful complex, which we have linked (Section 20) with the 'Christ-archetype'. This 'Christ-archetype' is the central factor in any psychotherapy, making possible psychotherapy for the neurotic, as well as for the analyst. In his search for a redeemer, the neurotic meets his therapist. It is by no means wholly neurotic to long for a healer, who could assume the burden of neurotic guilt, descend into the neurotic hell in order to redeem finally the neurotic through his triumph over guilt. It would be neurotic to project exclusively this archetype towards the analyst, or towards a myth explicable in terms of depth psychology. All human religions, but also all pseudo-religions, such as totalitarian political systems and scientific systems turned into dogmas, are ultimately inspired by the expectation of the future redemption of man. Individual expressions of this expectation are embodied in myths, and therefore can be psychologically interpreted and even distorted neurotically. But we are not justified in regarding this yearning expectation on the part of struggling and suffering humanity as a mere psychological superstructure of some difficulty in individual development, or even only as a neurosis. The longing for redemption is based on an eschatological, messianic archetype. Unless the analyst in some way answers to this longing, his work would be the confirmation of a total illusion, a temptation to total neurosis and thus anything but wholesome. The analyst, then, must in some way correspond to his patient's 'Christ-archetype'. And that he does. He is able to help in so far only as the 'Christ-archetype' is alive within him. It is reasonable to suppose that this archetype is not always and not immediately —not even with the analyst—connected with an objective saviour, but begins at first as a not wholly conscious complex which persuades the analyst towards his profession. The first theory about physical and mental suffering was a religious theory, because the problem of achieving freedom from suffering was ultimately a religious problem. These links between sanity and redemption are particularly intimate where it is a question of freeing from a delusion or 'life-heresy'; for true self-knowledge is like a spiritual renaissance or even resurrection.

Yet at the same time, the 'Christ-archetype' within the analyst may have an existence divorced from consciousness in the form of a pathogenic complex. Unless the training analysis has succeeded in making this complex more or less conscious and in converting it, for instance by explaining the complex, it can happen that the analyst also transfers on to his patient powerful streams of energy without being able to control them. And the very effectiveness of the 'Christ-archetype' will then tempt both parties to seek abortive, neurotic solutions, instead of retracing complexes to their archetype and then trying, if possible, to transcend that. It seems to me that counter-transference in connection with the 'Christ-archetype' can be still more active (and may be still more dangerous) than the counter-transference of other complexes on the part of the analyst, for instance any sexual complexes. In any case this complex makes it possible to look particularly closely to the positive and negative aspects of counter-transference.

Mrs J. N. (cf. pp. 37 and 77) tells her analyst: 'You are my God on earth.' After the rape incident (cf. p. 37) she pointed to a crucifix and said: *'He* didn't help me. *You* have been helping me for months.' On another occasion she says she has been reading the Sermon on the Mount, and adds in sudden agitation: 'Its beauty is purely apparent. No one can follow that. According to that teaching, a weak person must go down. With you I am learning the way not to go down. Anyhow, a God in Heaven is a strange God. The ancient Egyptians who worshipped crocodiles I can understand much better than the Christians.' This illustrates how deep and disturbing religious problems can stop short of transcendence. The patient ignores the Incarnation of the transcendent God and, for the time being, transfers it to the analyst. The power of this transference in a deeply 'heretical'—thus also deeply religious!—person eventually led, as we know, to suicide.

Another woman, Mrs O. P., nineteen years old, in a record of an analytical session, called the analyst a 'sketch of Christ'. 'The contours of the sketch are not quite clear and it is a little blurred, stained with alien colours. But he could still rise from the dead and lay his hand upon my brow. I wonder whether after two thousand years Jesus too would have set up as a psychoanalyst?' This projection arises from the grave problems besetting the nineteen-year-old's life among the relationship to good and evil. The Christ-image attracts her, but at the same time arouses strong feelings of aggression. In the same record she writes: 'One can be good even without God, but one can't be bad without him.

Goodness is autonomous; but evil is so intimately connected with *Him* that only *He* gives it life and meaning. Good is a reaction to God.' Three months later, she wrote: 'I had wanted to be a saint. Every night before falling asleep . . . First it was the stars, they served in God's antechambers and I always asked them first, and later I prayed to God about it, with a beating heart, and I was so close to him then. Once when I was eight, just as I had been feeding the squirels in the Augarten, the sky cleared and it was very bright. And two angels came down with the snowflakes and took me up with them. After that I walked around for weeks in a sort of dream. Of course, now I know that I was ill as a child, but sometimes I wish I still were. Later my father forbade me to go to church, and scolded me and locked me in because I still wanted to go. He was a member of the Nazi party, and was ashamed of me because I was always going to Communion. I remember how I lay behind the locked door and cried. Then I waited. I believed God would not allow it and would help me, and sometimes I used to wander about in the streets looking for him. And when God took no notice of me at all—I know I was being arrogant and, anyhow, childish. I sulked in a corner. Later I tried to replace God by art and philosophy and pantheism. Probably all this was due to my own development, and also to the general course things were taking. After all, my father alone was not to blame. Only it was too early then, and I was torn out of all my beliefs with such violence. Then, after the war, when Catholicism returned (immediately, so far as I was concerned) to Vienna, I became fanatically anti-religious. Mine was a hatred of God based on fear and inability to love God. I was nearly expelled from school for it, and the same thing happened at a convent where my father (now a good Catholic full of righteous indignation at my godlessness—he would slap me if I alluded to the past) had placed me in the autumn of 1946 . . . At the convent I had deliberately stamped on a host . . . Now I have thought and lived my way beyond all these problems. I am not anti-religious any more, because I have no feelings about religion at all. I know that it is rooted in longing and fear: but all this occurred to me in the course of my analysis. If I were a psychoanalyst, I would perhaps say to other people: 'Show a little more pride! Don't kick and struggle, only children do that!' With incredible accuracy, the patient had succeeded in relating her 'life-heresy' to religion. Thus clearly showing what significance her earlier projection of the Christ-image to the analyst must have had for her.

It may be said that not all patients show the redemption complex to this degree. We could, however, quote numerous instances of analyses which, although perhaps not emphasising the problem of redemption quite so dramatically—for instance, analyses of male patients—yet imply or even express the yearning for a redeemer. Indeed, the system whereby the patient records both single sessions and the whole course of his analysis might well receive wider application. Here is the analysis of a particularly reserved and unemotional, slightly neurotic patient, whom we have instanced already, namely Dr C. D. (cf. pp. 45, 52, 70, 80, 91, and 155).

After one year of analysis, when his symptoms had disappeared some months previously and Dr C. D. was largely freed from his fixations, the analyst invited him to write a retrospective account of his analysis. The analyst suggested that a severance of the analytic relationship may be imminent so that the patient's analysis dependence might be demolished gradually. The patient, indeed, seems to realise that this might be a sort of balance-sheet of his analysis. A few days after the analyst's proposal, the patient, perhaps not entirely by accident, developed a severe influenza, and although even during his illness he continued to make notes for the analysis on associations, dreams—he postponed writing the report for several weeks. This retrospect, which in itself contains nothing unexpected or sensational, is here summarised because even in this undramatic account the desire for redemption in particular emerges clearly. The analyst at one point is compared first with Christ and then with the Devil; here the transference is imbued with that ambivalence which characterises every fixation (i.e. every false absolute), because every fixation is both a libidinous tie and a restriction on development. Moreover, wherever a 'divine' image becomes relative, the first reaction is aggression against the former absolute: if in the course of the analysis the 'divine being' has been recognised as an 'idol', as Daim puts it, we may suppose this to be a personification of the demoniacal. The early Christians also believed the pagan idols to be demons. Only when a definite detachment has been achieved from the earlier fixation can the object be divested both of its 'divine' and 'demoniacal' aspects. Dr. C. D.'s report follows:

Psychoanalysis was a torture for me in the beginning. In the first session I had to speak about memories which I found it very distasteful to express, even when they were quite harmless. This was because I believed that everyone I had to do with immediately pronounced judgement on me, invariably an adverse judgement. I thought the same about you, and it frightened me. Every time I spoke of something which I thought deserved blame, I thought what an impossible, inferior person you must be thinking me to be.

'In addition I had no very clear conception of analysis, even after I had reached a fairly advanced stage. I always thought there must be something magical and unknown behind it. The notes I took after sessions, and then brought up with me, seemed to have no significance, and I could not see that they had much to do with analysis. I thought of analysis as the need to discover some single causal event which had brought about my "illness". The example of the philosophers' stone seems appropriate. My lack of understanding of the analytic method was the reason why I more or less failed in my attempts of associating freely during the sessions. I could not think of anything because I fancied that the things that passed through my head were, almost by definition, valueless and unimportant.

'I always endeavour to show my best side to everybody, that is, I often put on a show of qualities I do not really possess and conceal disagreeable things with which I cannot boast. I embarked upon analysis with this attitude. I did not want to utter the things I thought shameful. I closed up; above all, I was frightened that in the session, where I was supposed to give free rein to my associations, I would betray the impulse I thought shameful. Thus, during the critical period early in summer, I had not the courage to answer your question "How are you?" (always at the beginning of the session) truthfully, but always gave the stereotyped answer, "Quite well, thank you".

'I think that at the beginning of the analysis I must have transferred to you all the feelings I had as a child about my parents, the shyness and fear of telling them about what I felt. I remember the first session. You asked me why I was consulting you. I was doing so simply and solely on account of my speech defect. But I was ashamed of the defect, and therefore resorted to what I thought was a lie, I said I suffered from anxiety, and thought I was lying. I did not want to admit that I had come because of my speech defect. I trusted you profoundly from the very first. It is difficult at this late stage to catch the tone of my relations with you over the first six months of analysis. I remember that during the first months I looked forward very much to the sessions, and went to them gladly. On the other hand my fear of communication and my inhibitions had just the contrary effect . . . The method of free association did not suit me at all . . . I transferred feelings of jealousy, too. I remember the following incident: there is a colleague of mine who is also a good friend. In the spring of last year he too was facing certain professional difficulties, and in any case he is a very nervous, hasty sort of person. At the time he used to complain to me about his condition. I thought it would do him no harm also to consult a psychotherapist. But at the same time I felt stirrings of jealousy. I thought, or rather felt, that if he came to you too, I should in some sense have to share you with him. Probably this is connected with the fact that, as an only child, I unfortunately never experienced the necessity of sharing my parents' love with other children.

'Again, for a long time, I think as late as autumn of last year, I wished you and I would become more to each other than just doctor and patient. I wanted to win you over as a sort of fatherly friend above and beyond therapy. This may be connected with the following train of thought: a few weeks ago in the tram I saw a gentleman whose appearance inspired me with unmotivated fear, not a very strong fear, but I felt it. I began to associate from there. I thought of the time I was ten, when I went to boarding school. In those days any teacher or supervisor was a source of fear, particularly if he looked at me severely. I remember an elderly bearded gentleman; actually, he never taught me, but I had the prospect of having him as a teacher later on. I also remember that when I entered the university, I was frightened of the professors, who also acted as examiners. I used to try to make personal contact with them, partly in order to overcome my fear of them, and also so that they should get to know me, in which connection I also had the examinations in mind. Now, every time I actually managed to establish contact in this way, which in many cases was not difficult at all, my fear disappeared and was transformed into the opposite. I trusted them, even as examiners. The thought that one of them might examine me was not frightening, but on the contrary encouraged me. Of course, here too, I was keen on making the best impression possible, and indeed often had to make a pretence of what I knew.

'Perhaps it is like this: everything alien is a source of fear. I was not afraid of my parents, at least not consciously, because they were the people I knew best. Above all, my parents were a symbol of security to me when I was away from home, for instance at boarding school. In order, therfore to remove the source of fear, I had to achieve with you the same sort of relationship I had with my parents. Now, it may be a bold move to transfer this relationship also to you. Perhaps—I emphasise "perhaps"— I was unconsciously afraid of you, just as I was probably unconsciously afraid of my parents and teachers. And in order to overcome this fear, I wished for a closer relationship to you. Or did I perhaps wish it because I had overcome my unconscious fear?

'Last autumn, I realised that I could imagine Christ to be like you. Yet in my dreams, in my unconscious, you appeared to me as a sorcerer, my idea of you was not coloured by fear, so that perhaps the attribute "demonic" is out of place. For in my childish fantasies I imagine a demon as something that inspires fear. When, towards the end of the year, I felt I wanted to get certain things off my chest which awakened particularly strong resistance, I said to myself: "Why am I so inhibited, why is my resistance to the therapist so strong, why do I fear this man's unspoken judgment? After all, he is only my doctor, his duty is to help me, and nothing else. He can think what he likes about me in the process, why should I care?" It is also interesting, I think, that even in April of last year I was frightened of the end of the analysis. At the time I was afraid that the time would soon come when you no longer knew what to do with me. And I hadn't been helped yet! I was afraid you might dismiss me before the desired effects had been achieved. Later, in the autumn, when there were greater chances that the therapy might be successful, I thought with a certain nostalgia of the time when the therapy, even though it had been successful, would be at an end. At that period I resolved I would come to you as long as possible, as long as there was the slightest reason to ask you for help. I wanted to strike at the root of the evil. The sessions had long become familiar to me, I never wanted to do without them again . . .'

In the above examples which show the usefulness of patients' records and written reports, it is clear that the phenomenon of transference is not only conditioned by the transference, in the literal sense, of all childish fixations to the analyst. Moreover, every patient projects on to his analyst a nebulous idea somewhat on the following lines: 'The healer is bound to identify himself with the person in search of healing; he had to sacrifice himself and take on the burden of neurosis in order to be able to descend with the neurotic into the hell of neurosis and arise with him again.' It is of little use for the analyst to think that this unclear sacrificial process is in fact impossible. If the analyst has no support in the conscious cleansing of the 'Christ-archetype', he is in danger of becoming fascinated with his own role as redeemer. The psychoanalyst's terrible temptation, which is not made any easier by the fact that in most cases it remains unconscious, is to become God and play Christ.

On the other hand, the psychoanalyst led by the 'Christ-archetype', has to be healer and 'redeemer'. Unless his inner life thus corresponds to this vocation, he will be a false redeemer.

A psychologist undergoing training analysis dreamed of a little shabby, ugly hairdresser in Haifa, who put a halo around his head and was convinced he was the Messiah. Analysis of this dream-content showed that the patient's efforts to cure and 'redeem' people were still in flagrant contradiction with the stage of development he had actually reached. The interesting thing is that this psychologist was going through a very critical period, but had never before had any conscious misgivings reflected about the responsibility connected with his calling. He was a competent psychotherapist, who regarded the problems of psychotherapy as purely 'scientific'. His unconscious taught him a different lesson.

Another psychotherapist, also undergoing training analysis, recorded in his last analytical session:

'I am cycling across the countryside on a fine day and meet a group of people near a village. I get off and see Dr S. (a colleague of the dreamer, who works with him at a psychotherapeutic out-patient's clinic) dressed in priestly vestments and performing a ceremony. As always, he bustles, and performs his rites, which resemble black magic, with a slight self-satisfied smile. On the back of his vestment, in place of a liturgical symbol, was embroidered a pretty circular pattern which I—in my dream—identify as a "dream rosette". Dr S. explains it is a "cross rose". Then he continues with the ceremony and calls "his" wife over. I think, however, that I am not mistaken in remembering that it was not his wife, but Mrs A. Both tried hard to keep a straight face, but not always successfully. Mrs A. too was wearing a strange dress, like that of a pantomime Fairy Queen. That was the dream. Its interpretation follows spontaneously: "The doctor's role in pastoral care". The general, somewhat humorous and scornful undertone shows the problem of psychotherapy quite clearly. Dr S. is a "physician" in the literal sense of the word; he has a rather materialist outlook and in many respects regards psychotherapy as a kind of "magic" and tries to "divest" it of its non-natural elements. But what is the dream trying to tell *me*? The "priestly" element of psychotherapy should not be a "façade", a mere "vestment" covering what is typically "human" and thus presenting a sort of hypocrisy to the outside world. One ought to be able to fuse both aspects, to become a "physician of souls". No magic would be needed then.' There follow considerations about indentification with certain traits belonging to Dr S. and to the analyst, about the *mandala* on the back of the vestment (cf. pp. 199 and ff). Seen as a whole, the dream is a harmonious conclusion of a training analysis and a conscious defence of the 'Christ-archetype'.

We believe that the so-called 'training analysis' should not merely serve to make the future analyst conscious of, say, his sexual complexes, but also—especially in its constructive aspect of existential synthesis—to crystallize this tendency towards redeeming and being redeemed. The livelier the tendency, the more acute will be the specific psychotherapeutic impulse. It would be fatally dangerous to reduce this archetypal tendency to the early childhood stages of the libido. One-sidedness of this kind would turn the psychotherapist into a good technician, and also into a competent sorcerer; but there is no guarantee that he will not remain merely a sorcerer's apprentice. It is more than strange to hear an analyst declare at a conference : 'It is a matter of indifference to us whether the analyst is a good man; what matters is that he should have mastered the technique.' It is probably unnecessary to stress that the analyst should combine both ideals. What we have quoted is, in our view, just as one-sided and mistaken as the reverse opinion expressed by an existentialist psychotherapist, that all that was required in order to practice psychotherapy was to have one's heart in the right place and have a basic medical background. Unless it is itself to become neurotic, technique has to be taken very seriously and ought at the same time to be supported by a meaning or a general philosophy of life. If the analyst simply 'analyses away' or disowns the 'Christ-archetype' within himself, he will court danger both to his patients and himself. It may easily happen that he will be dominated by the redeemer part, but this will remain immanent and it will be transferred unconsciously, in a fallacious manner, to the patient's personality. For when the innermost core of a personality has been revealed, it will always be unique and fascinating. Many analytic patients radiate this fascination. V. E. von Gebsattel once told his students in the course of a control analysis: 'There are also psychopathic personalities in which the outward psychophysical layers may have worn so thin that analysis soon reaches the burning fire in their hearts. We may well be dazzled by the light of this fire.'

It will be seen that we are not concerned only with purely erotic deviations of counter-transference. The danger is a general one of 'penetrating the inner fire', the divine spark at the core of every personality. The danger may indeed be greater when this divine spark is found in a beautiful woman. The spark tends to burn particularly brightly in women because, in their passivity, they are more easily led towards good or evil, and less set in their ways than men.

To become an analyst, then, is not just a question of mastering a technique, and it is part of the paradox of psychoanalysis that even in a chapter dealing with psychoanalytic techniques we are once more led to this conclusion. Many 'technicians' of psychoanalysis may shrug their shoulders when they are told that neurotics cannot be cured without being loved.

We hope that this need for love will have emerged from this book. Besides, every sincere 'technician' of psychoanalysis will tell us that the analyst who, as everyone knows, sits outside the patient's field of vision during the session, should not make use of this situation to have a little snooze. Psychoanalysis is, after all, meant to be a living encounter between two unique and equally valuable personalities. But how can there be any fruitful encounter between two persons except through love?

Chapter Two

ON SYMBOLS

31. *Dreams and their multiple interpretations*

IT would be outside the scope of this book to deal at this
point with the techniques of dream interpretation. Dream
interpretation is of course central for psychoanalysis, and
without any doubt its surest and most important technical de-
vice; but what we have said concerning the interplay of psychoanalysis proper and meaningful synthesis, roughly determines
the technique of dream interpretation. Also relevant is what was
said about the neutrality of the analyst and the many senses in
which analytical material can be understood. All this indicates
the complexity of the work of interpretation.

Interpretation of unconscious activity is reductive, in so far as
it should enable us to regard the given psychic content as a cross-
section of the personality. Each content of the psyche has been
caused by countless others, so that the causal chain runs not
only from the cross-section to the first cause, but also includes
all the co-determining factors. For the causal experience too has
occurred within a complex human personality. Thus one may
say that a psychic content A can be traced back quite simply to
an experience B, because the experience B itself was already
correlated to psychic contents C and D. If in connection with the
interpretation of A, we discover B (by means of the associations
between A and B, which might be X, Y, Z and many others),
we see that B does not exist in splendid isolation, but is further
associated with C, D, etc. Yet in practice we can affirm that we
have reduced the symbolism of A, which we can understand, to
previous experiences. A was a cross-section taken at a certain
point in time, and in this cross-section we have managed to

isolate primarily cause B, but also a number of other contents (X, Y, Z, C, D, etc.).

Yet the analysis of a cross-section of the personality is not the kind of analysis performed in chemistry. The physical content A is not only caused by B and more or less directly connected with X, Y, Z, C, D, etc.; it also represents a value of its own. A psychic symbol is not only 'caused', it is also a unique and effective synthesis of human existence at the moment; it is also the cause of new experiences and new contents of the psyche. In this sense, content A, which is to be analysed, is a creative act, and the analysis has to discover its latent forces contained in A. Thus analysis also looks into the future; it is not *reductive* only, but also *prospective*.

Regarding reductive and prospective analysis, Jung, Maeder, Heyer and many others have made important contributions.

A fifty-seven year old woman dreams she is taken by the soldiers of an occupying power to be executed. The soldiers are quite nice about it, and they are sorry to have to obey orders. They take her out into the open, the priest is there already, and, weeping but without fear, she makes her confession in a loud voice. The reductive analysis of this dream is very instructive: it reveals almost the whole of the patient's past. Her fear of paternal authority also finds expression. This fear, by the way, is highly ambivalent, because it compels the patient, even in late middle-age, to elude complete adulthood, for her surrender to authority relieves her of responsibility. And here the prospective road of analysis opens up. It is high time she began to think of responsibility (general confession) and to proclaim it (loud voice). For many years she has maintained an attitude of reserve towards religion; but unconsciously she would like to be reconciled to religion, and to see more in it than an incomprehensible authority.

We see that this dream presents the dreamer's compensatory desires. It is, of course, another question whether these desires (for example the desire for a religious life) actually correspond to the dreamer's personal development. Not all unconscious desires are instinctively sound, even when they correspond to a philosophy of life. It would be the concern of analysis to pursue the question of how far the prospective tendency too can be integrated into the patient's personality, and whether it is not caused, for instance, by unconscious complexes (a tyrannical superego). We see, however, that the psychic content can not only be reduced (for instance, to the Electra complex), but also confronts the analysis with certain tasks which concern the synthesis of existence and must be regarded *prospectively*.

Like the neurotic symptom, the dream is an attempt at solution in a particular situation. It therefore concerns more or less wide areas of the personality. It reflects the 'left-overs' of the day in a wider sense than was formerly supposed. The dreaming personality is, after all, the whole human personality, but the dream is less under the control of a self capable of decision, and presents in a purer form than the waking state a summary of unconscious activity. Maeder, Adler and Jung have made profound studies of the compensatory function of dreams: the dreaming personality is given the opportunity of finding compensation for the one-sidedness of its conscious activity in the realm of the unconscious. Thus it is still the whole personality that dreams, even if certain aspects of the psyche's activity—for instance, the unconscious aspects—are more strongly emphasized than in the waking state; just as it is the whole personality that acts, but with the emphasis on consciousness. In this sense, the theory of the dreamer's complete 'irresponsibility' can be accepted only with reservations. Of course, the dreamer is not 'responsible' for his dream-production in a legal sense. Edward Grünewald, who has investigated this problem,[1] suggests that the common ground between the dreaming and the waking states is existence; dream contents are drafts of *our own answer to existential questions*. We are responsible for our attitudes to the dreams in so far as the development of our personality is likewise reflected, both causally and finally, in our dreams. Even the 'decision to be ill', to become neurotic, though it need not be fully conscious, is also an answer to a problem posed by life. Just like neurosis, the dream too may represent a wrong attitude to the problem of life. Beside the 'escape into illness', there may also be an escape into the 'irresponsibility' of dreams.[2]

---

[1] 'Traum und Verantwortung', *Wiener Zeitschrift für praktische Psychologie*, II, 1950, p. 117 and ff.

[2] Cf. also, Grünewald, *Flucht in die Krankheit?*, Tyrolia-Verlag, Innsbruck, 1947.

Precisely because dreams faithfully reflect the particular situation of the personality in some form, they are an excellent barometer of the psychoanalytic situation itself.

Dr C. D. dreamt, two months before the end of his analysis (cf. pp. 45, 52, 70, 80, 91, 155, and 166): 'I am walking with a friend along a gradually sloping dam. To the right of the dam is a wall that runs parrallel to it. Suddenly, the dam comes to an end and we must climb down. We climb down the left-hand side and go round the end of the dam to the wall to see if we can find a hole to slip through. We want to get to the fields beyond the wall. We go back a few yards, and find there are a few narrow holes in the wall, about the size of a man's body. But these holes are covered by barbed wire so as to be impassable. Besides, I have a tin of petrol tied to my chest, which would hinder my slipping through the holes. Further back, however, we discover two holes in the wall which are not blocked by barbed wire. My companion has already slipped through the hole and now I follow him. I lie down so as to be able to slide through the opening. In doing so, I am frightened for a moment, since the hole is not very big, that I may remain stuck fast to it, the more so since I am hampered by the tin on my chest. But I immediately overcome my fears and slip through to the free side of the wall without a hitch.'

Analysis of the dream shows the overcoming of the fixation at the oral phase (cf. pp. 70, 91 and 166), but at the same time the gradual loosening of the psychoanalytic relationship: the patient and his companion, the analyst, who always precedes him, have now made their way through every difficulty.

Shortly after the written retrospect of his analysis (cf. p. 166), Dr C. D. dreamt as follows: I am walking with my friend H. through the *Köhlerstrasse* in N. He stands still for awhile near some flowering bushes, probably lilacs. I have just washed my hair, and the bees flying about the flowering bush become entangled in my hair and buzz about me, so that I am afraid they may sting me. I ask my companion to go on, so that we may get away from the bees. In the end one of the bees actually does sting me on the finger of the left hand. While I am trying to remove the sting which has stuck fast in my hand, H. suddenly and brutally hits me in the back, so that I am disturbed in my efforts to remove the sting and the little wound is even infected with a little dust and earth, because while H. is hitting me, I am suddenly sitting on the ground. The blows on my back are painful, but I overcome my annoyance and do not react to this undeserved ill-treatment.

Then we are both pulling a cart, which H. later leaves standing in the middle of the road, as soon as there is some obstacle in the way, so that a car coming in the opposite direction has trouble in passing it. In the end we push the cart to the right of the road, in a place where the street is crossed by a bridge or some other obstacle. The street now turns into a river. Behind us there are children; they are carrying washing-troughs, which they float upon the water and use as boats. Now comes a critical moment. Shall we go into the water? What is the weather forecast? There are some soldiers too, who would also like to go into the water, but hesitate about it. They think there is bad weather ahead, and therefore it is not advisable to go into the water.

But now, someone else says, the Byzantine meteorological station has forecast good weather. On the strength of the Byzantine forecast we go into the water, probably H. is the ringleader. At first we remain on the surface. Then, probably as a spectator, I see H. and others go under the water to the bottom. I am under water now too, for I suddenly see H. walking on the bed of the river under water, but I hesitate. I wonder how all these people can breathe under water. They cannot get any air in the water, and they have no gills to enable them to suck up air from above. Perhaps it is a good thing they are not breathing, thus they will not make little bubbles and betray themselves. I see H. walking calmly, steadily and purposefully on the river-bottom under water, he has left the *Schöllerstrasse* and turns up another street.'

And now he comments upon his dream as follows:

'The beginning of the dream is fairly ambiguous. I am standing in front of the lilac and enjoying the flowers and the bees that visit them. This is pleasant. The obverse aspect is that the bees get entangled in my hair. This is unpleasant. Finally the unpleasant aspect gets the upper hand: a bee stings me in the finger. But as if this were not enough, my companion without any provocation, strikes me. Yet now something very odd happens: I do not react to this ill-treatment from him. (This means I have overcome my aggressiveness.)

The cart could be the symbol of the greyness of everyday life. It is no tragedy having to pull a little cart, but there are more pleasant experiences and occupations. Then comes the car; there is a sort of little traffic jam. This could be taken symbolically: I am frightened of life's difficulties and hate narrow straits which increase friction, they oppress me and take all the fun out of life (but, on the whole, I have got over this).

Then comes the break: the street turns more or less suddenly into a river. Children are floating on the river in washing-troughs. I used to like doing that as a child; it had a peculiar fascination for me. I always felt I was in another, more pleasant, better, more beautiful world. The children's troughs could be understood as a sort of continuation of the cart. This would be somehow encouraging, because it could mean that grey everyday life is not so grey after all, that *we* see the greyness, or rather imagine it. If one looks more closely, the grey dissolves into a more pleasant colour. And now comes the frightening question: should we, my companion and I, go into the water?

It is as if our decision about this had some fateful meaning. But it is not easy to answer the question; that is why we turn to the weather report. It is unfavourable. We are stopped short by events. There are the soldiers, who in the dream play the part of wild or half-wild men, untouched and unspoilt by civilization, who have kept their natural instincts. And even they hesitate to go into the water. What if even these people hesitate, who know natural things, as it were, in their blood? And then comes the encouraging news: the weather report from Byzantium. Byzantium, symbol of civilization. (Contrast with previous image!) Culture, enhanced by a certain aura of magic, does not mean natural instinct but—one might almost say—a scientifically based recommendation (For us lawyers Byzantium is the repository of Roman legal tradition, I might almost say a symbol of law itself). So now we embark upon the adventure, even though my companion is the leading spirit. But I do things only by halves. I enter the water, indeed, but somehow without committing myself (fear of ties and commitments) as a mere observer who takes no part in the proceedings. Perhaps I do not dare go into the water unreservedly; it is as if I did not want to burn all my bridges, I am wary; there seems to be some reason for my mistrust, however. I sense danger on the river bottom. This danger comes partly from above: otherwise how is one to understand the fact that I am glad the people under water do not breathe, because the bubbles might betray them? So one is safe under water, sheltered, the danger comes from above. But if this is so, why do I hesitate to go under water? Here my motives are just about turned inside out. What is also interesting is the changing role played by my companion in different dreams. Once he was an inhibiting factor, when I wanted to run away from my school (an earlier dream).

In this case I felt a prisoner and reacted like a wild animal, accustomed to freedom, who will batter its head against the walls even to the death; in just the same way, no sensible argument has power to move me. I have to break out. I am a prisoner, or rather I feel I am, and I just break away. The water was a different matter. Its depths attract me, it even seems reasonable to enter them, for my companion could be regarded as reason incarnate. But my complexes are no longer involved, so that my usual vacillation appears here as elsewhere. I remember that if, when bathing, I got into deep water and dived a few feet deep, so that the light grew dimmer, I felt somewhat caught, as caught as I used to feel as a child when I had to go down into the cellar and was afraid of all sorts of ghosts that might do me harm. When I was under water, I was driven up again by an almost elemental force, even if I still had enough air in my lungs to stay below the surface.'

Associations in the course of the session:
Companion = analyst;
Blows from the companion = resolution of transference; rapidly overcome disappointment;
Water = instinct, unconscious;
Hesitation = displeasure in the resolution of transference, instinctual uncertainty;
Favourable weather forecast from Byzantium = favourable prognosis, integration into the moral personality.

Miss E. F. (cf. p. 79) dreams hardly anything at the beginning of her analysis, until she is able to report the following dream: she is standing on the edge of a wood, and the psychoanalyst is sitting at a table outside an inn. Some people arrive who beat the patient severely. Then she goes up to the psychoanalyst and says to him: 'You're the most stupid psychologist in the world!' —This dream reflects great resistance, but it also opens the way to transference: the patient at last addresses her analyst, sharply but yet with a certain intimacy.

The sensitivity of dreams to the patient's situation, both in life and psychoanalysis, makes them the best possible means of checking whether psychoanalysis continues to be necessary. It is, after all, possible for the symptom against which the patient originally sought psychotherapeutic help to disappear long before the real problem is solved. So long as this fundamental problem is not solved, however, it may evoke other symptoms or revive the old ones, or, again, endlessly spin out transference. Conversely, the subjective feeling of deterioration during the analysis can also mean that the analysis has reached a new causal nexus, guiding it towards the realm of experience. No phase of development, no fixation find clear and unambiguous expression in symptoms; we have access only to symbols with multiple meanings. The reason is that, while a fixation reflects the corresponding phase of development, this phase potentially also contains subsequent phases; moreover, each phase of development is, in the cross-section of the personality, surmounted layer by layer by the subsequent ones (even if these have been deformed by the original fixation). Von Gebsattel[3] draws the special attention of analysts to the fact that 'the higher levels of development are already prefigured and implied in the lower'. On the other hand, the lower levels are shaped and transformed by the higher.

The deepest and most unshakable security is that of the maternal womb. The instinct of progression requires the developing creature to leave this haven of safety, and there can be no doubt that birth is the first great upheaval, the first great split. Analysis is now concerned with all experience. At the time of birth there is, of course, no 'I' with an individual re-action towards experience; but everything that lives for man is also experience, if only in the form of emotional functions, which become contents of the psyche, continue unconsciously to be effective, and after the formation of the self tend towards integration into the personality. Thus an old trauma may be actualised even after the attempt at integration; for at this moment man responds to the former emotional functions with the entire spiritual, psychological and physiological self. Serious problems can thus arise, which from a strictly physiological point of view would hardly be problems at all. Even though it is widely held that from a physiological point of view birth is no particularly critical moment for the newly-born infant (which is not quite in accordance with the facts); the turbulent emergence of the human person must not be neglected behind these quantitative measurements. The purely unconscious upheaval implied

[3] Criticism of a book by Daim, *Die österreichische Furche*, VII, 10.

in the necessity of having to adapt oneself for the first time to the surroundings must be reflected, owing to the unity of the person in later stages. Pure affects, without any individual attitude, which accompany the trauma of birth, are hidden for the empirical approach to psychoanalysis by analogies from later ambivalent layers of the psyche; but they can also be rediscovered in a more explicit form. Otto Rank,[4] an expert on the birth trauma, was careful to point out that such experiences would not be recalled in themselves because they lacked consciousness completely. However, Rank himself, and later G. H. Graber,[5] have stressed the deep significance of birth trauma for later stages of development. In many sufficiently advanced analyses there occur dreams and fantasies which can be satisfactorily explained only by referring them to birth trauma. They seldom appear in pure form; the primeval situation of ambivalence makes use of all sorts of ambivalent symbols, but the patient himself sometimes has a feeling of inherent certainty, since it concerns a primary experience and ambivalence itself and precedes all analysed phases.

This feeling of certainty appears somewhat more clearly and more often in certain dreams symbolic of the oral or the anal phases, although here too the unconscious sometimes makes use of rather far-fetched symbols. Most experiences of early childhood are heavily overshadowed by the symbolism of the Oedipus complex, analysis of which also produces feelings of certainty in the patient.

We reproduce below a few examples of dreams, mainly unclassified. Many authors have produced similar cases. We are giving a few instances only for the sake of completeness, and must emphasise that we have both reduced the account of the dreams themselves to the strictest minimum, and sketched only in a few words the sometimes quite lengthy work of analysis. Thus we do not claim to have even approximately exhausted the theoretical wealth of each dream. In a few rare cases we have added brief commentaries in brackets. (The dreams of men are preceded by a ♂ sign, those of women by a ♀ sign.)

[4] *Technik der Psychoanalyse*, Vol. 1. Leipzig-Vienna, Deuticke 1926.
[5] *Einheit und Zwiespalt der Seelenentwicklung*, Berne, Hans Huber, 1945.

♂ 'My parents are going away. They are going back to the town where I spent my childhood. I refuse to accompany them: I would not like to live in a small town. So I stay in Vienna, but at the same time I give notice at the office.' Increasing liberation from childhood complexes. At the same time, more mature relationship to work. Still some rigidity.

♂ 'A courtroom scene. I am acting as defence counsel. But the accused is identical with myself. The first defence counsel is Jean-Jacques Rousseau, and he leaves the task of speaking to me.' The time has come to look for the causes of life's difficulties in one's own soul rather than in the surrounding world. Naïve optimism is no longer adequate, but the dreamer still feels that he will win his case.

♂ 'I see a collection of extremely pornographic books. This collection bears the ironic title: *Histoire illustrée de la Morale*. Certain pseudo-ethical ideas of the dreamer's are based on untransformed tendencies to perversion. Problem of hypocrisy. (Problem of the Jungian 'Shadow'.)

♂ 'I am climbing up the façade of a skyscraper. It is dangerous and tiring. My analyst is with me. I refuse to go on climbing.' Analytic situation. The analysis is too active and encourages the tyrannical claims of the superego, which cannot be integrated.

♂ 'I am a patient lying in bed in a hospital. I am transferred from a private room to a ward full of women. I am indignant. I hit some man, whom I have first stripped of all his clothes.' Unwillingness to come to terms with femininity, both in the dreamer himself and in his relationships (problem of the Jungian 'anima'). Aggressiveness and homoerotic tendencies.

♂ 'An important gentleman with a big moustache is working in an office, but he is changed into a sickly child. Later, an elderly gentleman is walking with a poodle on a lead, but he trips over the lead and falls; he remains lying helpless in the street.' Childish instinctual claims are discussed in analysis and play tricks with the patient. Problem of outward respectability. (Jungian 'persona'.)

♂ 'Through some frivolous action I am in mortal danger, hanging on the outside of a building from a third-floor window sill. Dr N. N., the head of the institution where I work, frees me from my plight with the help of a fire-escape ladder.' The dreamer is undergoing a severe crisis and suffering from depressions. The analytic situation is dangerous. Dr. N. N. embodies the sense of duty. The dream is a warning.

♂ 'I have to send an empty envelope abroad. Because of military censorship I send it to the address of Miss X. Y.'—Problem of inner mission or vocation, which is inhibited by social ambition ('persona'), but furthered by clarification of relationships with feminine principle ('anima').

♀ 'I dream I have to become a soldier and march in an endless grey army.' Problem of mass conditioning, of mental impoverishment by falling a prey to insufficiently recognized masculine traits. (Problem of the 'animus').

♂ 'The stormy sea had suddenly frozen, so that the huge waves look like mountains. I am walking on the green ice. There are dangerous places and holes, too. I think that if the sea were suddenly to thaw, there is a danger of the flood overwhelming everything.' The vital forces of the unconscious are frozen up. Danger of a flood of psyche. Analytic situation. Fear of becoming psychotic.

♀ 'Fear of school certificate examination. I shall fail in mathematics.' (Dreams about examinations are among the most remarkable; but they cannot all be interpreted in the same way.) In this case: early infantile fixation on the father (mathematics is a masculine subject). This fixation threatens the dreamer's spiritual progress and her relationship to the masculine principle (Oedipus complex, 'animus', 'self' in the Jungian sense.)

♀ 'On the Boulevard St Michel in Paris. I am on my way to Africa. A big Negro stands up in front of me and shakes himself. I am frightened. I call my husband, but he is far away. The Negro grins and says that before I go to Africa I must cure the horse that is lying half-dead in the Boulevard St Michel.'—Danger from sexuality. Sexuality is over-stimulated. Vitality (horse) is diminished and sound relations to masculinity endangered.

♂ 'I am lying in a completely dark room. I have neither desires nor cares; I am neither happy nor unhappy. It is as if I did not exist, but before me a door opens, and an intolerable brightness shines through it. I am frightened; yet I know I must go through that door.'— Continual unrest on the part of the patient. The patient is very conservative, and yet is always wanting new achievements. Womb situation.

♂ 'Somebody says to me: "My knowledge is the consciousness of my ignorance." I reply: "There is an enormous force of liberation in this consciousness of ignorance. The level of consciousness is the fourth dimension which cuts across the corner at which the levels of the three other dimensions meet and thus opens a way into transcendence." ' —Association with birth, analysis also furthers a rebirth, a turning towards transcendent values.

♂ 'A woman's severed leg is lying on the pavement. Where it has been severed one can see the remains of the pubic hairs, pools of blood and vomit.' Aggressiveness (oral-sadistic traces).

♂ 'Quantities of chocolate and sweets. I stuff myself'. Greed (oral-fixation tendencies).

♂ 'I want to show someone what political freedom means, and I tell him that in the United States I could perfectly well shout in the street ". . . the President!" My interlocutor replies, "Yes, but what if you were married?" This objection does not seem absurd to me, because I know that, if it were, my wife would be punished for my words.' Associations: first touch upon memories of the anal phase (anal-sadistic remains). Aggressiveness against the father (President). The negative fixation on the father endangers free relations with the feminine principle (superego, 'anima').

♂ 'I dream I am excreting, and look for a cardboard box in order to pack my excrement attractively and present it to my mother.'—Numerous memories of childhood situations (anal-retentive traces and Oedipus complex).

♂ 'I am standing with my mother, who looks very young, in front of a peep-show. Behind a pane of glass one can see the canalization of Vienna with floating excrement.'—Associations as above; also memory of the idea that children come out of the anus (infantile birth-theory).

♀ 'The Emperor Maximilian of Mexico is shot. I miss a train connection with my father.'—Ambivalent relationship towards the father. Fixation and aggressiveness.

♂ 'I am bathing with a boy in the river. Perhaps the boy is a girl. The water is warm.'—Childish memories. (Traces of urethral sexuality.)

♂ 'A sea-shore. Some suburban-looking people wander up and down, paddling up to their ankles in the shallow water. I cannot swim but I am not afraid of the deeper places. The sea begins to get stormy, but I am still not frightened. There is a small boy with me, I tell him I will bite off his penis. He laughs and says his penis has not grown yet.'—Analytical situation: confidence towards the patient's own unconscious (sea). Overcoming his middle-class background ('persona'). Traces of castration fear (together with oral-fixation traits).

♀ 'I am travelling to the centre of town. I am to be employed by a very clever and beautiful woman.'—Analysis allows a more intensive inner life, but at the same time furthers activity. Vague homosexual desires (sublimation of homosexuality; balance between introversion and extroversion).

♂ 'I am sitting on the terrestrial globe, which is tied up with string like parcel.'—The dreamer has squandered too much spiritual energy on his business life. His urge towards self-assertion has become greater than his extroversion. Feeling of ambivalence: both exaggeration of extrovert tendencies and desire for introversion.

♂ 'I am travelling on the no. 67 tram. A boy is with me.'—67 associated with 69 (mutual *fellatio*): homosexual desires (latent homosexuality).

♀ 'I am swimming in clear water. It is very pleasant. At the bottom lies a small doll. I dive to fish it up, but it disintegrates in my fingers.'—Analytical situation: the dreamer feels she is moving about freely in her unconscious. But at the bottom she sees her own infantile image, which is hard to grasp.

♂ 'A blind dog is following me. I want to get rid of him, and throw stones at him. A little girl takes the dog under her protection. Perhaps it is not a dog, but a horse.'—The dreamer represses his instincts, which are blind and perhaps sickly. Something childlike and feminine protects and tames these urges (problem of the infantile 'anima').

♀ 'I see a dog biting its own tail in play. He looks very funny. But suddenly the dog becomes dangerous. He threatens me. To my right is someone who is apparently going to protect me, for suddenly I am no longer frightened.'—Another encounter with instinctual urges. This is first presented as harmless, there is something unburdened about it. The snake, too, bites its own tail (the 'Uroboros' according to E. Neumann: primary symbol of the awakening embryonic ego, a preliminary condition for the development of consciousness). Yet the development is not devoid of danger. The conscious masculine side of the personality ('animus') intervenes protectively.

♂ 'I see a pretty clock of white and gold, of the kind that are usually placed on mantelpieces. It is square, with a large round dial. It is seven o'clock. In front of the clock, down on the left-hand side, I think, there crouches an ugly animal, something like a newt or salamander.'—Time symbolizes development and growth. Seven is a significant number (sacraments, the ancient planets, etc.): a number representing wholeness (three and four addition). Similarly, the clock is both square and round (*Mandala*, cf. pp. 199 and ff.). The colours are preserved (white for the moon, gold for the sun). Down to the left ('shadow') is an ugly animal symbolizing the patient's own aggressiveness (dragon, basilisk).

♀ 'I think I dreamed of an embrace. I don't know who it was but everything was very peaceful and I was happy. Later on I remember a dance. Several figures were dancing in a circle on a meadow.'—The sexual event in this dream symbolizes a spiritual union (integration of archetypal images, re-birth, 'conjunction') The dance-circle is also an image of wholeness. Green (meadow) is the colour of fulfilment.

Other examples of dreams are to be found on pp. 81, 142 ff., and 170 ff. We should like to stress that the examples represent summaries of the work of one or several sessions, which were themselves prepared by a longer or shorter phase of psychoanalysis. An exact reproduction of the whole process in each case would probably take many pages.

Even in this very simplified form, however, which presents a mere skeleton of the dreams and their interpretations, our examples may well produce upon the reader an impression of chaos, *rudis indigestaque moles*. Yet such examples are not so much chaotic as complex. A principle of order can be derived both from sound psychological analysis and from the existential synthesis which we would advocate. The dreams can easily be classified from these points of view: each dream is so to speak at the point of intersection between instinctual development and the level of integration that has been achieved. Some sort of individual correlation could be established between the instinctual origin of a dream, and the existential attitude taken by the personality with regard to the particular stimulus, that is to say, a correlation between the ladder of psycho-physical development and the scale of a hierarchy of values. The lowest link in the chain of correlation could be imagined, ideally, as absolute narcissism; wheras the highest would be the point of intersection between Eros, in free surrender, and integration into the transcendental order.

Harald Schultz-Hencke[6] has proposed an 'approach to a systematic classification of dreams'. Dreams are analysed into component elements and are classified, according to certain criteria, in almost tabular form, by a system of co-ordinates which indicates the correlation between the types of stimuli and the emerging level of development.

In this section we merely wish to point out that modern research on dreams, which owes its fundamental principles to Freud, has made great advances in the last half-century. The multiple significance of dream symbols is infinitely more complex than Freud supposed. Dream-life is the realm of almost total projection. The whole of the dreamer's mental and emotional life is projected on the dream mirror, and particularly those contents of the psyche which in the waking state have not been fully realized. The dreamer's entire life-history plays a part in determining his psychic life; but at the same time the dream is a permanent creation tending towards a teleological synthesis of existence. The analysis of dreams clearly cannot be a mere analysis of the parts, but must be a kind of chain reaction which affects the whole of the psychic contents subjected to analysis. The significance of a dream is, as a rule, greater than that

---

[6] *Lehrbuch der Traumanalyse*, Georg Thieme, Stuttgart 1949, pp. 163 and ff. One of the best summaries of our present knowledge concerning the scientific interpretation of dreams.

of the sum of its parts. This does not mean, however, that dream-interpretation is mere 'fantasy'; it is, on the contrary, a science of fantasy, which takes the fantasies produced by the patient quite seriously, because creative forces are mobilised through them.

32. On analytic reports

As we have seen, absolute non-intervention on the part of the analyst is impossible, for analysis, after all, is an intervention in the patient's mental life. There is considerable misunderstanding about the limits of this intervention. We believe that any 'activation' of analysis should, as far as possible, be avoided, in so far as it does not correspond to the stage of development actually reached by the patient. We welcome, however, anything that can actually promote activation and acceleration of analysis, anything that can favour the process of re-experiencing and becoming conscious of the hidden strata of the soul. Even the classical analysis of dreams is, after all, an 'activation' of the process of auto-therapy to which the dreams open the way. Jung made a decisive advance when he asked his patients to write down their dreams, without discussing them. Such series of dreams slowly led to the solution of many spiritual conflicts. Every analyst knows that patients will tell him that they are unable to have dreams. In this case the first 'activating' step is to induce them to dream and bring the dreams to their attention. The interpretation of dreams is but a second, though decisive, step in the direction of 'activation'.

The technique of analysis, therefore, has to stimulate if possible both the production of every level of the unconscious and the integration of this production into the personality. Analytic technique is active, in the true sense of the word, when it promotes first an abundance of symbols and second their emergence into consciousness. A forcible method, such as used by Stekel, which attempts to interpret the products of the unconscious by purely rational means, fails, as we have seen, in many cases. But other 'active' methods have often proved successful; one of the most remarkable is that evolved by Robert Desoille[7] which

[7] *Le rêve éveillé en Psychothérapie*, Paris 1945, and *Psychanalyse et rêve éveillé dirigé*, Bar-le-Duc, 1950.

encourages the direct productivity of the pre-conscious waking dream. Doubts are possible, however, about the immediate integration of this production.[8] Considerable work has been done by Marguerite A. Séchéhaye on the therapeutic liberation and development of the ego in schizophrenics:[9] this method, quite different from shortened therapy, promotes the symbolic realization of instinctual desires in order to lead them towards integration.

After many years of experiment, we are convinced that part of the necessary encouragement is for the patient to keep records of analysis. We started with accidental experience collected in the course of training analysis. No fundamental distinction was made between didactic and therapeutic analyses, but it was intended to give learners an opportunity of collecting material derived from their own experience, so that they might have authentic records of insights that were empirically obtained, which they could use for their own analytic practice. We therefore encouraged those who were undergoing training analysis to make a record, not too extensive but as accurate as possible, of each analytic session on the same day, and also to compose written reports about turning points in their analysis. It was found that this activity constitutes, so to speak, an analysis of the second order. Free ideas in the course of the session arise in connection with dreams, and themselves represent a spontaneous activity of the psyche which, while it helps to bring dream symbols to consciousness, could itself be brought more clearly and decisively to consciousness by being recorded subsequently. The reports written by the patient on his analysis seemed to deepen, strengthen and accelerate its effect.

Having been influenced ourselves by 'non-interventionist' technique, however, we were not without misgivings about this method. We wondered whether the writing of such reports might not foster a harmful rationalization that would strengthen resistance, or whether it might not lead to an excessive preoccupation with mere analysing.

We collected experiences, for instance, by interrupting the

[8] Cf. the sessions of the seminar held by the Vienna Depth Psychology Study Group during the winter term 1950/51.
[9] *La Réalisation Symbolique*, Berne 1947.

recording process for a while, or intensifying it, by asking patients to reproduce the sessions almost word for word. In this way it was gradually possible to establish experimentally that by keeping records the analysis was not fundamentally influenced, but the insights gained could be more clearly displayed and a growing consciousness of the contents of the psyche quickened and confirmed. Such 'recorded' analyses generally require fewer sessions than others of which no records are kept; months of work can be saved in this way.

In our experience, patients tend during psychoanalysis to brood over their problems more than usual, to go on analysing themselves (and, unfortunately, other people) and to protract the analytic situation into their daily lives. Now we have ascertained that written records serve to round off the session, and give the patient an opportunity of making his habitual brooding more objective. These records also enrich the analysis by capturing new ideas in black and white instead of forgetting about them over the day.

At the same time, the patient will be enabled to gain a certain distance towards the recorded event, and especially after some time has passed, the written report begins to show clear traits which were at first veiled. From the repetition or further development of certain ideas the patient gradually acquires a clearer view of his complexes and—a special advantage of written records—of the analytic situation as such, for example resistance and, later, transference. Resistance, by the way, is sometimes expressed in the manner in which these records are being kept, whether they are handed in too late or written with distaste. In general, however, patients will become interested in these tasks, and will carry them out without difficulty.

In most cases patients very quickly find their own way of expressing themselves by using certain key words or detailed reports. They rarely complain about the additional time involved. Typewriters tend to be used increasingly and carbon copies of his reports can be kept by the patient.

Analytic reporting also permits confrontation at certain points with the analyst's impression of the same event; stubborn repressions, hesitations in the growth of consciousness are clearly documented when the analyst compares the patient's records with his own notes and impressions. We have quoted enough examples of this on pp. 154 ff.

One final advantage of this technique is the possibility of collecting internal evidence for the value of the analytic method by gathering authentic material. Only too often (but not always unjustifiably) various schools of depth psychology, and indeed depth psychology as such, have been charged with interpreting all sorts of nonsense into the unfortunate patient.

The more widespread use of the recording technique during analysis would make it possible to undertake the publication of analytic processes on a broader basis. Of course, such publications would do justice to only one aspect of the psycho-analytic process: the subjective aspect as seen by the patient. But is this not the most important aspect? To help the patient and guide him further is what matters. After all, what he says is decisive. In any case such publications would serve to contradict the charge that the material published has been selected by the analyst's subjective point of view.

In this book we have frequently used the analytic reports of patients, for instance those dealing with the phenomenology of neurosis (cf. Mrs G. H., pp. 57 ff., and Dr C. D., pp. 45, 52, 70, etc.) or with pecularities of the analytic situation: resistance (pp. 151, 167), transference (pp. 164, 167) etc. Records are particularly useful during the final period of analysis. In lengthy analyses of patients who manifest dramatic symptoms, records may serve to draw attention to the gradual development of positive traits of the personality.

For instance, a forty-seven-year old school mistress, who undertook analyis because of a general feeling of depression, largely due to gland trouble, wrote:

'I try to make myself consciously notice, hold on to and enjoy pleasant experiences (e.g. if I wake up in the morning without feeling the usual pressure, or feel a momentary liking for a stranger). I sometimes make the effort to be positive towards life —I try not to give in to my tendency to be closed in. In the evening, when I think back over the day, I try to find what was positive in it. Or I consider that I have been spared many of the sorrows which others have to bear (but that causes anxiety and takes me back to a negation of life). At times, when sadness or tension overtakes me, there is no "good deed" for me at all.'

In the case of other patients symptoms disappear early, but, as we have seen, their conflicts remain latent. Analysis can be said to be completed only when the synthesis of existence has been arrived at, which, on the strength of the symptoms alone, neither analyst nor patient could have foreseen. The patient's reports can be very informative on the attained synthesis. As an example we shall only quote a brief report from Dr C. D. (*passim*):

'On Sunday in church I saw some little boys, who had dared to sit down in a pew, being driven away rather harshly by the owner of the seat. I would never have dared to sit in a pew as a child; I did not know whether or not it was allowed and did not dare to do so. I did not even dare to ask whether it was allowed. If I had done and had been chased out like those boys I would have felt hopelessly ashamed. My parents were far too authoritarian in my upbringing. I was much too frightened of any authority. Why, as a child, I saw every grown-up as a sort of God who could not be contradicted. I felt exactly the same when I regained my religious faith three years ago. The last thing I felt was relief. I took this step instinctively, partly because in so doing I hoped to find peace; but at first I found just the opposite. I had to acknowledge new laws, accept a new authority; new guilt feelings arose, I felt ashamed before my acquaintances and my parents of going to church on Sundays when I was alone. I gained nothing but a new set of difficulties. But now psychoanalysis and faith work in unison. I often think about the meaning of life nowadays, and I no longer find the problem a difficult one to answer. By acknowledging God and his law I am achieving a proper relationship to secular authority and its laws.'

Let us repeat once more that the only analytic technique that can do justice to the human personality is one which reminds the analyst that the symbols used by reality are no mere signs but genuine symbols. But the significance of symbols is always much greater than that of signs of conditions, because the symbol expresses simultaneously several levels of being.

33. *On analytic drawings*

We hope to have emphasised that it is essential for the technique of analysis that activation and deepening of analysis should not at all be linked with the transmission of ready-made truths. On the contrary, all such ready-made truths which the analyst would like to infuse in his patient, whether causal or existential explanations, are basically undesirable interventions.

We have seen, however, that it is possible to activate analysis by stimulating the production of spontaneous knowledge and subjective abreactions.

Certain 'active' methods in psychotherapy also serve such a promotion of abreaction. Such methods are, for instance, Moreno's 'psychodrama' and Robert Desoille's 'directed waking dream', which may also produce excellent results. Fundamentally these are forms of that activity long forgotten by civilized man, play for play's sake. We cannot here go into a detailed description and critique of these methods; we shall say only that their primary purpose is to further the abreaction of dammed-up emotions, and that they are far less concerned with the deepening of spontaneous knowledge. It would appear, by the way, that Marguerite Séchéhaye, the Swiss psychologist, has combined both aspects of activation in her ingenious method of 'symbolic realization' for the treatment of psychoses.

What particularly interests us, however, is the combination of active techniques with the sure method of the large analysis. In this connection we have already mentioned analytic reports as a means of activation.

Analytic drawing should, however, be assigned at least some importance. C. G. Jung has introduced this technique and has perfected and investigated it. It has also been taken over by analysts from other schools, in particular by Gustav R. Heyer.

As a rule, the patient is requested to draw between the analytic sessions whatever occurs to him. He is not supposed to think too much, but simply draw what his fancy dictates, without—especially at the beginning—attaching much importance to the artistic merit of his drawings. The patient is to draw 'from imagination' and express his feelings in this way. To this end, he must overcome any initial resistance, and draw regularly, whether or not he feels like it. Nearly all patients, particularly those who think they have 'no talent' for drawing, regard this task with distinctively negative feelings. They are for ever trying to excuse themselves on the ground that they are 'not good at drawing'. Most people nowadays have lost the enjoyment of apparently purposeless visual presentation. They believe only in what is 'useful', 'purposeful'—in other words, 'conscious', forgetting that 'consciousness' too is influenced and co-determined by the unconscious psychic contents. Some patients at first try to get out of it by very 'conscious' drawings, they copy some object or other and remain caught in a meaningless, purely externalised 'reality'. In such cases the patient should be told that, even if nothing occurs to him, he could start with aimless doodles, which unless he gives up, will begin to take shape by and by. In fact, the doodles eventually acquire subjective significance.

A colleague of ours, already mentioned (pp. 143-4), begins by a series of apparently confused doodles on white paper. Eventually, however, on looking at these apparently meaningless drawings, he himself begins to project certain images into the confused tangle of lines, much as one projects images on to ink-blots in the Rorschach test. Soon he begins to retrace certain lines with the pencil. Thus a few odd pictures begin to emerge as from a puzzle, which, while they remain fairly obscure to the objective beholder, have already acquired shape and meaning for their author. For instance, the patient himself discovers certain images in his tenth, apparently quite meaningless drawing (Plate I, Fig. 2), which he brings out more clearly by going over their outlines again with his pencil. In the background he sees a lion, which reminds him of his wife, born under the (astrological) sign of Leo, who also stands in the background of his present problems. In the foreground to the left he sees a figure wearing a magician's pointed hat: this, he says, is the analyst. On the right is a rider on a tall horse, the patient himself. What is depicted is a lively conflict between analyst and patient—or rather, between opposite trends within the patient himself. Eventually, by the way, the patient also ventures on real drawings, the first of them being a sort of compromise between a jumble of lines and a clear presentation (Plate II). The patient comments on this drawing as follows, in one of his records:

'I intended a kind of self-portrait at first, but without any definite purpose or idea, I just let the pencil and my mood take over. The picture shows a room at night. On a chair that stands on a carpet sits a cat, partly a little uncertain, partly proud and also a little surprised. Behind it, to the left, an oil-lamp and a bookcase, one book is just falling down. On the right above the chair floats a little spirit, not an evil one, and there is a moth flying about the room too; through the window one can see the moon and one star. A huge fire is burning in the fireplace and making faces. In front of it stands a little open box with a snake in it; on the mantlepiece a clock, it is making rather a wry face too; above it a portrait of a general, perhaps Prince Eugene. On the extreme right, a broom and logs for the fire. The atmosphere is fairly strong —lonely, uncanny, concealed tensions, expectation.'

Soon he ventures upon more detailed drawings. As is often the case, he begins with the representation of his dreams and draws the dream we have already quoted (pp. 143-4) (Plate 1, Fig. 1).

Dr C. D. is unable to do symbolic drawings for many weeks, and begins by drawing pictures from memory of various places connected with his childhood. He does so fairly clumsily, but even these drawings are not devoid of value for purposes of analysis, since each of them is the starting point for a whole series of memories during the session. As the analysis progresses the whole mode of drawing changes, and Dr C. D. develops a rather remarkable ornamental style. In these drawings the ornamental motifs increasingly take the form of squares and circles.

One day Dr C. D. arrives with a drawing (Plate III) which develops the now familiar circle-square patterns and fashions them into a very striking whole. This drawing recalls certain exotic ornamental motifs and comes as a great surprise to Dr C. D. himself. The patient now spends months elaborating on various isolated elements from this drawing; sometimes the whole structure seems to fall apart, sometimes there is a struggle between unity and dispersion, with a new triangular motif appearing (Plate IV), sometimes structural unity returns. Dr C. D. says that the restoration of the unity produces upon him an impression of strength. The angular and unharmonious elements disturb him, and he takes them to be the expression of his own aggressiveness. Similarly snakes and flames are the still unconquered neurotic impulses. One day Dr C. D. buys himself a box of coloured pencils and makes two drawings (Plates V and VI). The latter drawing, particularly, seems to interest him. 'The remarkable thing,' he says, 'is the point in the middle and the way the drawing is split into four. Everything irradiates from the centre to the periphery. Four is a convenient number. The four seasons . . . The four rays go straight to the outermost points. From the centre the whole structure can be dominated . . . Yet there is still one tension, there was a mediaeval torture that consisted in having men torn apart by four horses.' Dr C. D. had never heard of the *mandala*—of which we shall have more to say later—or read the works of C. G. Jung.

Gradually, patients begin to acquire confidence in their own drawing. In any case, they notice that it mobilizes certain unconscious forces which strive to be given shape.

A woman patient, on bringing two drawings (Plates VII and VIII), says: 'It is amazing how one simply has to draw things one does not oneself understand. To me, this proves that people who talk about the necessity and effectiveness of analysis without having gone through it themselves simply do not know what they are talking about, because analysis is not a medical technique but a process that cannot be described.' These drawings show the patient's inner difficulties. Plate VII represents her infantile desires: in the middle is the symbol of the deepest regression into intra-uterine life, but at the same time the promise of re-birth. Plate VIII shows the divided heart, but at the same time promises a return to inner unity: the heart here plays the part of the combined circles and squares; it is a *mandala*.

Analytic drawings have great emotional importance for the patient. We have seen that some patients report that they are simply compelled to draw. In addition, they realize that the drawings are connected with various emotions, sometimes very powerful ones.

G. G. records the following dream: 'All the symbols in my drawings are moving up and down in a circle before me. Feeling of anxiety or constriction. Vision of the analyst. Sarcastically reproachful expression? At the last session I concealed the fact that I had really shown the Szondi pictures to Henrietta (the patient's mistress) and not merely intended to do so, as I said. Therefore bad conscience in dream. Drawing I brought with me showed island in water; water represents my psyche, that is to say I am being secretive towards the analyst.'

In passing we may, in connection with this observation, touch upon the much-discussed problem of 'dishonesty in psychoanalysis'. There is no such thing as dishonesty in psychoanalysis, because psychoanalysis concerns itself with all the patient's fantasies, including 'lies'. Besides, contents passed over in silence always emerge again, as in this case the Szondi experiment.

Analytic drawings are extremely illuminating in content, but also in the form of their presentation. The colours used, the arrangement of the drawing in space, the thickness or intensity of the lines, the symmetry or asymmetry and many other factors are important in their interpretation.[10]

The central problem posed by analytic drawings is, however, the shaping, that is, the integration of forces from the unconscious. The shapelessness of the wild, unrecognized, unconscious forces threatens to overwhelm the conscious part of the personality. Analytic drawing gives the patient a chance to shape these forces, also to recognize them to some degree, or at least to direct them away in an ordered form.

An artist of our acquaintance began his career with drawings which still contained more or less recognizable shapes—generally uncanny machines and edifices. One of the first pictures, called 'My Fear', is as yet an attempt to give objective expression in this way to the artist's fear of the threatening unconscious. According to him, his first pictures still in some sense reflect 'nature'. The artist believes something can still be 'recognized' in these pictures. The later pictures show an increasing shapelessness. They represent a series of adjacent grey-black surfaces; they are somewhat reminiscent of a geological cross-section and could be extended in any direction, because they have no centre. The artist says 'nature' bores him to death, he hates 'nature'; he adds that he is now consciously following the path of total introversion, and trying to lose any remaining 'distance' from his inner image. Total introversion, he says, also means total shapelessness.

This example shows an uncanny attempt to follow, apparently consciously (and yet under compulsion) the path trodden by so many psychotics, which leads at last to the total disruption of the capacity to shape. Not only fear of 'nature', but, behind it, fear of one's own emotional life emerges. Analytic drawings are basically intended to serve the opposite purpose. As far as possible, the patient should accept his emotional life, give it form and thus achieve abreaction. Yet every graphic production has an analytic, or at least a symptomatic value. The disintegrating figure in analytic drawings always suggests a severe crisis of the personality.

[10] Among recent articles on the subject, we might mention: Jolan Jacobi, 'Erfassung und Deutung der "Bilder aus dem Unbewussten" '; and Hugo Debrunner, 'Mandalasymbolik und asymmetrische Ausdrucksformen in der Phantasiezeichnung', both published in the *Schweizerische Zeitschrift für Psychologie und ihre Anwendungen*, IX, 1950.

A crisis of this kind is shown in a particularly moving way in a series of fourteen drawings produced by a girl during adolescence (Plates IX-XIV). These drawings were made in the course of one month, during which her condition had become so acute that electro-shock treatment was being considered. The danger is shown in the progressive distortion of the human image in the sketches. Faces become more and more uncanny, but also seem to be falling apart, until the human face is eventually reduced to chaos. On 22nd of November six drawings are made, each of which strengthens this impression of chaos. On 23rd of November, the crisis reaches culmination, and no more drawings are made. The crisis is resolved, and on 24th of November there is the last drawing, a self-portrait, the serene and harmonious features of which recall nothing of the former chaos.

Analytic drawings, therefore, have considerable symptomatic value. They supply thereby innumerable associations which facilitate analysis and the interpretation of which resembles that of dreams.

The patient G. G. (cf. p. 196) makes a drawing (Plate XV) and writes about it in next day's record: 'Drawing: portrait of Henrietta (the patient's mistress). Hair, nipples, pubic hair, nails and mouth red. Linked with shooting-target, at which a penis-shaped pistol is fired. Green body. Green is a colour about which I have obsessional feelings. On the one hand it is my favourite colour (clothes). On the other hand, I associate it with ex-crements: faeces, saliva, urine, pus, mucus, gonorrheal secretions, etc. Also poison and the fields at home. The wallpaper in my parent's bedroom was green. Mother wears a lot of green. Green eyes always seem to me the sign of a 'peculiar' personality. I my-self have green eyes, and at the time I insisted that this be specified on my passport. If I had to assign a colour to Henrietta, green is exactly what I would choose. Even though she has red hair—but to me the verdigris shows through!—and blue eyes, pink and blue seem to me symbols of sentimentality, virginity, softness, etc. Red reminds me of explosion, blood, wounds. Henrietta cannot stand the sight of blood. Also associations with my desire for anal inter-course with Henrietta. For sadistic reasons, because a homosexual once told me it was painful and that a lover who permitted it was trying to make some kind of sacrifice.'

It is easy to see how quickly the drawing leads us to the patient's own highly emotional, insecure, problem-ridden and ambivalent attitude to his own sexual life. The drawing's colours, style and intensity of line are very revealing. Moreover, the drawing yields important chains of association for future sessions.

A woman patient, already mentioned (cf. p. 196), produces seven paper cuttings in the form of a mask, one on top of another, and fastened with a paper-clip; they represent—behind the impassive but mysterious social mask or 'persona'—the secret layers of her personality. Each of these little drawings affords manifold opportunities for interpretation (Plates XVI and XVII). With them, a larger explanatory drawing (Plate XVIII) which represents the patient's renunciation of the mask-like 'persona' and the beginnings of an integration of the secret layers into the heart or 'self' of the personality—the same heart that has already appeared as a *mandala*.

We refer briefly in connection with the above drawings to the *mandala*. The *mandala* is an image, usually round, sometimes round and square, used in the east, particularly in India, for purposes of meditation. The concept of the *mandala* was introduced by Jung into analytical psychology. He sees the *mandala* as representing a concentration upon the 'self'; when produced in analytical drawings it is a mechanism and the product of the unconscious, which comes up compulsively.

Analytic drawing indeed will produce the *mandala* with almost absolute certainty, though there are patients incapable of producing it. Thus the patient referred to on p. 191, who has already undergone three years of analysis.

Perhaps Jung has unintentionally exaggerated its significance, in as much as his writings give the impression that the production of the *mandala* is the culmination of the analytical process by the discovery and release of the 'Self'. But it seems more likely that the production of the *mandala* is no more than a sign of progress; it shows the patient's ability to grope his way towards his own Self. The *mandala* may be taken as a sign that the analysand might now be ready to correct his own problems, do without the 'scapegoat', withdraw his projection and admit that the most important problem is that set by the self in need of salvation. In some analysands this turning-point is reached fairly quickly, even at the beginning of the analysis. This is by no means unimportant, because the release of the problems connected with the Self is a condition for integration (Jung refers, significantly, to 'individuation'). Conversely, the prognosis for integration is less favourable if after much analysis and drawing an unmistakable *mandala* is not produced. It appears that the *mandala*, particularly the quadruple *mandala*, points towards the patient's feeling of his own need for salvation, and suggests that he has correctly placed the neurotic problem within the Self. The quadruplicity of the *mandala*, then, stands for a need for salvation and not, as one might think, for the completed integration. It constitutes therefore a great advance and at the same time an expression of deeply-felt needs, indeed of profound disturbances.

Dr C. D. quoted on p. 195 referred to the domination by the centre of the quadruple *mandala*, yet he also recalled the medieval torture by which the victim was torn apart by four horses.

The patient who supplied the drawing in *mandala* form (Plate VIII) (cf. p. 196), commented upon it as follows: 'The heart is crucified. The horse at the bottom left-hand corner is crucified too. The cross is an instrument of torture, and the sign of salvation.'

The division of the *mandala* into four sections is, therefore, certainly also connected with the positive aspect of neurosis, which is the Christ archetype. The quadruple *mandala* includes the 'shadow'. As yet a state of tension, a 'crucifixion' obtains. We do not really know whether the rarer combination of the *mandala* with a triangle (as it appears, for instance, in Dr C. D.'s drawing, IV, later giving place again to the quadruple *mandala*) stands for successful integration, and whether it should not, accordingly, be regarded as an advance over the quadruple *mandala*. Jung holds the opposite opinion, but he has been influenced excessively by Buddhism and Gnosticism. He maintains that the triangle could stand for the repression of the shadow; also possible is an illumination of shadowy regions. Yet much difficult research remains to be done. We know of cases where the triangular *mandala* in fact represented the peak of the process of integration, but whether this is a general rule cannot as yet be said with certainty.

What is quite certain is that the *mandala* stands for an image of the 'Self'; Jung has warned against prematurely interpreting it as knowledge of God. He even wrote: 'A modern *mandala* is the unconscious admission of a particular mental state. There is no divine being in the *mandala*, nor is there a suggestion of submission to, or reconciliation with, a divine being. The place of the divine being seems to have been taken over as a total entity.'[11]

This last sentence clearly shows the barrenness of an exclusively human system of reference. For man, too, can become an absolute. The *mandala* always points to the discovery of this human self, and the human self as a 'divine archetype'. It is in the Self that the decisive drama is enacted. Crucifixion, if referred to absolute values, betokens a need for redemption. In the same way, man as a total whole is in need of redemption, but if he merely replaces God, there can be no redemption in the immanence. If it points towards transcendence, it leads to recognition of the hierarchy of true values.

[11] *Psychologie und Religion*, Rascher Verlag, Zurich 1942, p. 147.

Chapter Three

THE ANALYSIS OF THE ANALYST

34. *On training analysis*

WHILE medicine became separated from religion many centuries ago, it is only comparatively recently that psychotherapy followed the same development towards autonomy. For psychotherapy to declare itself to be exclusively a discipline of natural science, it needed probably the superstition of the nineteenth century. This superstition required that all knowledge should be traced back to the pattern of natural science, and denied the scientific character to any system of knowledge that could not be arranged in terms of quantitative causes. Extreme 'secularization' of knowledge is expressed in the dictum: 'No soul has ever yet been found under the scalpel.' It was therefore believed that it did not exist, save perhaps as a mere function of matter. Such conclusions, arising from questionable premises, testify to the poverty of the anthropological thought in that century. Only today psychology seems to be prepared slowly to reject such notions.

And yet even the age of the great superstition produced some partial truths which must not be discarded. But for them, our knowledge of man would be the poorer. Perhaps even now the time is not yet ripe for a complete integration of all these partial truths into a universal system of anthropology. On the contrary, however great the need for a universalist anthropology, it is as yet too likely to lead to temptations of totalitarian thinking. The universalistic approach is all too often confused with a totalitarian, and universalism is likely to emerge from the pangs of dying totalitarian thought. The defection from the hierarchy of values thus led anthropology to the totalitarianism of science. It was then countered by a reaction in the form of a totalitarianism of subjective thinking, followed by psychologism and solipsism. Traces are noticeable still in the existentialist systems. Yet gradually even subjectivism seems to be on the way out.

Obviously the history of psychological ideas (cf. Introduction), which, incidentally, is one aspect of the history of ideas as a whole, has a decisive effect on the claims which the *zeitgeist* makes on the psychotherapist.

Of all the disturbances of the human personality, neurosis is the one which most decisively affects both the mental-spiritual and the psycho-physical aspects of the human person. A thorough consideration of the mental problems involved in neurosis, in both their positive and negative aspects,[1] led us to the conclusion that neurosis can be grasped and treated only by a therapy which can see the spiritual core behind psycho-physical signs and symptoms. Starting out from the general nature of the problem and from an analysis of the required method, we have defined the task of psychotherapy[2] as a restoration of the hierarchy of values, by which we mean an openness towards absolute values. Psychological analysis is thus necessarily linked with a meaningful synthesis of existence.[3] Any attempt to practise psychotherapy either from an exclusively causal-determinist angle of the practical biologist or physician, or from the exclusively spiritual angle of the priest is, therefore, necessarily incomplete. The medical aspect in so-called psychogenic disorders will, indeed, be subordinate to the spiritual; but the point is that neurosis, as an expression of the sickness of our age, is *par excellence* a dual phenomenon, and any simplification risks singling out in this twilight one aspect as against another and thus adding further weight to the equivocal nature of neurosis.

Moreover insufficient account is taken of this equivocal character of neurosis in the practical training of doctors and priests. Nowadays there is simply no ideal training for psychotherapists which could prepare them sufficiently to understand and influence mental-spiritual problems and their psycho-physical expression.

The spiritual problem inherent in neurosis is given almost always, as we have seen, misplaced expression, sometimes even

[1] Part I, Chapters II and III.   [2] Part II, Chapter I.
[3] Part II, Chapter II.

in the physical sphere. It is therefore absolutely necessary that only the physician should make the diagnosis; his object being chiefly to differentiate between organic diseases. What is more, even pure psychoneurosis tends to take cover behind organic symptoms during treatment. Analysis of resistance often leads to functional disturbances. Even analytic progress in certain spheres connected with malignant fixations may give rise to symbolic psycho-physical expression.

The analysis of the anal phase in Ch. L. (pp. 87-90), for instance, is accompanied by anal eczema and constipation. C. D. reacts with severe 'flu to the eclipse of transference (cf. pp. 166 ff.).

Vegetative disturbances are quite normal with many patients in the course of analysis. Because of the phenomena of resistance and transference, the analyst must not also undertake medical examinations. The patient's medical care is someone else's job.

Differential diagnosis, indication and finally medical treatment of physical effects during psychotherapy are obviously and necessarily the physician's province. But this does not mean that psychotherapy itself—in the personalist sense, which takes into account the spiritual-mental aspect—should be exclusively the physician's domain. Medical training cannot always justify this claim. It is acknowledged rightly and widely that the physician's calling is to minister to the living person, not just to symptoms. This new conception of medical duty has been adumbrated in 'psychosomatic medicine', and further developed in 'anthropological medicine' (V. von Weizsäcker), 'personal medicine' (Paul Tournier) and in 'universalist medicine' (A. Niedermeyer). It remains, however, an ideal, still frequently contradicted in actual practice under the influence of the old generation. Specialization all too often culminates in a mechanistic conception of symptoms, without regard for the living human person. Admittedly, the physician who treats neurosis is in a difficult position. He should be both a specialist, since his subject differs considerably from the general scope of medicine, and an anthropologist, indeed a philosopher, since he has to be a 'physician of souls'. For it is the very essence of neurosis to be a peculiar 'disease of the bad conscience' and to reflect deeply personal phenomena. Yet some of the admirable medical efforts which aim at a spiritual approach to psychotherapy cannot but give rise to doubts whether present-day medical training can provide the necessary preparation, especially since a method which claims to be, for instance, 'analysis with a spiritual approach and an existential orientation', far exceeds therapy in the usual medical sense of the word. In any case it is inconsistent, and probably due to social and professional prejudice, that just such efforts should lead to the formation of exclusive groups of medical psychotherapists. It would be desirable, on the contrary, that these efforts should lead to a universal solution, both in the interest of suffering humanity and of sincere experts who may come from any university faculty, but who will largely come from the humanities, especially from studying psychology. In Austria legislation permits attempts in this direction which are both generous and professionally unobjectionable. Austrian law reserves to the physician 'the *prescription* and *supervision* . . . (of) psychotherapy'.[4] No sound psychotherapist could ask for more; only a quack will feel endangered by the physician's powers of prescription and supervision. *Abusus non tollit usum*: the dangerous misuse of psychotherapy by ignorant men cannot serve as proof that it would be used properly by physicians only, or by any physicians.

In this connection it needs saying that the concept of 'lay analysis' requires drastic changes. A 'lay analyst' is, quite simply, any person with insufficient analytical training, whether or not he has a doctor's degree. The truth is that neither physicians nor non-physicians, especially psychologists, are fitted by their official training to try their hand at psychoanalysis. Attempts to provide an adequate training for analysis have largely been made only in the margin of, or complementary to, the actual course of study; yet, wherever these attempts have been made seriously and honestly, the apparent conflict between 'medical' and 'non-medical' psychotherapy was spontaneously resolved. Physicians and non-physicians complemented each other, by learning from one another. In practice this collaboration has proved much more fruitful than the unscientific segregation into exclusive groups.[5]

[4] Federal Law of 30 March 1949, Section I, Article 1, paragraph 1.
[5] Some recent German publications in this field are A. Niedermeyer, *Handbuch der speziellen Pastoralmedizin*, Volume V, Section on psychotherapy, Chapter on 'Lay Analysis', Herder, Vienna 1952, and W. Daim, *Umwertung der Psychoanalyse*, Herold, Vienna 1951, pp. 317–326.

H

More important than the degree for the future analysts, however, is the training in actual analysis. Besides the acquisition of theoretical knowledge (philosophy, depth psychology, general psychology, psycho-pathology, clinical psychiatry, etc.) this training must be based on practical experience, in the so-called 'training analysis', and 'control analyses' performed under supervision. Freud already recognised that training analysis was far more important for the analyst than specialised university study. But Freud was faced by a tough medical opposition, and he may well have been driven into a position of resentment, so that Freudians in particular could be widely accused of producing 'lay analysts' who practised without adequate theoretical background. The term 'lay analyst' should be reserved, as we have already stated, for those persons with or without medical degrees who lack either training analysis or an adequate theoretical background. In any case, a university degree, whether in medicine or psychology, ought not to become a sort of bonus on resistance against training analysis. It must be admitted that professional psychologists usually spare neither effort nor money to complete their training analysis, in the hope that it may provide them with at least some title for the practice of psychotherapy. Matters are worse in the case of the medical profession. In Austrian law, for instance, every qualified physician, however little he may know of depth psychology to treat neuroses, and many physicians concerned with these treatments, neglect to undergo the necessary training analysis. Others honestly believe that all that is needed for the successful practice of psychotherapy is a sincere disposition. We have witnessed some very curious things; for instance, young internees who, after a few days' hospital residence, were put in charge of difficult cases of neurosis. Such an attitude is not only in contradiction with the very demand for an exclusively medical psychotherapy, it endangers above all any medical training for the therapy of neurosis.

The technique of analysis cannot be learned from books and lectures. Since psychoanalysis inevitably mobilizes the deepest forces of the unconscious, no amount of rationalist preparation can replace personal experience. That is why the arguments against training analysis that are usually advanced by people who have not themselves been analysed are quite worthless and unscientific. Nothing can be proved at all with logic if one has not oneself undergone this experience. Of course, the completion of analysis is in itself no kind of guarantee for the achievement of a new form of existence; it has no sacramental character. Much harm is done by analysts who look down upon the un-initiated herd and regard themselves as a kind of analytical free-masonry. The requirement that all psychotherapists should undergo analytic training can gain ground only with patience and by avoiding excesses. One of the objections against it is the opinion, held by neurologists, therapists and psychologists, that training analysis is necessary only for 'full-scale', 'intensive' psy-chotherapy, but could well be dispensed with for the practice of 'small-scale' and 'extensive' psychotherapy. This is an error. We have seen this so-called 'small-scale' psychotherapy; small-scale psychotherapy should never be attempted on the basis of only a little knowledge of depth psychology : it presupposes as much experience or more than full-scale therapy. Small-scale psychotherapy must not be allowed to become a cover for in-creasing the activities of amateurs and dilettanti. Intimate ex-perience of resistance and transference is on the whole rather more indispensable in 'small-scale' than in full-scale psycho-therapy, because in 'small-scale' psychotherapy these phenomena occur, so to speak, in hot-house conditions. And it is not enough to know that there are such things as resistance and transference : these dangerous dynamic factors, which occur in every psycho-therapy, are more or less recognizable only to experience. Hence the unreal air of so many theoretical polemics against training analysis. They are advanced by people who have not troubled to fulfil the basic condition in order to judge what they are talking about. We value greatly the report of a physician who had resolved to endure three months of psychoanalysis. He re-ported that this short period afforded him no particular know-ledge excepting the fact that the three months were exclusively devoted to a painstaking analysis of his own resistance.

The basis of analysis is the uncovering of desires and the re-arrangement of feelings, and these processes cannot be taught by theory. A man born blind cannot be expected to know what colour is; the emotions of a man who is in love, who despairs or who has passed hours in a dark cellar during air raids, can be understood only by someone who has had the same or similar experiences. Nor can there be any theoretical and rational communication of desires which, in addition, resist any attempt to make them conscious.

There is an important additional consideration. A man may feel called to become a psychotherapist because he seeks to overcome in this way his own mental difficulties (of which he himself at first is usually unaware). Many people are apt to regard psychiatrists, psychologists and psychotherapists with some indulgence, thinking that their dealings with the psychologically deranged might add to their own eccentricity. They are quite right. Psychopathologists are somewhat odd, but not because they have to do with other odd people. The reverse is the case. Some psychotherapists choose their profession because they may unconsciously hope for the integration of their own complexes; they actively project their own need for salvation to their fellowmen. Yet psychotherapy must not stop short at projection; the need for salvation has to be integrated and illuminated within the therapist's own personality. This also explains the difficulties and dangers of training analysis, which is in fact far more of an analysis than a merely didactic exercise. The analysis of fellow-psychiatrists especially produce most unexpected examples of resistance. They are usually slower in learning the technique of free association on the threshold of spontaneous consciousness; stubbornly they will look for rational explanations, and in thinking continuously about a process deprive it of all spontaneity. We might remember that the synthesis of existence attained in each particular case is being questioned in analysis. Of course, this synthesis is also a way towards self-knowledge. But psychoanalysis endeavours constantly to analyse the spontaneous synthesis and to incorporate the experiences of this synthesis that have determined it. Everyone is, however, tempted to build up the synthesis of his existence without sufficient knowledge of the determining influences. Each step of psychological analysis leads to a new pattern of existential synthesis; but how unwillingly some of these steps are taken!

In the course of this book we have taken a few examples from training analyses (cf. pp. 142-4, 151-3, 159-60, 170-1, and 194-5), which suggest not only the need to free the budding analyst through psychological analysis from his more or less neurotic fixations, but also the importance of the process of existential synthesis, of significant orientation, for people who find their vocation in the spiritual guidance of others. In the psycho-analytical setting, the psychoanalyst is no exception as regards the contradictory development of spiritual dynamism. In the existential and synthetic setting, however, this development in the case of the analyst, is of possibly even greater significance, since the analyst is to follow a vocation particularly influenced by the 'Christ-archetype'. We notice, accordingly, in most train-ing analyses that the importance of the *metanoia*, the 'change of heart' or 're-birth' must not be under-estimated. To quote finally from the records of the last six sessions of a young psychotherapist's training analysis:

U. T. dreams of a cave in a small wood. In the course of a struggle of some kind he reaches the entrance of the cave, which is guarded by a gnome. Through a narrow passage, U. T. alone manages to enter the cave; but it has already been occupied by enemies, whom at first he takes for allies. So he has to fight his way out again, even though he felt comfortable in the cave, which seemed familiar to him. At some time he seems to have slept there with a woman—a being that symbolized both the maternal and the feminine: it was wonderful, no consciousness, a sort of nirvana.

A few days later, U. T. produces a drawing which also repre-sents a cave; inside the cave is a cradle; above it a halo with a cross in it (quadruple *mandala*). He records: 'I spoke of the drawing, and said that the cave at the same time symbolized a cosmic birth: birth from the earth. Mary thus represents the whole of nature. The halo is meant for Christ; it floats above his head. It occurred to me that fish are a symbol of life in the womb and of death. My dream is about birth and death. Actually it is un-Christian, because the Christian conception of death is really dif-ferent. Caruso once said that, while it was quite true that *anima naturaliter* was *christiana*, yet *Christ* had risen and only thus did we have a guarantee of the resurrection; we would have none without his resurrection. Therefore, he said, there could be no *natural* philosophy of death. I think this is very important. Caruso also spoke of the inscription of the tombs of martyrs: Born . . . and there follows the date of death. This speaks for the extra-ordinary dynamic force of early Christianity, which thus experi-

H*

enced death, and thereby opened up the deepest layers of the soul.

'I had a dream. All I can remember is that someone—I think a man—was pulling me out of the water. I may have been in a lake, and he took hold of my chin with both hands and thus pulled me out of the water . . .'

The analysis proceeded towards its end. During these last days U. T., almost as if under compulsion, began to make sketches of an ornamental motif until at last, during the last session, he was completely satisfied by a triple *mandala*. 'This', he writes in his record, 'is a symbol of the concentrated interplay of biological and spiritual aspects.'

We can see that training analysis is not so much a teaching method as a means of understanding the liberating effect that can result from an honest attempt to carry out both the analysis of the psychological data and their meaningful synthesis.

CONCLUSION

HAVING arrived at the end of our investigation, it is not our intention to undertake a large-scale theoretical synthesis. The foregoing analysis of the data resulting from neurosis, as well as the solutions proposed by depth psychology, cannot communicate what Jaspers would describe as 'total knowing', but merely a few important and, up to a certain point, new vistas. The reader will have noticed that we regard totalitarian ideologies with some scepticism. Accordingly, we shall let the facts and material we have collected, and also our own hypotheses and comments, speak for themselves.

This caution, however, should not prevent us from drawing certain conclusions and opening up new perspectives. Reasoned thinking is both a human privilege and an obligation. We would prefer to exercise this privilege consciously rather than, by apparent abstention, as it were, to suggest our conclusions in an underhand manner. If to 'philosophise' is to meditate about facts, arrange them in order and draw conclusions from them, we are unable to share Freud's dislike of it; he spoke of his 'constitutional incapacity' for philosophy (cf. p. 4), which did not, however, prevent him from setting up a pseudo-philosophical system of his own. Nor do we conform to the strict condition laid down by Jung, that psychology must remain within its own proper sphere, without exceeding it 'by such things as metaphysical assertions or other confessions of faith'. It is, of course, meritorious if a scientific investigator confines his method to the strictest empiricism; but after giving solemn assurance of this methodological limitation, he is not entitled to propound 'metaphysical assertions' in a roundabout way, under an empiricist cover. On the other hand, nobody may stop the scientist from arranging his empirically acquired data into an orderly and significant whole by means of a logical process, and this applies even more to the psychologist, for the object of his research, as we have seen, is also a subject, related to a meaningful transcendent order. This is precisely why even those psychologists who, frightened as they were of 'philosophising' as of an embarrassing disease, could not help, as it were unconsciously, drawing conclusions which, under the guise of objectivity, constituted a distinct philosophy. Yet to draw such conclusions is of particular importance in psychology; because the object of its study is man, an object itself capable of drawing conclusions, thinking and of value judgments. Thus psychology, and particularly depth psychology, which is the science of the hidden motives of human behaviour, plays its part in the philosophical thinking of our times; it is far better that it should play this part consciously than allow its influence to remain unrecognized.

We have shown in the Introduction how psychology is dependent on the *zeitgeist*, and how, conversely, it also largely determines the philosophy of an age by presenting to it a certain image of man. The concept of man is, obviously, of the greatest importance in the thinking of any given period; and particularly at the present time, when so many of our philosophies are being reassessed because man had come to occupy the centre of all our intellectual preoccupations. A critique of our attitudes towards the universe must necessarily lead to a radical transformation of anthropology; but the transformation of anthropology must also lead to profound changes in our general outlook.[1]

Every 'layman' is nowadays more or less aware, particularly in the present crisis of humanism, that psychology occupies a point of intersection between knowledge of self and knowledge of the universe. Public opinion, art and literature are concerned with almost paralysing monotony with the problems of psychology, particularly with depth psychology. Even the spokesmen of established traditional philosophies seem to feel somewhat unsure of themselves in the presence of the psychologist.

---

[1] This twofold process has been recognized among philosophers by A. Dempf, *Selbstkritik der Philosophie*, Thomas More Press, Herder, Vienna 1947; *Theoretische Anthropologie*, A. Francke A-G Verlag, Bern 1950.

Any psychologist who does not regard psychology as the centre of the universe will sometimes have the disagreeable experience that he appears to cause a feeling of insecurity, not only among the snobs, but also among serious people. The psychologist has in our society become a sort of secularized priest or even a modern magician. This attitude certainly illustrates the impoverishment of our disjointed sensitivity, but it also illustrates the longing of mankind to restore a valid image of man in order thereby to regain their bearings.

Depth psychology, as a descriptive discipline of the submerged realms of anthropology, ought to make an important contribution towards a sane view of man and of the universe. It may contribute towards a new synthesis, a new universality of knowledge. It is thus neither in the interest of depth psychologists, nor in that of the representatives of other anthropological disciplines, that depth psychology should remain an esoteric science. Naturally, emotional resistance is an obstacle to the integration of its discoveries; but it cannot affect their importance in principle.

It is therefore understandable that depth psychology itself ought not to be considered in isolation. Its discoveries indeed, can be misused to 'prove' anything. We have seen that one-sided theories of depth psychology reflect one-sided views of the world in general. Thus the materialist psychology of urges rested upon the assumption that the findings of physics and mathematics were binding upon all other sciences, and that only those aspects of reality were valid which could be represented according to these findings. The findings of natural science led to false absolutes and to fallacious 'nothing-but' conclusions. In reaction against this materialistic conception, depth psychology was turned into a kind of spiritualist doctrine, an irrational theory of freedom, in which such exaggerated freedom was sometimes definitively compared to grace.

The exaggerations of the first thesis and of the subsequent antithesis illustrate the fact that philosophies of man and of the universe exert a mutual influence. An optimistic conception of endless progress through the expansion of natural science was followed by a disillusioned and pessimistic view of man and the world, which in its turn led to a crisis. The beginnings of a synthesis are now just emerging. A. Dempf has pointed out in this connection that a sociology of decline and doom is gradually replaced, at the end of the crisis, by a sociology of survival, that existentialism leads to essentialism, and that a psychology of the 'id' tends to be followed by a psychology of the conscience. However, neither the theses nor the antitheses are as yet entirely spent. Both are revivals, in different forms, of ancient heresies. The rationalist-optimist view largely corresponds to an older tradition of man as the centre of things, which at the outset of Christianity appeared as Arianism and Nestorianism. In modern thought, such 'Nestorianism' is at work in placing natural, and indeed physical man, at the centre of observation. Enlightenment, moralism, historicism and relativism are the results of this tendency. Christianity is being re-interpreted philosophically and the figure of Christ rationalized into myth. The 'Monophysite' reaction despises natural, and especially physical, man. He is seen as a shadow, an insignificant epiphenomenon, without spiritual individuality and the 'magic of the soul' (Ed. Spranger).

Unfortunately, the conflict between modern 'Nestorians' and 'Monophysites' is not seen in its proper context, which is that of the *Incarnation*. The ancient heretics were much closer to the hierarchy of values: they knew that their conflicts concerned the *Incarnation*. It is interesting to find that the present-day conflicts are concerned with the same problem in a different form. The object of the struggle is no longer God-Man, uniting in himself the fullness of human nature and of being itself, but relative autonomous man—and, all too often, only one aspect of man, is emphasized and turned into one absolute.

Erected into an absolute, the 'Nestorian' view led to the belief that what is specifically and essentially human in man could be distinguished only quantitatively from the psycho-physical being of animals. The 'Monophysite' outlook on the contrary conceived of human nature as spirit and freedom alone by suppressing all aspects that were unfree in man. Both views were totalitarian in their one-sidedness. Neither the psycho-physical factor nor the spirit is the specifically human characteristic of man. What is specifically human is the incarnation of the spirit: the spirit become flesh and the flesh become spirit. The solution of the central problem of anthropology—conscience as the specific characteristic of man—is to be found in the recognition of the intimate and inextricable union of spirit and matter.

The conscience is man's ability to be mindful of a hierarchy of values which was not born of the laws of the flesh. Thus conscience serves as evidence of the incarnation of the spirit. It is, therefore, the central characteristic of man; there can be no true knowledge concerning man unless there is knowledge about his conscience. Recognition of the conscience, however, leads to personal responsibility, the imputability of man. On the other hand, science is concerned with the unbiased (i.e. non-evaluating) observation of phenomena. Is this criterion not in flat contradiction with the very function of knowledge about man? Depth psychology without value-judgment is not commensurate to its task; but if there are value-judgments, might there not be the danger of arbitrary judgments?

We have already described the paradoxical ambiguity of depth psychology. Strict separation of knowledge and value-judgments is essential in psychological analysis. 'Every psychopathologist must distinguish absolutely between knowledge and value-judgment. He must be capable of dispassionate investigation of the facts of the soul without at once taking up a position, he must be able to meet his patient freely, interested in him unconditionally and without prejudice. It is easy to see the difference between knowledge and value-judgement in principle; in application it requires so high a degree of self-criticism and factual objectivity that it is still far from being self-understood.'[2] On this analytical-scientific level, 'diagnosis is at the very end of the psychopathologist's approach'.[3]

Applied psychology and applied ethics meet only in the truth as it is experienced by the 'subject', in the meaningful vision of his latent potentialities of what ought to be. Value-judgments are being applied as yardsticks for action. We have gone beyond diagnosis, and knowledge occurs on a completely different level, that of *metanoia* or conversion.

That is why it is misplaced to accuse personalist depth psychology, for instance, of blaming people for their early childhood

[2] Karl Jaspers, *Allgemeine Psychopathologie*, 3rd edition, Julius Springer, Berlin 1923, p. 14.
[3] Op. cit., p. 16.

fixations. Such fixations are merely diagnosed, and it is the business of synthesis to go beyond the diagnosis and to achieve conversion. Analysis can never regard infantile absolutes as a matter of personal guilt, since they are the results of an impersonal, generally human frailty—characteristic of fallen nature (cf. pp. 126-8). There can also be no confusion with the sacrament of Penance, although it is part of the tendency of our psychologistic century to attach a perhaps exaggerated importance to subjective intentions. 'The objective offence against God's order in our conscience of sin is perhaps too far hidden behind the subjectivity of the sinful will: he who is not aware of his sin is held not to have sinned'.[4] Psychotherapy might not be needed at all in a less subjectivist age, nor would it be possible to confuse the psychologist with a secularized priest.

However, as personalist depth psychology emerges from the crisis of our thinking, it will be seen to be devoted to freedom and life.

It serves freedom. Since the personality which seeks to free itself from its own absolutes is not the *object* of liberation (like people living under a dictatorship), but always the *subject*. Psychotherapy is the means of attaining freedom—not a compulsion towards freedom, or a violent process for freedom's sake. We have discussed the temptation of wanting to instruct that besets inexperienced psychotherapists. His task is not to win victories or to annex conquered territory; he is to be a witness.

It also serves life, since this is the purpose of life itself. But this cannot be an immanent purpose, for, immanently considered, life leads to death and is absurd. In the last resort, therefore, death itself must be overcome. This is where depth psychology can do no more than to point the way, and to reveal the archetype of redemption alive within us. Whether this archetype is also referred to a personal redeemer, who has overcome death by his resurrection, is a question which lies outside the proper province of psychology. In any case, the more successfully the soul is freed from its immanent false absolutes, the closer it will come to experiencing the living truth of this Christ-archetype.

---

[4] Gotthard Montesi in a review of a book by Thomas Mann in *Wort und Wahrheit*, VI, 1951, p. 382.

The liberating and life-giving purpose of depth psychology is admittedly modest. It can but point out to man the beginning of a long and arduous task; which to accomplish is ever to be ready to begin it again. Man, as St Gregory of Nyssa said, goes 'from one beginning to a new beginning, until he reaches a beginning that has no appointed end'.

INDEX OF AUTHORS

INDEX OF SUBJECTS

221

SELECT BIBLIOGRAPHY

Adler, A., *Practice and Theory of Individual Psychology*, Routledge 1948, Humanities Press 1951.

Baudouin, C., *Myth of Modernity*, Geo. Allen 1950, Macmillan 1951.

de Beauvoir, S., *Second Sex*, Knopf 1953, Jonathan Cape 1953.

Frankl, V. E., *Doctor and the Soul*, Knopf 1955, McClelland.

Freud, S., *General Introduction to Psychoanalysis*, 1920, Boni, New York, and Garden City Publishing Co.
New Introductory Lectures on Psychoanalysis, Hogarth Press 1933.

Jaspers, K., *Reason and Existence*, Routledge 1956, and Longmans (Toronto).

Jung, C. G., *Collected Works*, Routledge 1953, Harper, McClelland.
Psychology of the Unconscious, Routledge 1957, Dodd.
Undiscovered Self, Routledge 1958, Atlantic Press.
Structure and Dynamics of the Psyche, Routledge 1960.
Psychology and Religion, Yale U.P., Oxford U.P. 1960.

Köhler, W., *Dynamics in Psychology*, Faber 1942.
Mentality of Apes, Universal 1948, Routledge (also available in Penguin series).

Mounier, E., *Be Not Afraid*, Rockliff 1951, Harper 1954.

Piaget, J., *Judgment and Reasoning in the Child*, Humanities Press 1952.

Sartre, J-P., *Existentialism and Humanism*, Methuen 1948.

Tournier, P., *The Meaning of Persons*, S.C.M. 1957.

1

2

IV

V

VI

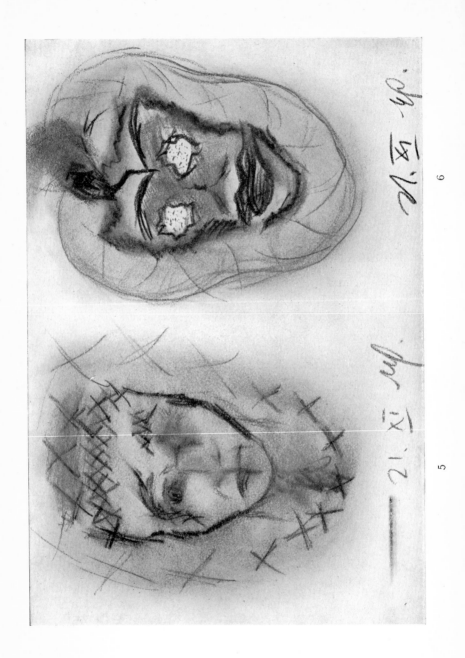

21. XI. ref.

21. V. 40.

5

6

X

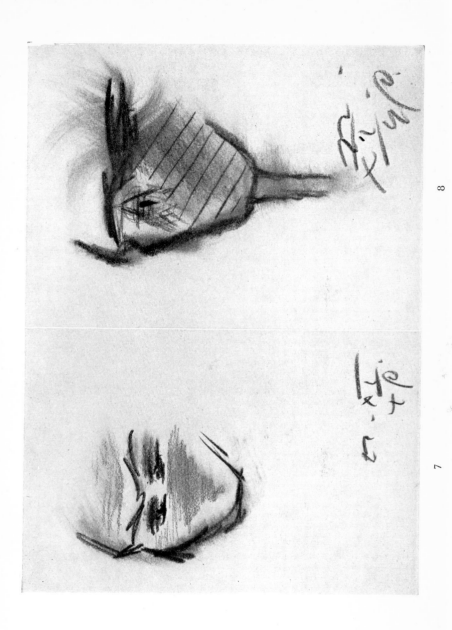

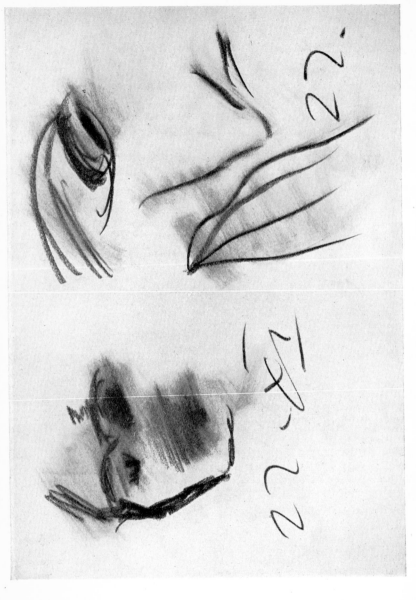

11

12

XIII

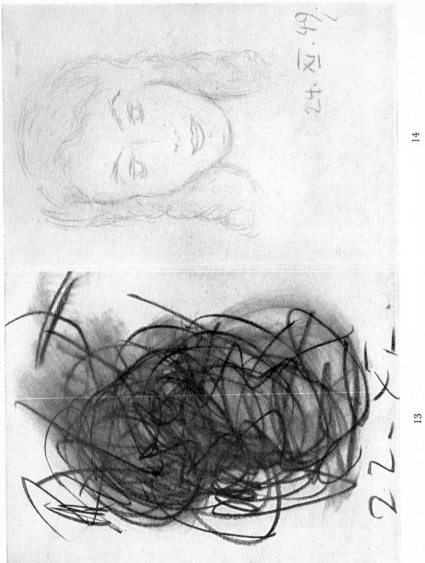

14

13

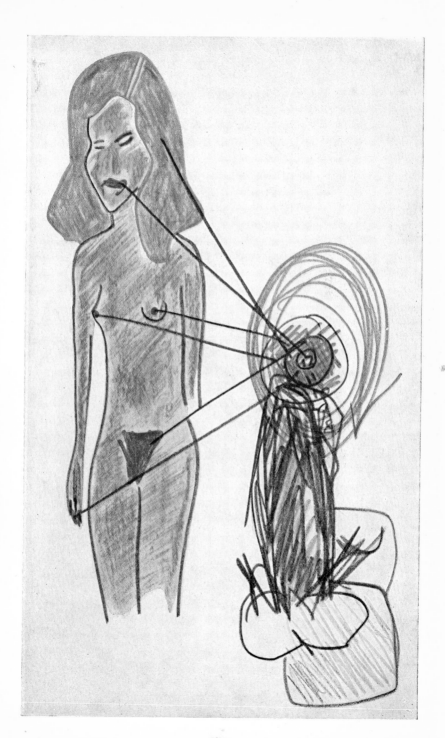

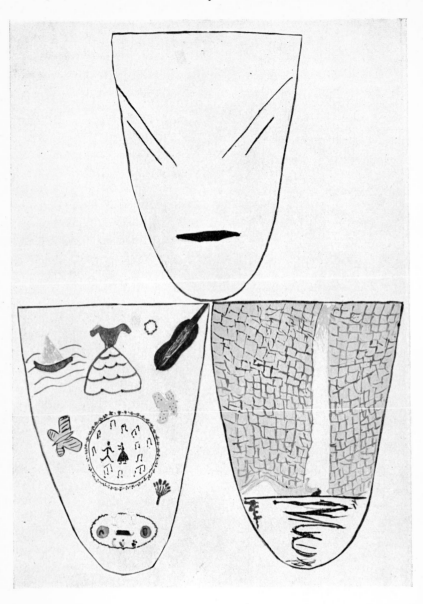

2   3

XVIII